Charles Godfrey Leland, Mary Alicia Owen

Voodoo Tales

As Told Among the Negroes of the South-West

Charles Godfrey Leland, Mary Alicia Owen

Voodoo Tales
As Told Among the Negroes of the South-West

ISBN/EAN: 9783337005528

Printed in Europe, USA, Canada, Australia, Japan

Cover: Foto ©Thomas Meinert / pixelio.de

More available books at **www.hansebooks.com**

VOODOO TALES

AS TOLD AMONG THE NEGROES
OF THE SOUTHWEST

COLLECTED FROM ORIGINAL SOURCES

BY

MARY ALICIA OWEN

INTRODUCTION BY CHARLES GODFREY LELAND

ILLUSTRATED BY

JULIETTE A. OWEN AND LOUIS WAIN

G. P. PUTNAM'S SONS

NEW YORK
27 WEST TWENTY-THIRD STREET

LONDON
24 BEDFORD STREET, STRAND

The Knickerbocker Press
1893

INTRODUCTION.

As leaves are seldom gathered till they change colour and begin to fall, nor made into bouquets and wreaths till brilliant colours begin to show themselves in their dying beauties; so, all the world over, folk-lore stories are but little noticed by the cultured world until they begin to assume romantic lines of association, nor are they gathered till they have fallen, so to speak, from the lofty trees of religion, and lie on the ground, or are driven about by the playful wind, as mere legends or nursery tales. It is in this state when "prettiest"—but unfortunately driest—that the relics of tradition are most admired by children or the general reader; and there are indeed too many folk-lorists who care to go no further.

This very remarkable collection by Miss Mary A. Owen takes us more deeply than those which are made on the Grimm principle of "pleasing tales for the nursery"—back to the fresh green and growing leaves. It is indeed entertaining and amusing, but nothing has in it been sacrificed to the latter element, nor are the narrators of the tales in it made of more real importance than the subject. This *subject* is as curious as it is entirely novel. There is in Missouri, as "all along the Border," a mixed race of Negro and Indian descent, who have

inherited a vast stock of the traditions of both races, and
combined or blended them strangely into new life. As there
is in them, however, a very great predominance of red Indian,
we get therefore a clue as to the mysterious origin of American
negro tales. The *stories*, in fact, all agree almost to identity
with those found in the collections of Schoolcraft, Kohl, and
many others. But in the vast amount of sorcery, magic, medicine, and fetishes recorded, we find the African Voodoo ideas
very strangely mixed with the *Indian*. Here, by the way, the
term "Indian" may be used to indicate the Aryan, for it is
one of the most extraordinary coincidences known, that the
American, or Hindu, hold and carry out to an extraordinary
identity the doctrine of acquiring magic power by means of
penance.

The real or inner nature of *Voodooism* is as yet almost unknown, even to the learned ; and I am glad that Miss Owen,
who has been initiated sufficiently into its mysteries to divine
and grasp its full scope and nature, has carefully recorded, and
will at some time publish, her very extensive knowledge of the
subject. Unlike the Aryan and Red Indian magic based on
fasting, contemplation, and " prayer," it relies on daring that
which is horrible and repulsive, and, above all, in a perfectly
subjective iron *will*. It also acts greatly by the terror or influence inspired by the conjuror himself. And its cures and
means are fouler and far more revolting than those of Indian
" medicine." Guided by these simple hints, the reader will
understand and detect for himself the predominant elements
of the folk-lore in these tales. And doing this he cannot fail
to observe that there is in this collection, and on almost every
page, items of true folk-lore, earnest, clear, and well-defined,
while, at the same time, ancient, mysterious, and strange. I
have been tempted at almost every passage to step in with
footnote observations—as, for instance, that while it might very
well be mere chance coincidence that Woodpecker was a red-

capped dwarf magician in ancient Italy, and a red dwarf
sorcerer among the Negro-Indians, this by no means explains
the other *numerous* coincidences between the tales told of the
dwarfs, which are manifestly of the woodpecker stock, in
Europe and America. I mention this because Miss Owen's
contributions to the folk-lore of the Woodpecker, who is the
most ancient and important of all fairies, are very valuable and
original.

The superstitions as regards informing the bees of a death,
and much more relating to them, are identical with Norse
beliefs, but are expressed most clearly and fully in the Finnic
Kalevala ; [1] of which work I may here be allowed to say that
I have seldom been more gratified by any contribution to the
literature of translation than by the admirable version of Marion
Crawford, which has given to Anglo-American literature something which has long been wanting. The Finnic traditions
bear to the Norse, in a great measure, the same relation as the
Indian to these Missouri transmissions, and the Norse, in all
probability, to the Algonkin. But whether all such lore be
" tradited," or due to the action of like cause and like effect,
it is equally clear to me that in the immense collection, published or unpublished, made by Mary A. Owen, and derived
directly from true believers, we have a vast amount of material
for discussion. It is this which must be chiefly borne in mind
in reading this book, and not the mere *form* in which it has
been cast. The fact that this work bears the title of " Rabbit,
the Voodoo," and that in it old women communicate to a white
child their stories, will naturally suggest an imitation of " Brer
Rabbit," while in reality it deals with altogether different
material. The mere general reader, for amusement, may
judge of the book by this coincidence, but no folk-lorist can

[1] I commend to every folk-lorist as the most exhaustive and valuable com-
mentary on this subject, " Il Kalevala o la Poesia tradizionale dei Finni"
(Rome, 1891), by the Senator Domenico Comparetti.

fail to perceive its true value. It is in this inner or true character that the value of this really remarkable work consists. As regards novelty and originality of subject, it ranks among the most important contributions to Folk-lore.

Mary A. Owen was not only born and brought up, as her writings indicate, among the most "superstitious," race conceivable, but had from infancy an intense desire, aided by a marvellous memory, to collect and remember all that she learned. In reading her letters I have often been reminded of the title of an imaginary work called "Travels among the Savages, by one of their Chiefs." In all my experience I never met with but one person so perfectly at home in the subject, and that was a full-blood Passamaquoddy Indian, who had, under some strange inspiration, collected all the folk-lore, even on the most trifling subjects, of his tribe. As regards the inexhaustible extent of her acquisitions, I may mention that in the letters which I have received from Miss Owen there is perhaps as much traditional lore of the most interesting and valuable description as would make another volume as large as this, which has not been given in it. It was sent to me under the impression that I might find it of some use. And here I may remark that the writer had no idea of publishing anything on the subject till I suggested it.

Though I have in justice exalted the subject-matter of this very valuable and curious book above the form, I cannot refrain from declaring that the latter has decided merits. The separate characters of the old Aunties, who tell the tales in it, are admirably described and clearly presented. The "real old Guinea nigger," who had been a slave, was not unknown to me in my boyhood, and I well remember one who was more than a hundred years old, who could speak only Dutch and African. That she had long passed a century, and had really seen General Washington was proved by a well-educated lady, eighty-four years of age, who could remember the old negress from her own earliest infancy. The triangular character, Miss Boogarry, who is equally Indian, Missouri-French, and Negro, shows her grim yet childish nature with its strange mixture of Catholicism and heathenism in every sentence which she utters. The author shows tact and truth in translating her difficult dialect into plain English.

Apropos of which I would remark that while American readers will readily understand the Negro-English of this book, though it differs greatly from that of other parts of the United States, this may not be the case in England, and I have therefore taken the liberty of giving in parentheses and in plain English the correct form of many words which otherwise have been, though perhaps only for a moment, unintelligible. That the dialect is really correctly given, is shown by the consistency of the spelling. But as it is as natural to the author as Platt Deutsch to a Hamburger, or native of Bremen, its correctness can hardly be questioned.

When the paper by Miss Owen on Missouri-Negro traditions was read before the Folk-Lore Congress in 1891, it received the great honour of a distinguishing complimentary notice in an editorial article in the London *Times*. Upon which she modestly expressed to me the hope that her forthcoming book would show that she deserved it. Much allowance should always be made for a first work by a young writer ; I can only add that I sincerely trust that the readers of this volume will kindly admit that the author has shown herself worthy of the very favourable impression caused by her first appearance in England.

CHARLES GODFREY LELAND.

CONTENTS.

—⋆—

LIST OF ILLUSTRATIONS.

—•—

THE BEE-KING AND THE AUNTIES.

WAS not a convention of witches, though it bore the outward seeming of one ; it was Aunt Jinny's " company," and a " good time " the guests were having, too.

Aunt Jinny, or as her intimates called her, " Granny," sat in the middle of the semicircle drawn round the great fireplace

THE BEE-KING. ablaze with the conflagration of a quarter of a cord of hickory logs, and felt herself as important a mistress of the situation, there in her cabin, as any queen could in her palace of carved stone. A great authority in her way was Granny. She knew the value of every herb and simple to be found in the state ; she was an adept in the healing art ; she could " set " hens so that they never lost an egg ; she could out-general the shyest turkey that ever " stole its nest " in the weeds and brush ; she could tell when to wean a calf or baby and when to plant " craps " by the age and position of the moon ; she could " lay out " the dead and usher in the living ; she could interpret dreams ; she knew the " sign " of every-thing from the spilling of salt to the flight of birds ; she had seen ghosts and withstood devils ; she knew legends and tales without number ; she could, as actively as a girl, " pat Juba "

2   1

"SHE COULD TELL WHEN TO WEAN A CALF."

and " jump Jim Crow " ; and, last and most important, she was, to quote her own words, " bornded at Culpepper Court-house in Ole Feginny an' hed seen Gin'al Washington wid my own eyes." " An' I ain't no common ole nigger," she would add, not boastfully, but with the calm assurance of one born to high estate, " I mos'ly ain't no nigger 'tall. Ise come down fum dem Lenny-Lennype Injuns dat hilt de kyentry (country) 'fo' de w'ite folks come dar ; an' I wuz sold wunst an' fetched er heap o' money an' I would ergain, Ise bound, dough I'se mo'n er

GRANNY MOVING IN S'CIETY.

hunderd yeahs ole. 'Deed I would, kase Ise spry. Hit's only shif'less critturs dat's cheap fum de start dat wears out 'arly." Her claims to aristocracy were always acknowledged by her associates. She had been bond and now was free, and they agreed with her in thinking that all the past glories and dignities of her former owners, "the folks up at The House " a few rods away, were centred and kept alive in her own proper person. Her lineage, too, was believed in without a demur. She was accepted as a child of the Werowances, although her

abundant grey wool was of the woolliest ; no broader, flatter
nose was ever seen ; no pure-blooded African ever had thicker
lips with a more decided curl outward.   As to costume,
Granny's tastes were evidently simple.   Although she was
supposed to have a fortune in second-hand finery laid away in

GRANNY TENDING TO BIZNESS.

the various trunks and boxes beside and under her bed, she was
"saving o' gear."   Only Fourth-of-July, Christmas, circus-day,
or camp-meeting ever brought out the splendours of be-flounced
and be-ribboned gowns, or any one of the two or three dozen
bonnets of all ages, shapes, and sizes that snugly reposed in her

biggest " big chist." Ordinarily, she appeared, as on this evening, in a short costume of faded blue-and-brown cotton, a Madras turban very much awry, and a pair of men's boots much the worse for wear. Whene'er she took her walks abroad—not to see the poor, for she despised human " trash," but to hunt eggs—she donned a man's chimney-pot hat. " Yis," she would explain to impertinent questioners, " I w'ars ole master's boots an' hats. Wut's good 'nuff foh him is good 'nuff foh me, an' ef yo' don't lak (like) hit, yo' kin lump hit an' look t'urr (the other) way." As Granny always carried a stout hickory staff, and had a nervous motion of her right arm when answering superfluous questions, if her auditors " lumped " her raiment they were usually discreet enough to do it in secret.

On Granny's right hand was a woman fully as dark as she, but the darkness was of a different sort altogether. Granny, good old soul I looked with her century of gathered wrinkles as if she had been carelessly covered with coffee-coloured crape, while the other was of the brown of old leather burned by the sun and dried by the winds ; a tall, strong, gaunt, fierce-looking woman of eight-and-forty she was, with the nose of an eagle, the eye of a hawk, the mouth of a cat, and hair like the tail of a black horse. This was Madame Angelique Bougareau, generally spoken to as " Mrs. Boogarry," spoken of as " Big Angy." Big Angy sat before the blaze, scowling, and knitting at a red mitten as savagely as if the insensate body of yarn had done her a personal injury. Perhaps some one had ordered mittens or socks and then ignored the order ; perhaps she had allowed an insolvent customer to get possession of a great share of her precious " garden-truck " ; perhaps an impertinent housewife had dared to affirm that her soap wouldn't " suds " or her brooms shed straws—for Big Angy was a dealer in some of the luxuries as well as the necessaries of life, and was also the primitive type of that product of a supposedly *very* modern business method, the commercial traveller. She owned a little brown house set in the midst of an acre of good, rich soil, better even than the average black loam of North-west Missouri. On that acre she raised pretty nearly everything good for man and beast, and, at the same time, illustrated the freedom and lack of caste in frontier civilisation. " Touch-me-nots," " unprofitably gay," were not more prominently in view of the passer-by than the cabbages ; the beets were as honoured as the "four-o'-clocks" ; the onions were in bed with the pinks, the marigolds with the radishes, the larkspurs with the lettuce ; the garlic was cheek-by-jowl with the delicate musk-roses, and the prince's-feather and the broom-corn nodded their tall heads together. Everything was as good as everything else, and a pretty show the collection made too, from the time the first parsley and crocus appeared through the melting snow till the last dahlia and tomato were gathered. When its season of growth and fruitage was over and all things not plucked and garnered were shrouded in straw, old coffee-bags, and cast-off garments, Angy's weekly rounds from house did not cease. Instead of the flowers that bloomed to fade, stiff bunches of " bachelor's buttons," " everlastings," and bittersweet-berries peeped from under her great basket's-lid, and the place of the vegetables was taken by bars of " hard," and gourds of " soft " soap (Granny had taught her the art of civilisation known to them both as " soap-bilin' "), hearth-brooms, socks, mittens, grated horse-radish, and little jars of a villainous sweet compound of pumpkin stewed with water-melon-juice and known to all as " punkin-butter." She drove good bargains as a rule, and might have been a person of independent means if she had not allowed her worthless little Creole French husband, " Lame Joe," to gamble away the greater part of her earnings. When advised against yielding to this amiable weakness, she defended herself by saying, " Me daddy was gret French hunter, me mammy was chile ter de big chief de Iowas. Dey not putt by lak de squir'l in de

THE AUNTIES AND TOW HEAD.

hole, w'y me do so ? " " Des (just) please yo'se'f 'bout dat,"
Granny would make answer, with offended dignity. " Ef yo'
lak (like) dat Joe drink up all dat hahd wuhk (hard work), let
'im drink um, dat's all !—but ef enny ob my ole mans (husbands)
wuz a-libben, I boun' yo' see sumpin diffint ! " " Me hab save
alway some silba piece foh de mass," Big Angy would say, half
in apology. Granny considered that as great a waste of good
money as making a banker of Joe, but she was too discreet to
challenge religious prejudices—of which Big Angy had many ;
her faith, indeed, being of as many hues as Joseph's coat, as was
evinced by her keeping her medicine-pipe and eagle-bone
whistle along with her missal and " Key to Heaven " ; by
carrying a rabbit's-foot and rosary in the same pocket, by
wearing a saint's toe dangling on her bosom and the fetich
known as a " luck-ball " under her right arm.

On Granny's left, sat Aunt Em'ly, a woman about Big Angy's
age and stature, but of a different avoirdupoise and temper.
Her jolly soul was enveloped in billows of fat, and her round
eyes looked on the world with childlike content, in spite of her
hard labours, day in and day out, at the washtub, the merciless
scoldings she received from her rheumatic old husband, and the
various tribulations brought upon her by her worthless sons.
Like Angy, she was a half-breed, as her high cheek-bones and
shiny black ringlets falling to her shoulders proved beyond
dispute ; but she was of another class altogether, her mother
having been a negress and her father a Fox Indian. Nearly
every night, after her labours were done, she trudged the two
miles between cabins to visit Granny and smoke her tobacco,
and talk of the good old times, the like of which they should
never see again—those times when the thriving city, growing
so rapidly towards their country cabins, had been only a cluster
of shanties on the banks of the Missouri, and had not encroached
on the virgin forest, alive with mysterious whisperings and
strange wild songs, nor on the grassy plains swept into waves

like the sea's by the winds, and jewelled as the sea never was
by an unreckoned multitude of wild flowers.   Ah ! those *were*
good old times, when the forest meant more to the human
intelligence than its price in cordwood and lumber, and there
was another valuation to the plain besides its capacity for
raising hay.   Each had its voice and its story, in the good old
times, when the heart of Mother Nature beat in unison with
her children's, and she did not in the depths of her scarred
bosom and sapped arteries feel herself a Lear despised of the
children she had enriched.   The good old times ! the good old
times ! others besides Aunt Em'ly look back on them with
regret and longing.

On her knees, close to the fire, knelt Aunt Mary, an oily,
dark woman of forty, of middle height, well proportioned and
strong.   Like all the other women, except Granny, she wore a
calico frock of a dark-blue ground sprinkled with white stars.
On her head was a snowy turban, but, white as it was, it was
no whiter than her great eyeballs and polished teeth.   She
looked the typical darkey, but was accustomed to assert that
she was "some Injun," "thes how it comed in " she did not
know, but was sure of it, nevertheless.   She was the cook of
" The House," slept in the cabin with Granny, and was assis-
tant, not associate, hostess.   According to her own account, she
was " bornded in Tennissee, but mos'ly brung up in Mizzury."
In both states she had had some ghostly visitors and serious
encounters with his Satanic majesty, but, while her experiences
were usually considered as doing pretty well for one of her age
and opportunities, they were accounted trivial in comparison
with those of her friends.   Her occupation, which necessitated
her lowly and devout posture, was the roasting of eggs by tying
strings round their middles and dangling them before the fire, a
delicate feat in which many failed, but she was an adept. She never
let an egg fall, nor lost its " meat " by an untimely explosion,
but years of uninterrupted success never palled her enjoyment.

Each egg, as it had a neat little hole pecked in its side and was girdled by a twine loop, received the rapturous grin accorded to its predecessor.

Opposite Aunt Mary, and half in shadow, was a little, bent woman more important even than Granny. Nobody knew or could guess her age. As for her looks, they are best described as a recent acquaintance once spoke of a celebrated literary lady —" Plain ?—she'd be better looking if she *were* plain !" The little woman was Aunt Mymee, the only pure-blooded African in the room, and, oddly enough, the only copper-coloured person present. Aunt Mymee was the child of a Guinea sorceress who had fled on board a slaver to escape death at the hands of her countrymen. Like mother, like daughter— Mymee was a great " cunjerer," and would fain have had her acquaintances believe she had the devil for a father. She was treated with great respect, tempered with a hypocritical cordiality, by her neighbours of colour, and was a valued servant of the whites, owing to her skill and tenderness in the management of children. In her lap at that moment was a tow-headed white young girl who followed her about like a shadow, and was supposed by the aunties to be "charmed." The influence at that particular time seemed to be reversed, for Tow Head was giving evidence of perverseness. Aunt Mymee was expostulating, coaxing, even threatening, in a low tone, all to no purpose.

" I *won't*," Tow Head at last said, decisively. " Grandma and Mamma know I am here, and they don't care. I'm not sleepy ; I won't go up to the house. If you fuss at me I'll break your pipe ; if you let me stay and hear the stories I'll buy you a head-handkerchief with my own money."

There was nothing Aunt Mymee desired less than a " head-handkerchief," as she wore her hair (except on Sundays, when it was carded out in a great black fleece) in little wads the length and thickness of her finger, each wad being tightly wrapped with white cord. She scorned to conceal these efforts to " take de kink outen de wool," as did other ladies of colour with their kerchief-turbans, but as the proffer of the present she would not wear was accompanied by many vigorous hugs and pats, she weakly yielded to bribery and allowed her charge to remain.

Granny looked at the two sadly. She knew a charmed child when she saw one, and was resolved to do what she could to relieve the unconscious victim. Oh ! she knew Aunt Mymee, and so did the others. Although they visited and received her in turn, although she had lived in the cabin a few rods from Granny's for years, not one of them ever went to bed at night without hanging up a horse-shoe and pair of wool-cards at the bed's head. Not one of them failed to pour a cup of mustard or turnip-seed on the doorstep and hearth, so that she would have to count all those seeds before she could go in at the door, or down the chimney to tie their hair into knots ; to twist the feathers in their beds into balls as solid as stone ; to pinch them with cramps and rheumatism ; to ride on their chests, holding by their thumbs as by a bridle, while she spit fire at them till cock-crow. Not one of them had any doubt as to her ability to jump out of her skin whenever she pleased, and take the form of owl, black dog, cat, wolf, horse, or cow. Not one of them merely suspected, she *knew* Mymee could appear in two places at once, ride a broomstick or a bat like a charger, and bring sickness and bad luck of all sorts on whomsoever she pleased. No wonder the aunties sighed in secret over the recklessness of white folks in turning such an uncanny body loose among the children. If Aunt Mymee knew what they thought she gave no sign ; for when not engaged in confidential discourse with Tow Head she smoked in silence. Perhaps she was thinking of the stalwart sons killed in the civil war ; perhaps of the Negro husband, the Mulatto husband, the Indian husband, and the virtues that made her take them, and the failings that made her "turn 'em all loose"; perhaps she was meditating some awful "trick," or magic curse. Whatsoever the thought was, she kept it locked in her own cunning brain. The child's caresses she received with secret delight at Granny's uneasiness and jealousy, but that light emotion made no ripple the eye could detect, she smoked on and on in seeming peacefulness and innocence.

Big Angy broke the silence with a French oath, accompanied by an angry gesture. She had snapped her clay pipe in twain, and as she flung the fragments among the blazing logs she anathematised it stem and bowl.

Granny kindly made good the loss by taking from one of her many pockets a pipe made from a corn-cob, and fitted with a sugar-cane stem, which she handed her guest without a word.

Big Angy received it with a grunt that might have meant thankfulness, put it in working order, and went on smoking.

Granny watched her with great concern.

"Ain' yo' sorter out o' sorts dis ebenin', Miss Boogarry?" she inquired.

"Yes, me is," answered Big Angy, in a dialect similar to her friend's, but garnished with patois and a few Indian gutterals. "Ise out o' sorts fum top to toe. Dem bees"—she qualified them with an adjective not necessary to repeat—"am 'stractin' me."

"Wut dey done?"

"Me dremp 'bout um."

"Dat er mighty good dream—

' Dream o' honey, lots o' money ;
Dream o' bees, lib at yo' ease.' "

"Na dishaway dat my dream go. Hit bin dat de bees wuz all daid, an' de hibe (hive) chock full o' mots (moths)."

That was serious. All the aunties sighed in sympathy.

"Dat ain' all ne'er. Dey's mo' ahine. In de swa'min'-time

dey run off, dey pay no 'tention at me. Hollerin' an' poundin' on de dish-pan ain' do no good. Off dey go ! "

" An' yo' bees bin oncommon good twell (till) now ! I 'low yo' done mek un mad somehow or ur nurr," said Granny.

" Dat's de truf," groaned Big Angy. " W'en my sister's darter die an' dey sent atter me, hit slip me mine dat I otter tell de bees an' putt mo'nin' (mourning) on de hibes. Dey bin mad hand-runnin' sence dat."

" I ain't s'rprise none," said Aunt Em'ly, cheerfully. " Ef yo' don't tell de bees 'bout all de bornin's an' weddin's an' fun'als dey gwinter (going to) cl'ar out ur else sorter pindle (pine) an' die. How come dat I know dat, I done lost de lastest bee I got w'en my Jake merry Aunt Kate's big yaller Sally. Hit comed on me dat suddint dat hit ain' cross my mine dat I got er bee, twell I wuz a-settin at de table, an' Aunt Kate, she holler 'cross at me, will I gib de young folks de two fust swa'ms dat come off. I wuz dat skeered dat I mighty nigh cussed ! ' De good Lawd ! ' sez me, an' drapped de vittles dat wuz on de way ter my mouf. ' De good Lawd, Aunt Kate ! I ain' tole dem bees dat Jake an' Sally wuz a-merryin' dis night ! ' Aunt Kate, she des fell back in 'er cheer lak someun hit 'er wid er dornick (stone). ' Well ! ' says she, ' I 'low de young folks ain't gwine ter tire deyse'fs out, takin' keer o' all de bees yo' gwine ter hab fo' um.' An' dat wuz de troof too. I ain' got nair bee ter my name by de nex' spring. I bin puttin' my pennunce (dependence) in de honey dat I find in de woods sence dat. Dey ain't no use o' me a-trying ter raise bees."

" Ef yo' steal some new hibes an' leabe de price in dey place, yo' kin raise some ergin (again)," said Mymee, oracularly.

" Reckon I could ? "

" Sholy. Hit's de finest kind o' luck ter steal bees an' de worsest in de world ter sell um, dough yo' kin fa'rly buy um widout crossin' de luck if yo' leabe de price on de bench whah yo' steal um fum."

"Honey!" cried Aunt Mary, suddenly, as she critically examined an egg and seemed to be addressing it instead of the company. "Honey is good ter eat an' good ter drink an' good ter wear."

A chorus of laughter greeted her remark.

"Dat's so," she insisted, stoutly, after joining in the laugh. "Hit's good ter eat, all um yo' knows dat. Hit's good ter drink ef yo' putt de hot wattah an' de spice wid hit w'en yo' got de sore th'oat, an' hit's good ter wear ef yo' got chap'd han's, ur ef yo' am 'fraid o' ghostes. W'y, I knowed er 'ooman dat did de milkin' foh er milkman, an' she hatter (had to) go home arter (after) milkin' through er big holler whah de ghostes wuz ez thick ez gnats in de summah-time. Fust time dat 'ooman go through dat holler, she skeered twell she kyarn' (cannot) squall. She tell't (told it to) witcher 'oomen. Witcher 'oomen say, 'rub fum head ter heel wid new honey, an' I boun' yo' don't see nuttin mo'—not eben ef de moon am on de wane an' a-ridin' on 'er back up in de sky.' 'Oomen do dat, regler. See nuttin no mo'; but, man suz! her close (clothes), dey des (just) wuz er sight fum dat out, an' de flies, dey foller 'er round lak de little niggahs foller de sukkus-waggin (circus-waggon)."

"It's good for something else," said Tow Head, sitting up. "It's good to per-oph-e-sy."

"Wut dat?" asked Granny, with a suspicious glance in Aunt Mymee's direction.

"That's to know what's going to happen," explained Tow Head, importantly. "Mamma told me the big word for it, and I found out the rest from Aunt Mymee. Yes, I did, Aunt Mymee! Don't you remember that time you coaxed me to get you some of Grandma's amaranth seeds and told me that amaranth seeds, honey, and whiskey made into a cake and eaten in the dark of the moon would make people know when things were going to happen?"

"I wuz des a-projecking (projecting—experimenting) wid yo',"

mumbled Aunt Mymee. " Des (just) keep still mungs dese
niggahs an' I'll sing ter you, torectly."

" But twasn't projecking," piped Tow Head, getting shriller
and shriller with each word, " for I ate some when you were
not looking, so as to see if Uncle John would bring me the doll
he promised me, and I couldn't tell, but he came that very
afternoon and he did have the doll. Before that he always
forgot. Oh, yes ! and you made a love-cake too."

" Dat chile gwine ter git pizoned, some day," said Granny,
after an embarrassed pause, " ef she go dippin' an' projeckin
hither an' yon', bedout axin' leabe o' dem dat's older."

Aunt Mymee's eyes snapped.

" I 'low," she remarked, with deliberate emphasis, " dat dem
I got er intrest in ain't gwine ter drap off, suddint, ef *I'*m dar."

" Truf, truf, Aunt Mymee, ef yo' *dar*," Granny made haste
to answer. " Hit wuz de times yo' wuzzent dar dat gimme de
worrymint. Missey, she's a mighty free hand 'bout a-dippin' in
an'——"

" Oh, stop fussing, Granny ! and tell some stories. Tell a
bee-king story," interrupted Tow Head. " Mamma scolds me all
I need. You tell me a pretty story."

" Yes, Aunt Jinny, tell my lil lamb er putty tale 'bout de ole
bee-king," urged Aunt Mymee, sweetly.

" Law, now ! my tales dey's sech *ole* tales," said Granny,
modestly. " Ef yo' ax Aunt Em'ly now, ur Miss Boogarry, I
lay (wager) dat yo' git er tale yo' kin putt by in yo' membunce
(memory) medout a-grugin' de room hit tek up."

A chorus of protests from the parties so honourably
mentioned.

" Well ! " said Granny, at length, " ef yo' sesso, I gwine ter
mek de start, den de res' mus' foller wid dey tales. I fetch on
de pone (maize bread), de res' fetch in de sweetnin'."

Having thus poetically defined her rank, and at the same
time paid her friends a compliment, Granny filled her mouth

with smoke, blew it out through her nostrils like an amiable dragon and began :

" In de good ole times w'en de trees an' de beasts wuzn't feard ter talk foh fear o' bein' sot ter work, dey use ter be a heap o' spressifyin' (expressing opinions) in de woods. Special dat wuz de way mungst de bee-trees,[1] kase (because) dey wuz feelin' mighty sweet an' peart wid dey eensides all fill up wid honey in de comb. De trees wid honey in dey hollers wuz all sot up, lak chilluns (children) whut am got de sugah-tit in dey moufs, or sugah-plums in dey braid-bastets (bread baskets— stomachs). Dat's de way dey wuz. Dey wuz thes (just) dat high in dey tops dat day mos' fegit dey use ter be nuttin but saplin's a-switchin' in de wind, an' atter dat ole holler logs twell de ole king ob de bees, he say unter de new swa'm dat came off, ' Git in dis tree ! ' Oh, yes ! de favour*ites* o' de ole king, dey jounce dey limbs up an' down an' fluster dey leabes a *heap*, des de same ez fine ladies toss dey heads an' swish dey skyurts."

" Oh, Granny ! what does the king look like ? Did you ever see him ? "

" Now ! Dat show yo' ain't ne'er seen 'im, an' dat suttinly am a shame, kase he's de finest king a-gwine. He am brown lak de bees deyse'f, an' he eyes am des de colour ob honey, an' he ain't got no ha'r on he head, an' he nose an' he eyebrows an' he eye-winkers bin mek out o' stone, an'—oh, my !—he got er crown on he lil bald head mek out o' bummle-bees ez long ez brack-buhds (black-birds) an' all a-stannin' up on dey tails."

" Oh, Granny ! " breathed Tow Head, squeezing her knee in her two little hands because she must do something, or die of a repressed ecstasy of satisfaction and anticipation.

" Sidesen (besides) dat," continued Granny, with the unelated air of genius conscious of its own powers, " I ain't done name ter yo' dat he got er mighty quare suit o' close (clothes) mek

---

[1] Bee-trees, those which bees inhabit.

out o' bee wings ; nur I ain't say dat he kyar (carry) round er long paw-paw stick wid er whustle in de eend foh ter whustle de bees back ter wuhk (work) w'en dey go a-traipsin' (strolling) off, a-playin' in de field stiddier (instead) o' tending ter bizniz. Oh, he wuz de fine genterman, suz ! He uster gq a-paradin' thu the woods an' a-hyeahin' (hearing) eb'ry libbin' ting dat de crittuz (creatures) wuz up ter, *eb'ry* ting, kase he c'd hear de grass grow an' de fedders a-sproutin' on de lil young buhds in de nest, let 'lone de sorftes' whispeh dat kin be talked. One time—'twuz de night time an' de big clouds wuz a-rollin' in de sky—ole king, he stop by de big oak dat got two hollers an' two swa'ms o' bees. Now, dat oak he bin mighty proud dat he sich a favour*it*e dat he got two swa'ms w'en de rest o' de trees, dey ain't got but one, but, at de same time, he allus bin sorter high-strung (high-tempered), an' now he gittin' ole he wuz dat cranky an' cross ! Ole king, he lissen foh ter see how de queen-bee behavin' 'erself in dar. She wuz 'havin' mighty nice time, but ole oak, he grummle an' grummle. He say, 'I des sick an' tired ob dese bees gwine hum ! hum ! twell (till) Ise plum 'stractid. Fust dis side ! den dat side !—hum ! hum ! hum ! Hit's wuss den de locust wid dey hollerin', ah-zee, ah-zee, ah-zee, w'en de sun stan's high. An' I don't lak dat honey—sweetnin' a-ropin' around an' a-dribblin' out on my bahk (bark) an' 'tractin' de bugs an' varmints, dat I don't ! Ise a mine to drap whole heaps o' bittah sap on ter 'em some o' dese days, dat I has ! '

" W'en de ole king hyeah dat, he wuz des ez mad ez fiah (fire). He mek one grab," cried Granny, raising her voice and suiting the action to the word so effectively that all her hearers jumped, and Tow Head screamed in addition, " an' he scoof dis lot c' bees out o' de oak wid one hand, an' nurr grab an' scoof dat lot wid turr hand, an'—*bim !*—he gin dat servigrous (fractious) ole tree des one peck wid dat big stone nose o' hissen a', de laws an' de lan' ! dat ole oak bin petterfactid. Hit bin mek in ter stone thu an' thu. Dat am sholy de fack kase I'm

3

got a piece ob er tree dat bin done dataway, my ownse'lf an' lo an' beholes ! hyeah 'tis, dis same piece dat I rub ginst my arm w'en hit git de rheumatiz ; hit mighty good fer dat."

" Oh, granny ! " burst in Tow Head, " is that a piece of the very same tree you've been telling about ? "

" Hit's des ez possumble ez not dat hit is," said Granny, gravely. " Ef 'twuzn't dat tree hit come fum, hit bin one dat wuz cotch (caught) de same way."

" Dat's so," agreed Aunt Mymee, rousing up. " Dey use ter be heaps o' dem stone trees round in de kyentry (country), an' dey all bin sarve dataway kase dey wuz sassy ter de king, ur he tuck up de notion dey wuz."

" Granny, dear, sweet, sugar-pie Granny, please, *please*, PLEASE, let me hold that stone in my hand a minute. I'll be very careful."

" De aigs is all did," announced Aunt Mary, to create a diversion, for she knew Granny would never trust that precious piece of petrified wood so near Aunt Mymee as Tow Head's eager hands were at that moment.

" Den we gwine ter eat um hot," said Granny, briskly. "Fetch um ter de table, Aunt Mary, w'iles I fish out de res' ob dat cawn-pone (corn bread) an' er smidgin o' cole bile shoat (piece of cold pork)."

" May I have two eggs, Aunt Mary ? "

" Oh ! honey, yo' can't hab none," said Aunt Mary, as she set the dish of eggs on the table. " Yo' ma, she say dat ef yo' git sumpin 'sides milk, ur mush-an'-'lasses out hyeah, she ain' gwine ter let yo' come no mo'. Ain' she say dat, Aunt Mymee ? "

" O' co'se," said Aunt Mymee, " but dat ain't no diffunce. Missey don't want no aig. She wuz des a-projeckin' wid yo', wuzn't yo', missey ? " she asked, turning her charge's face around in her hands and smiling insinuatingly.

" I wasn't ! I want an egg ! I want two eggs—big ones, too ! "

" No, no, honey ! "

" Yes, I do, too! and you're a mean, hateful old thing. You're all mean, hateful old things," continued Tow Head, noting the resolved expression of her friends. " I don't like you ; I don't like anybody in this cabin."

" I reckon I mought ez well tek de chile back ter de house," said Aunt Mymee, thoughtfully. "She feelin' so mighty 'bused dat she betteh hed go lay de case 'fo' huh ma."

Instantly Tow Head's demeanour changed. That veiled threat of conducting her into the presence of her parent was as potent as soothing-syrup. The presence of mamma meant bath and bed. Tow Head's aversion to water was equal to a mediæval saint's, and she had long ago resolved that when she was grown she would never, *never* go to bed again ; if *she* could have heard a voice cry, "Sleep no more," she would have received the mandate in a very different spirit from that which animated the breast of the Thane of Cawdor. " I was just funning, Aunt Mymee," she declared, with an embarrassed giggle.

Peace was restored. The supper, served in Granny's best china, progressed with that tranquillity and steadiness peculiar to well-cared-for cows and ancient dames.

When the last egg was eaten, the last bone picked, the *débris* cleared away, and pipes were restored, Aunt Mary announced with a perfect shower of grins that she " des natchelly honed arter (yearned for) one o' Aunt Em'ly's tales."

Aunt Em'ly modestly declined " ter put fo'th any lil triflin' tale twell Miss Boogarry done tole sumpin wuth w'iles."

When Big Angy felt disposed to talk she needed no urging ; when she was in a mood for silence she heeded no importunity. This evening was one of her times for communicating, so, without any make-believe bashfulness or preliminary angling for compliments, she told the story of " The Snake's Daughters."

It was a very long story as she told it, and plentifully garnished with original comments, given in language that set at
nought all known rules for the personal pronoun, first person
singular. The nominative " me " and objective "I " of her
discourse added nothing to its quality and much to its quantity,
so they may well be omitted here, and only the sum and
substance of it all be given as Tow Head repeated it in after
years to other children :—

There was once an old witch who had a snake for a husband,
and even he was too good for her. She lived in a lodge by
a stream, and he under a rock hard by, and nobody but the
moon and the owl knew that they were married. In time
they had two daughters beautiful in the face as the most
beautiful of maidens, but with cold and scaly bodies. The
daughters played on the land and in the water, happily and
without knowing that they were not as other girls ; but their
mother knew, and if strangers appeared, covered them closely
with fine garments curiously embroidered. When they were
grown no man could see them and not love them, no man
could touch them and not hate them, so their lovers all became
enemies, and they raged furiously and came to hate all human
kind. No man took them to his lodge, therefore, in accordance
with their father's advice, they married snakes. After that
they laid all day in the sun and smiled, that they might entrap
the unwary, for each had a poisoned arrow given her by her
father on her wedding night—an arrow endowed with such
deadly cunning and power that it never failed to kill whosoever
it was aimed at, and always flew back to its owner's hand after
it had done its deadly work. Each had also a bow strung with
her mother's hair. This bow told her who was coming, and,
if he was a charmed man, the one spot where he could be
fatally struck. Now, this was very terrible, so after awhile all
knew of the witch's daughters, and hated them exceedingly
because of their hapless victims. Everything in the land went

on very badly, for when one place was shunned the snake's daughters secretly removed to a new one. Finally, the king of the bees went by. He was ruler of the trees as well as the bees, so those bows of wood dared give no warning of his approach, nor tell his name and title, for he held up his hand before them in token of silence. The strings of the bows hissed like serpents, but that told nothing but that an enemy was by.

When the sisters saw him they smiled and beckoned.

He approached, smiling in turn. Instantly they fitted the venomed arrows to the strings, but the bows bent like grass and the arrows fell. Hissing louder than the bowstrings, the sisters picked up the arrows and flung them like darts.

The strange, ugly man before them laughed till the sky and the earth rang with the sound, and caught the arrows in his hands.

When the sisters saw their weapons were powerless they tried to fly, but were given no time to get away, for the king had a stone nose, and the breath from it worked enchantment. He breathed on the arrows, and flung them at the sisters. They were pierced to the heart, but did not die as women do. From their wounded bodies came no blood, only water, stagnant and dark. As it poured out they fell. Their fall was heavy, the ground shook under them, the trees near by staggered as if their roots were loosened from the soil. Where the sisters fell they laid. No one buried them, but no matter, they did not harm the air. Their father and mother did not bury them because they did not know where they were, and did not find them for a long time ; neither did their husbands ; but the birds did, and the wolves and the worms ; nevertheless, none of these creatures molested them. The reason was, the sisters were changed into stone by their own arrows. Many have seen them, and know this to be true.

Granny nodded approvingly.

"Dat am er mighty fine tale," she said, turning her face

from the fire to her friend, and puffing tobacco-smoke about her like incense.

" I seso, too," chimed in Aunt Mymee, with animation. "Am dat de tale yo' laid off ter tell arter frost 'way back yondeh in de summer-time, Miss Boogarry ? "

" Dat him," replied Big Angy. " De Lawd know me tell no tale de lil booggers is froze up in de ground. I de one dat know hit gwine ter bring bad luck ef so dey hyeah me tell tales on um." [1]

" Dey is cu'us 'bout dat. I ain't e'er tell no tales befo' fros', my own se'f," Mymee answered.

" Now it's Aunt Em'ly's turn," cried Tow Head, impatiently. "Do go on, Aunt Em'ly, that's a good, sweet aunty. Mamma · may call me before you're through, if you don't hurry."

Aunt Em'ly smiled delightedly, but hesitated.

" Hit's er sorter, kinder skeery tale, honey," she said. " Ef so be dat yo' git all wuhkt (worked) up an' a-cryin,' yo' ma gwine ter lick ole Em'ly."

" 'Twon't hurt but a minute, if she does," said Tow Head, with an air of knowledge born of experience.

"Missey's des a-projeckin'," said Granny, jealous of the family. " Dat chile ain't nurr yit feel de weight ob no han' in de worl'. Huh! I t'ink I see Miss Agnes a-whuppin' chilluns. Miss Agnes ain't come o' no wuhkin' (working) fambly. She ain't got no strenk (strength) in huh lil wristes (her little wrists)."

Tow Head had neither dignity nor family pride. Her mother's adherence to the precepts of Solomon she considered a joke. Her answer to Granny was a meaning smile and a closing of her eyelids.

" Hurry up, Aunt Em'ly," she said. " Tell an old, old story."

---

[1] This tale appears to be of Red Indian origin. The habit of never telling stories till after the first frost is widely spread among the American-Indians, and certainly never could have come from Africa.—CHARLES GODFREY LELAND.

"Tell nurr ole tale!" exclaimed Aunt Em'ly, valiantly sup-
pressing a chuckle at Granny's discomfiture. "Well, de laws
he'p my soul! Ef yo' ain't the beatenest chile. I s'pect yo'
reckon ole Aunt Em'ly des mek out o' ole tales, des kase she
ole she own se'f. I lay I done tell yo' mo' a'ready den yo' lil
membunce kin tote (memory can carry). Howsomedevvah, er
tale I done promiss an' er tale I gwine ter tell, an' hit gwine
ter run 'bout the aspums (aspens), wid de 'count ob de way dat
hit happen dat dey be 'way up de hillside 'stid o' down in de
sandbank whah dey use ter be. H-m! h-m!—whut wuz I
gwinter say next? 'Pears lak I done fegit sumpin. Lemme
scratch dis hyeah ole noggin (head) an' see ef hit be so I kin
scratch up dat 'count o' dem trees an' de bee-king. Uh-huh!
—oh, yes!—*now* I got um! Hit bin dishaways :—In dem ole
times dat wuz such a mighty mich (much) betteh den ourn am
ebbeh gwine foh ter dare foh to set up ter be, de ole bee-king wuz
a-rampagin' eround an' car'in' t'ings wid er mighty high han'.
Co'se he wuz! Wuzn't he a-ownin' all de woods an' all de
bees—honey-bees, bummle-bees, sweat-bees an' all ; an' wuzn't
dey des miles an' miles ob de woodses in dem days, an' all de
trees in de woodses des chock-full an' a-runnin' ober wid de
finest kind o' honey? W'y, my chilluns, de hunks ob de
comb wuz ez big round ez de top o' er cawn-bastet (corn-
basket), an' dem lil vidgins (divisions) o' de comb wuz ez long
ez dis hyeah fingeh, an' 'most ez big round ez one o' dem
chaney teacups yondeh. De ole bee-king wuz mighty high-
steppin' an' proud 'bout dat time, an' he do des prezackly ez
he a-mineter (precisely as he was of a mind to). Ef he feel lak
fillin' ole holler tree wid honey-bees, he fill um ; ef he don't, he
lef' um foh de squir'ls. Now, some de trees, mo' special de
cottonwoods, don't lak dat, don't lak dat '*tall*, but dey know
'nough, bress Moses! dat dey don't say nuttin'. One time,
dough, w'en de lil willers, an' de lil young cottonwoods, an' de
cattails, an' de flags down anigh de ribber (river), git a-chattin'

'bout dis an' dat an' turr t'ing, dem cattails 'low hit kine o'
quare dat w'en the woods all round is des a-bustin' wid honey,
an' some o' de trees got much ez two swa'ms in um, hit kine
o' quare dat none o' de ole willers an' cottonwoods got no
swa'ms whatsomedevveh. Dat rile de cottonwoods, an' dey
fling up dey leabes lak es ef hit gwine ter rain, an' dey mek
lak dey gwine ter tek up foh dey 'lations ; but de willers dey
mo' careful, an' dey sorter simper out, 'Hu-ush, hu-ush,' ter de
cottonwoods, an' so all hands let de 'miration o' dem mischevyous flags an' cattails pass by. Well ! so hit go dat time, but
toreckly dem ornery, gabblin' weeds tuk de text ergin. 'Whut
de bee-king got 'gin yo' daddies an' mammies dat they don't
hab no bees an' honey ? ' dey say. Dat rile dem young cottonwoods, an' dey des gwine ter say sumpin sassy, w'en de willers
dat wuz ol'er an' not nigh so high-strung (high-tempered), dey
simper out ergin, 'Hu-ush, hu-ush ! ' des lak de win' wuz a-
stirrin' in dey leabes, kase day don't want dat de flags an' de
cattails hyeah um. Dat pass by, an' dey all tork 'bout dis an'
dat, an' lis'en at de buhds (birds) gwine, 'Cheer-up ! cheer-up !
peep ! peep ! ' ez dey mek dey reddymints foh baid (prepara-
tions for bed). Toreckly de flags an' de cattails at hit ergin.
' Am yo' folks so mighty onsound in de bahk dat dey kyarn't
be trustid ter hole no honey ? Is dey maggitty, ur w'at ? ' say
dem pesterin' weeds. At dat dem forrid an' biggitty young
cottonwoods des tuhn deyse'f loose, dey did, an' my lan' ! sech
busemints dey 'wuz nebber de likin's ob sence de worl' wuz
made. Dey 'buse de ole king, dey say dey 'spise the bees, dey
ain't got no use foh honey, an' sidesen dat, heap mo', I dunno
des wut. Den w'en dey git dat off dey mine, dey whirl in an'
gib de flags an' de cattails one good tounge-lashin' foh dey
imp'ence in axin' ef the ole cottonwoods bin er lot o' no-'count
ole half-strainers. Oh, dey des lit inter dem flags an' cattails !
—'n' sarve um right too, fur ez dat go, but dey ain't bin strong
in de haid (head), dem young cottonwoods ain't, w'en dey

don't lef' ole bee-king out o' dat disco'se. Co'se de flags an'
de cattails tole 'im all dat de cottonwoods say, an' ar plenty mo'
dey ain't say *tall*—dat allus de way wid de tattlin' o' dat kine
o' trash. Well, den ! old king, he come down dar, des a-rippin'
an' a-snortin'. He 'low he gwine ter peterfy dat crowd—an' de
Good Lawd know dat he c'd do dat berry same, ef so be he
could a-cotch um, but dat de pint ! Dem young trees mighty
soople, an' dey seen 'im a-comin'. Dey run, dey did—run lak
de Ole Boy (Devil) wuz arter um, an' he run lak de Ole Boy
hisse'f, twell he chase um plum outen ribber-botton an' 'cross
de perarer (prairie), an' up de lil hills, clean ter de flat place 'twixt

"HE RUN LAK DE OLE BOY HISSE'F."

de lil hills an' de big ones. Dar he lef' um, kase dat wuz out o'
his kyentry, an' mighty close ter Tundah (Thunder) Land.[1]
Dar he lef' um, an' dar dey is ; but, po' t'ings ! dey ain't ne'er
grow no mo'. Dey wuz skeered outen dey growth, an' dey
wuz skeered twell dey bahk tuhn pale. Mo'n dat—dey wuz
skeered twell dey leabes trimmle, trimmle, des lake de wind
wuz a-blowin' mungs um, w'en de win' ain't blowin', not de
least lil teenty, tinty bref. Dat the way dey do yit, all de
time. Dey don't git dey colour back, ter dis day, in dey bahk,

---

[1] Thunder-land is apparently of Algonkin-Indian origin.—C. G. L.

an' dey trimmle, trimmle, night an' day. Big wind, lil wind, no wind 'tall, dey trimmle, trimmle, trimmle."

" How did their name get changed to 'aspens,' Aunt Em'ly ? "

" Oh, go 'long, chile ! Hit *bin* change, dat all we 'bleeged ter know. Ef some folks change dey name an' dey ain't no 'miration 'bout hit, whyso kyarn't some trees ? Ef yo' bound ter know, ax Miss Boogarry. W'en I fust knowed 'er, she wuz call Angelique Beaumais, now she Miss Boogarry. 'Splain dat, den I 'splain how cottonwood tuhn aspum."

Tow Head looked at Big Angy.

Big Angy looked at the fire, and seemed about as likely to make satisfactory explanations as a totem pole.

The youngster gave up in despair, and turned her mind to actions instead of names.

" That was a beautiful story," she said, approvingly, " but are you quite, *quite* sure it's all true ? My mamma read to me once that aspen leaves tremble because our Saviour's cross was made of wood from that tree, and the poor thing has trembled ever since that first Good Friday."

" Like ez not, like ez not," said Aunt Em'ly, with the magnanimity of one great mind towards another. " I ain't 'sputin' de word ob him dat mek yo' ma's book ; but ain't yo' fegit, honey, dat dese aspums ob mine bin *young* aspums, an' dat un dat bin mek inter de cross must a-bin er ole un, kase hit 'u'd tek er mighty big tree ter mek the cross dat hilt up de Good Lawd A'mighty."

This seemed reasonable to Tow Head. She thought about it a long time. The flames roared in the chimney, the aunties talked, smoked, and sang, but she interrupted them no more. Presently the flames twisted into snakes, the blackened rafters swayed like trees in a hurricane, the bee-king came out from behind a tall cupboard and gave her head a push that nearly threw her out of Aunt Mymee's lap.

"Ef dat chile ain't drapped off ter sleep, an' I ain't noduss hit !" exclaimed Aunt Mymee.

The snakes, the trees, the king, all vanished.

"I wasn't asleep ; indeed I was not."

"All right, honey ; but I'll des tote yo' up ter de house so dat in case yo' do git er mine foh er nap (a mind for a nap), de baid'll be handy."

So Tow Head was carried away. As she and her "charmer" went toward "The House," Aunt Mymee sang this song, which the child considered entirely too summery for such frosty weather :—

"De peaches am ripe by de ole souf wall.
O, honey, don't yo' hyeah me?
Dat yal-ler gal, she shuffle an' call.
O, honey, don't yo' hyeah me?

O, come ter de haht (heart) dat lub yo' so!
Come, honey, come ! Do yo' hyeah me?
O, come to the haht that lub yo' so !
Come, honey, come ! Do yo' hyeah me?

I tuck holt de limb ter grab yo' er peach.
O, honey, don't yo' hyeah me?
De plumpes' ones, dey growed out o' reach.
O, honey, don't yo' hyeah me?

O, come ter de haht dat lub yo' so !
Come, honey, come ! Do yo' hyeah me?
O, come ter de haht dat lub yo' so!
Come, honey, come ! Do yo' hyeah me?

Hit's des lak dis all troo my life.
O, honey, don't yo' hyeah me?
De gal I want won't be my wife.
O, honey, don't yo' hyeah me?

O, come ter de haht that lub yo' so !
Come, honey, come ! Do yo' hyeah me?
O, come ter de haht dat lub yo' so !
Come, honey, come ! Do yo' hyeah me?" .

"Don't say any more about honey," whimpered Tow Head, sleepily. "I'm afraid the bee-king will get after us."

II.

CONCERNING A GOOSE, A BLUEBIRD, AND OTHER FOWLS OF THE AIR.

THE evening was cold and gloomy, so much so that Granny, when she went to the door to welcome Aunt Em'ly, remarked that the night was dark as the north-west corner of a nigger's pocket, and that she smelt snow in the air.

Aunt Em'ly stumbled in, puffing and blowing.

"De wild geese is a-kickin' up er turrible ruction," she panted. "Dey's a-headin' souf ez hahd (hard) ez dey kin flap, an' a-squallin' wuss'n er yaller-laig rooster wid er litter o' pups a-chasin' 'im. Dey's a-flyin' low too, an' dat means fallin' wedder, ez well ez de way dey go mean cole (cold)."

"Dat's de sakid (sacred) troof," assented Granny. "Oh! I knowed hit wuz a-comin', kase I seed dem ole win'-splittehs (wind-splitter)—the name in the vernacular of a species of long, lean hog that ranges half-wild, and feeds on the mast in the oak woods of Missouri), kyarin' (carrying) straws ter dey beds, two, free days back. Sidesen dat, de breas'-bone ob de goose we hed yestiddy, hit wuz all motly wid w'ite spots. Co'se, ef de wedder promuss fair dat bone u'd a-bin fa'r, an' ef hit promuss rain dat bone u'd a-bin dahk an' motly. Dat bone say, 'snow' *plain!*—an' snow hit boun' ter come."

"Hit mighty quare 'bout dem gooses," giggled Aunt Mary in the faces of her serious elders.

"Whut mighty quare?" inquired Granny, severely.

"How dem gooses is good foh ter tell de wedder, ef so dey be

28

libbin', ur so dey be daid. Libbin', or daid, dey tells de wedder
—pintedly."

"So dey does, so dey does," agreed Aunt Em'ly, taking out
her pipe and lighting it by a coal she picked from the hearth
in her bare fingers. "Gooses is smart. Dey 'zerves er heap o'
credick dey don't ne'er git. Den ergin," she continued reflectively, "dey ack des ez foolish ez de folks dat name arter um,
an' den dey git dey come-uppunce (deserts) des lak folks, too.
I wuz tuhnin' er case lak dat in my mine ez I wuz a-joggin' thu
de bresh dis ebenin'."

"Tell it, Aunt Em'ly, tell it right now ! "

It was Tow Head, who spoke from the billowy depths of
Granny's feather bed.

Aunt Em'ly turned in the direction of the voice, and looked
at the small damsel with a quizzical eye.

"Whutcher bin a-doin', missey ? " she asked. "I lay dey's
er peach-tree lim' ripe foh er lil gal 'bout yo' size up ter de house."

" 'Taint nuttin wuss'n tumblin' inter de big watteh-buckets
dis time," said Granny. "Hit mought easy a-bin wuss'n dat,
dough ; some folks, dey rampage round so. Ef yo' know er
tale 'bout *good* chilluns, Aunt Em'ly, hit won't huht none dat
yo' tell hit, w'iles *dis* chile's close am a-dryin'."

"Dat ain't my tale, Aunt Jinny. De tale I hab in han's am
de tale of de meddlin', mischevyous goose dat done got change
inter er chicken-louse 'pun 'count o' he foolishness."

"Tell um, Aunt Em'ly, tell um ! " cried Aunt Mymee, from
her seat by the fire, as she shook and turned a damp little red
flannel dress and anxiously felt of its tucks and gathers.

THE STORY OF THE BAD GOOSE.

" Ef 'twuz er goose dat clumb evvurwhurs dat hits mammy
say hit mustn't, ef 'twuz er goose dat putt 'lasses in hits daddy's
slippers, an' waked up de baby-gooses, an' slipped hits gran'ma's
specs, an' busted um an' let all de bran outen de big pin-cushom

in de spare room, an' dug de eyes outen hits wax doll dat wuz brung unter hit clean fum Ole Feginny, Ise des a-honin' (yearning) ter know de awful jedge*mint* dat come 'pun dat goose."

There was an uneasy stirring among the feathers, but nobody said anything, so Aunt Em'ly proceeded to tell the fate of the goose.

" Wunst, in de ole times, dey wuz er fine ole wild goose dat riz er heap o' goslin's, an' dem goslin's, dey wuz all good an' mind dey ma (their mother) ceppin one, but dat one, mine yo', wuz turribler den er whole fambly o' des middlin' bad goslin's.   He des wuz er limb o' Satan, dat he wuz !   He gobble up all de greens ; he flounce in de watteh twell hit wuz all muddy an' riley, froo an' froo, an' he bite de odeh goslin's w'en he ma wuzn't a-lookin'. Oh, he des kyar on (behaved) shameful ! Bimeby, w'en he grow up, he wuz de berry wussest t'ing dat e'er flap er wing o'er de ma'sh. De geese, dey 'spise 'im ; de cranes, dey 'spise 'im ; de frogs, dey 'spise 'im ; de brants an' de ducks an' de pelicans, de snakes an' de wuhms an' de mud-turkles, dey all 'spise 'im, too. De mud-hens, dey ain't noduss 'im, at de fust, kase he got de sense ter lef um 'lone. Bimeby, he git so biggitty (conceited) dat he 'gin ter peck um on de shins an' touzle up dey haid-fedders. Dat show he suttinly wuz er fool, kase dem mud-hens, dey got er ole granny w'at wuz er cunjerer an' lib down, *down*, DOWN, in de deep yaller mud undehneat' de watteh.   Well, dem mud-hens, dey don't want ter mek no sturvince (disturbance), so dey say, sorter easy-lak, ' Misteh Goosey-Gander, we des plain folks, we ain't no jokers, so des please lef us 'lone.' Dey des let on lak dey t'ink he wuz jokin', kase dey t'ink dat mek hit easy foh he ter 'pologise an' ax dey pardin. But hit don't. Hit mek 'im mo' sassy. He bite um 'gin, dis time on dey necks an' dey laigs, an' gib dey wings er pull, too. Oh, he hit an' he bit whatsomedevveh he c'd ketch a-hold !

"Den de ole witch comed up, des a-r'arin' an' a-pitchin' (scolding and storming).

"' Whacheh doin' unter my gran'-chilluns ? ' she holler out dataway dat it fa'r mek de watteh bile up. ' I l'arn yo' mannehs, Misteh Young Goosey-Gander.'

" Wid dat she s-s-s-spit on he back !

" *Dat se'f same minnit* he 'gan ter wizzle (shrink) an' wizzle. Fust, he wizzle up ter de size ob er duck ; den he wizzle ter de size ob er croppy-fish ; den he wizzle ter de size ob er baby-turkle ; den he wizzle ter de size ob er sand-fly ; den he wizzle ter de size ob er chicken-louse ; den he *wuz* er chicken-louse—nuttin mo'.

"' Dár now ! ' say de ole cunjer-witch, ' fum dis out, yo' gwine ter be peck at an' chase up an' down by de chicken's bill, stiddier doin' de chasin' an' werryin' yo'se'f.'

" Dat wut happen sho 'nuff. W'en yo' see de mud-hens come out o' de watteh an' pick, pick, picketty wid dey bill un'-neat' dey wings an' down in dey j'ints dey am a-chasin' dat se'f same grey goose."

When the proper compliments had been administered to Aunt Em'ly by her little circle, Granny, with a look toward the occupant of her bed, announced that she bethought herself of a bluebird story wherein was set forth the rewards bestowed by Providence on " dem dat' 'haves deyse'f putty an' nice ".

Tow Head cared nothing for innuendoes, but she cared a great deal for stories, so with a cheerful air she stated that she was " just dying to hear the story of the bluebird." So were the aunties, as they hastened to add.

Granny, quite sure of the sympathy of her audience, told the following tale of—

How the Bluebird came by his Colour.

" Hit mek me plum sick w'en I see er norty chile a-flingin' rocks at de putty lil bluebuhd, kase dat buhd bin fix up out o' er piece ob de Good Lawd's own heb'n. Deed he is, hit's de plain troof, and I gwine ter tell all de fax an' de mattehs ob de case. Dishaway de way dat putty buhd git dat fine blue coat o' hisen, stiddi er dat ole grey un dat he use ter w'ar. One time dey wuz er man dat wuz meaner'n gyar-broth (soup made of the gar-fish), pizoned at dat ! an', in co'se, he pick out de like-liest gal in de kyentry, an' git 'er, too ! Well den ! He des ack skannelous all de time, an' de older he grow de wuss he ack, twell he git at de pint ter dribe dat po' 'ooman an' huh (her) two lil chilluns plum off de place an' out o' de township. Den, de po' 'stractid critteh, she hundertuck ter git back ter huh own folks. Ter do dat she 'bleeged ter go thu de turr'blest lot o' woods dat grow dat t'ick dat yo' kyarn't skursely see yo' hand befo' yo' face in de daytime, an' w'en hit come night—good lan' !—hit bin mo' brackeh (blacker) in dar den de eenside ob er witch's pottit (pocket) in de daid ob de cloudy night. Well suz ! dem misfortnit crittehs, dey mek out foh ter go good ways. Den dey git lost. Den de chilluns say—

" ' Oh, mammy, gimme sumpin ter eat. I *so* hongry ! '

" But she ain't got nuttin, an' she 'bleeged ter say so. She a-honin' arter vittles huh own se'f twell she fit ter drap, mine yo', but she ain' say nuttin 'bout dat.

" Arter w'iles, dey say—

" ' Oh, mammy, I *so* dry, gimme des one gode (gourd) full ob watteh ! '

" She 'bleeged ter say she ain't got no watteh. She bin a-wantin' er sup o' watteh dis long time huh own se'f, but she ain' say nuttin 'bout dat.

" Den dey all fall to an' dey hunt watteh an' dey hunt watteh, an' dey hunt an' dey hunt, but dey don't find none. Dey look in all de gullies an' 'long side de lil risins, but stream dey don't see, spring dey don't see. Arter dat dey hunt berries. Heap o' briers scratch um, but dey don't find one berry.

" Den dey set down pun de ground an' cry.

" Bimeby, dey hyeah sumpin. Dey look up sorter joyful.

Oh! dey 'd be proud ter see anybody 'way out dar whah dey a-dyin' in de wilderness.

"'Taint nuttin, dat am, 'taint nuttin 'cep' dat lil grey buhd a-peepin' down fum de tree.'

"Dey all hang dey haid (head) an' cry des lak de rain wuz fallin' down.

"Hih! hih!—shuh! (be quiet)—wut dat?

"Dat se'f same lil buhd.

"Dis time dey take noduss dat hit say, 'Come! come! come!'

"Hit say dat in de sweetes' way, an' hit look right inter dat po' (poor) mammy's eye.

"'Come! come! come!' dar 'twuz ergin' (again).

"'Come on, chilluns,' de mammy say, a-jumpin' up an' a-grabbin' dem chillun's hands. 'Ise gwine ter foller ef he lead.'

"Seein' dat, de buhd struck out, a-hoppin' 'long mighty slow, kase dem folks wuz weak an' hit know dat. Hop, hop, hop, he go an' 'long dey foller arter. Hop, hop; foller, foller. Bimeby all han's, dey come ter de puttiest lil spring a-gugglin' an' a-dribblin' out. Dey drink an' dey drink; den, hop, hop, ergin; foller, foller, ergin. Den de 'ooman an' de chilluns see heaps o' paw-paws ¹ hangin' ripe on de trees. Den po' starvin' crittehs eats dey fill o' de paw-paws.

"Den de night come on.

"De buhd ain't fergit um. Hit mek out ter lead um ter er big ole tree wid de limbs startin' out mighty low down so dey could climb hit, kase dey wuz mons'us 'fraid ob de wolves an' turr varmints. Dey clum dat tree, des ez I tell yo', an' w'en dey reach de crotch dey stop dar an' go right off ter sleep, kase dey wuz plum tuckered (worn) out.

"Nex' day dat buhd feed um an' watteh (water) um, same lak dey bin cattle. Nex' day arter dat, same t'ing. Nex' day arter dat, same t'ing, an' so hit go, day come in, day go out. Hit

---

¹ A kind of wild fruit, somewhat resembling the banana in taste.

tek keer o' um in de night-times, too. In co'se, hit do dat
a-pintin' out de trees dey could h'ist (hoist) deyse'fs inter.

" Well, at de last, dat 'ooman an' de two chilluns com thu de
woods an' git ter dey kinfolks, an' de kinfolks dey mek de
bigges' kine ob er 'miration o' er um, an' all dey troubles, dey
wuz at er eend, an' seein' dat, de buhd flewd off an' nobody
kyarn't stop um.

" But dat wuzn't all ! No, suh !—De Good Lawd He seed
dat whole bizniz an' hit tickle 'Im so, dat right off, He change
dat good lil buhd's feddehs fum de dimmes' kine o' grey ter de
bluest kine o' blue, des de same ez de sky, an' dat yo' kin prube
ef yo' look at de sky an' look at dat buhd, tuhns (turn) an'
tuhns erbout."

With waiting a second Tow Head forestalled the comments
of her elders by stating that Granny's story was as nice as the
one about " The Babes in the Woods " that mama knew. The
robins in that story saw two little children die in the woods
and buried them " bea-u-tifully " in leaves.

" Huh ! betteh a-feeded um an' a-fetched um fo'th a-libbin'.
Some buhds, des lak some folks, is fools. De Good Lawd ain't
colour up no robins."

" He did colour a thrush's eggs—grandma said so," cried Tow
Head, nettled at Granny's tone, and determined to tell something to equal the story of Bluebird's reward. " That's the way
the first Easter eggs came."

" Huccome dem yeaster-aigs urrways (otherwise) den fum
a-dyein' ob um wid ingun-peelins, ur logwood-bahk, ur green
oats ? " asked Granny, rolling her eyes around the group to
intimate that she was merely giving her pet an opportunity to
" show off," and was not really ignorant of the legend referred
to.

" Why, don't you know, Granny, don't you, really ? "
questioned Tow Head, in perfect good faith.

" Yo' reckon I know all de tales in de worl' ? "

"I thought you did, but if you don't I can tell you this one. It is a thrush story. The thrush, you know, had a nest very near the place where the cross was set up that Good Friday when our Jesus was crucified, and—oh! Granny—the poor little bird grieved and mourned so that her four little eggs turned black, quite black. They stayed so until Easter morning, but then, when the dear Lord rose again, the little bird burst out singing and sang so beautifully that the angels themselves stopped to listen. And, oh! when the song was finished and she looked at the poor little black eggs, they had turned silver and gold and crimson and purple. Wasn't that grand, Granny? and aren't you glad it happened? If it had not, you know, you could never have had the fun of dyeing my eggs for me," added Tow Head, with naïve egotism.

"Dat suttinly would a-bin er mons'us pity," said Granny, gravely, and Tow Head wondered why the rest were so rude as to laugh at her.

"I know of another bird, too," said Tow Head, anxious to divert Granny's attention and save her feelings. "A wasp-bird, Granny. I'll tell you about him if you like."

"Des yo' git dese hyeah close on fust, honey," said Aunt Mymee, rising and going toward the bed. "Dey's dry now, an' pray de Lawd yo' flannin dress ain't swunk twell yo' kyarn't git eenside o' hit."

The raiment was adjusted. Tow Head, meanwhile, noting the fit of each piece in anxious silence. She heaved a sigh of relief when her frock was buttoned. "It didn't shrink!" she exclaimed, gleefully.

"Hit swunk de wedth o' my two fingehs," Aunt Mymee answered.

"Oh, I guess not! I think I've grown that much since tea time. Mamma says I grow like Jonah's gourd. Now for the story, Granny. Big Angy told it me, that day you took me to her house and we had such a good time."

"Er good time ! Dellaws ! des lissen ter de chile. Dat wuz
de day Miss Boogarry's big brown slut a-most bit de laig off o'
huh foh foolin' wid de young pups. Huh ! dat *wuz* er good
time, sholy."

" So it was. Angy tied my leg up in a big handful of brown
sugar and put a beautiful piece of red calico outside of that, and
she let me have the prettiest pup in my lap when we went into
the house. Besides that, she whistled a tune for me on her
eagle-bone whistle, she gave my two hands full of prawleens
and told me to eat them all, and, when I was through crying,
she told me the story of the wasp being changéd into an oriole.
O, let us go to see her again, right away, Granny ! "

" Nemmine, nemmine ! Ef yo' want yo' laig gnawed inter
sassidge-meat we kin git hit done nigher home. Le's (let us)
hab de tale, dough."

Tow Head immediately seated herself on Aunt Mymee's
knee and, with a close imitation of big Angy's manner, which
sent Aunt Mary into a dark corner in a perfect spasm of giggles,
and caused the other three to choke on their tobacco-smoke
more than once, she told this story, which is best reproduced in
a dialect more nearly akin to the King's English than Madame
Bougareau's :—

" When the big black witch from Thunderland came sweeping over hill and hollow to fight the witch of the bright Corn
Country, the world rang with the sound of her terrible voice
and the trees bowed themselves to the ground in terror. In her
anger she danced, she whirled, she whistled. She smote the
trees, she trampled the prarie-flowers, she scattered the corn-in-
the-ear as if it had been blades of grass plucked by a child. She
fought the witch of the Corn Country, striking her fiercely.
She would have prevailed and destroyed the witch and her
country utterly had not a wasp, flung from his nest hung from
the bough of an ancient crab-apple tree, stung her in the eye,
so that her tears fell, and then she became calm and weak

as the weakest of old women. Then it was that the witch of the bright Corn Country was able to chase her back to her own land.

"Now the witch of the Corn Country was not forgetful, nor ungrateful. She took her benefactor, the wasp, in her hand and besought him to ask for whatsoever he desired, promising, at the same time, that it should be granted him. Immediately he answered that he and his wife wished, exceedingly, not to be wasps, whom every one hated, but birds, well-beloved by all.

" At once the wasp and his wife had their wish and became orioles ; but, because some of the wasp nature was left in them, they did not build their nests as other birds do, but made grey pockets to hold their eggs, which from afar looked like wasps' nests ; and as they did, so do their children to this day."

" Dat's er fine tale," said Granny, glad of an excuse to talk and laugh a little. " I 'clar' ter gracious, ef yo' keep up dat lick, yo' gwine ter beat yo' po' ole Granny all holler, honey."

"Sez me, dat chile am gwine ter tek de bizniz ob yo' folks right out o' yo' han's ef yo' don't hustle yo'se'fs," cried Aunt Mary, strangling the last giggle.

Aunt Mymee chuckled and made a tight belt of her arms round Tow Head's waist, but paid no mock compliments. She kept silent a long time, musing, doubtless, on the strange adventures of the various birds mentioned during the evening, for she suddenly began to sing of a " speckled " bird and the "Ole Boy." Her song was new to the child, but evidently familiar to her coloured sisters, for they at once joined in the queer exclamatory chorus :—

"Speckle buhd a-settin' on de ole daid lim'.
　　Hoodah !
Look mighty peart an' young an' slim.
　　Hoodah, hoodah, hum !
Look out lil buhd, de Ole Boy come.
　　Hoodah !
Fiah in he eye, he look mighty glum.
　　Hoodah, hoodah, hum

Look out, lil buhd, he gwine foh ter shoot !
           Hoodah !
Flap yo' wings an' git up an' scoot.
           Hoodah, hoodah, hum !
Oh, sinneh, sinneh, dat des lak you !
           Hoodah !
De ole Bad Man, he gotter gun, too.
           Hoodah, hoodah, hum !
He shoot yo' front an' he shoot yo' back,
           Hoodah !
Down yo' go, plum daid, ker-smack !
           Hoodah, hoodah, hum !
Run, po' niggah, run an' run.
           Hoodah !
Debbil, big debbil, a-aimin' he gun.
           Hoodah, hoodah, hum !
Run, run, run ; run, run, run !
           Hoodah !
Run, run, run ; *run*, RUN, RUN !
           Hoodah, hoodah, hum !

BIG DEBBIL.

III.

BILLS OF FARE—THE CROWS—LITTLE DOVE'S SON.

When Tow Head dashed into the cabin in advance of Aunt Mymee, a delightful odour greeted her nostrils. She knew it well. It was the fragrance of prawleens,[1] that compound of New Orleans molasses, brown sugar, chocolate and butter, boiled together and enriched just before leaving the fire with the meats of hickory nuts, hazel nuts, pecans, almonds, and the never-neglected goober [2] dear to the sweet taste of every child, adult creole and darkey.

" Prawleens ! " exclaimed the maid, delightedly, as Big Angy poured the bubbling mass from a little glazed iron pot, usually kept sacred for the boiling of partridge eggs, into a buttered pan. " Prawleens !—and nothing in the world is as good."

Big Angy showed all her white teeth. " Punkin-sass is betteh," she said, slowly. " De punkin-sass dat ain't got no stow (store) sweet'nin', mais am biled down clost (close) wid watteh-million (water-melon) juice."

" Chitt'lin's [3] is betteh," amended Granny.

" Schewed cawn (stewed corn) t'ickened wid dried buffler-meat (buffalo-meat) pounded inter dust am de t'ing dat mek de mouf dribble," cried Aunt Em'ly.

---

[1] *Pralines.* Burnt almonds. So called from a Duke de Praslin of the time of Louis XIV., who is said to have invented them.

[2] The *goober* (*arachis hypogea*) is the pea-nut or ground-nut, which still preserves the name (*gūba*) by which it is known all over Africa ; even in Cairo.

[3] *Chitlings*, an old English word.

" Shoh, honey l shoh ! " exclaimed Aunt Mary.   " 'Pear lak
yo' done fegit bake 'possum an' sweet-taters wid coon gravy."

" I stick ter de cawn," answered Aunt Em'ly, with decision ;
" dough I ain't kick up my heels at 'possum.   Torkin' 'bout
cawn 'minds me, Miss Boogarry, dat I seen yo' bilin' an' dryin'
er heap las' summeh.   Wut yo' done wid um, seein' dat yo'
ain' got no suller (cellar) ? "

" *Cache* um."

" Cash um ?   De Good Lawd !   How ? "

" W'en," said Angy, with dignity, " de roas'in'-yeahs (roasting-
ears) is in de milk, me git um, bile um, dig de grains offen de
cob wid lil stick, spread um on de big rush mats me mek'
twell dey dry lak sand, den me dig hole in de ground—*deep*,
putt in de mats all round, den tek de cawn, putt um in de big
bag mek outen de eenside bahk o' de linn-tree, fling dat bag
in de pit, putt on de top mo' mat, shubble on de dirt, smack
um down flat.   Dat *cache*in'."

" Uh-huh !   uh-huh !   dat de rale Injun way."

" Torkin' 'bout cawn," said Aunt Mymee, who had not
before spoken, " mek me fetch up de membunce ob how hit
come out dat de crows, dat use ter bin ez w'ite ez er tame
goose, wuz all tuhn brack."

" Tell dat tale !   Le's hab dat tale," said every one, eagerly,
for it was not always that Aunt Mymee would impart her
garnered knowledge.

" Hyeah 'tis," said Mymee.

" In de ole time, de crows wuz w'iter den de driben snow
a-stretchin' 'long de perarer (prairie).   Dey might a-bin dataway yit ef dey wuz boss by de stren'th o' dey haids stiddi er
de gnawin's o' dey stummicks.   Dishaway hit happun : De
time o' de yeah come 'round w'en dey hilt dey big meetin'
whah dey tork 'bout all dey done in de time back an' lay off
wut dey gwine ter do in de time for'a'd.   One day dey 'low
dey gwine ter hab er big bank-it."

"What's a bank-it?" asked Tow Head, promptly.

"Hit's de biggest an' de finest kine o' er big eatin'. Ise s'prise yo' don't 'membeh dat, kase I hyeah yo' ma read 'bout um unter yo', (unto you) des yistiddy."

"Oh, a banquet! I didn't know that anybody except the people that make poetry had 'em. Go on with the crows, please."

"De crows lay off ter had um," continued Aunt Mymee, avoiding a repetition of the doubtful word, "kase one de ole crows done fotch in word dat er strange 'ooman dat ain't got de sense ter hab out her skeer-crow wuz des got thu de plantin' ob her big fiel' ob cawn. Dey 'low dey ain't gwine ter leabe nuttin foh de cut-wuhm (worm), dey gwine ter tek de lastest grain. Dey didn't know dat 'ooman wuz de ole 'ooman ob er cunjer-man. Dat whurs dey miss hit. Dat cunjer-man wuz tell dat 'ooman er chahm (charm), an' ez she plant she say :—

> 'Sprout foh me,
> Come out foh me,
> Mek um drunk dat steal fum me.'

Dem crows ain't know all dat an' dey dat hongry dat dey ain't keerin' w'y dat fiel' ain't got no clacker-boy, no skeer-crow, no nuttin. Dey pick an' dey eat an' dey gobble an' dey stuff. Bimeby dey laigs 'gin ter trimmle an' dey eyes 'gin ter budge (bulge), an' dey fetch one squawk an' down dey flop right 'side de cawn hills. Den come de ole 'ooman fum ahine er big hick'ry stump, an' she ketch up all dem crows an' fling um inter er big splint bag, des lak dem bags dat Miss Boogarry done putt huh cawn inter. Den dat 'ooman, she mek 'er big pile ob sticks an' dry wood-moss an' grass an' leabes an' de lak o' dat, an' she fling de bag 'pun top o' dat, an' den she scrub two sticks tergedder an' strak 'er light an' set de pile afiah. Some dem sticks wuz green an' some wuz rotten—she wuz dat mad w'en she wuz pickin' um up dat she don't skursely know

ef she pickin' up limbs ur pickin' up snakes—so, arter de fust
flash, de fiah smoke an' don't buhn good. Dem crows wuz smoke
turr'ble, an' swinge *some* (somewhat singed), but dey wuzn't buhn
up. Dey lay dar twell dat slow, swomickey (smouldering) fiah
buhn er hole in de bag, an' by dat time dey wuz dat skeered dat
dey git o'er de drunk dat de chahm gib um. W'en dey see de
hole, flap ! smack ! whis-sp ! dey go thu an' fly clean off an' leabe
de ole 'ooman a-cussin'. My ! wuzn't dey glad dat dey all git
away ?—dat is, at de fust, w'en dey feel so good dat dey ain't all
brizzled inter coals ; but, bimeby, w'en de smoke git out o'
dey eyes, an' dey look dishaway, look dataway, at fust de one,
den de turr, den down at deyse'fs, dey dat 'shamed dat dey
kyarn't hold dey haids up. My ! my ! my ! dey all des ez
brack ez de bottom ob er soap-kittle. Den dey plume an' dey
preen an' dey pick an' dey wash ; dey ain't e'en 'bove tryin'
cunjerin' deys'fs, but 'tain't no use ; brack dey wuz, and brack
dey is, an' brack dey gwine ter be. Deah suz ! yo' all know
dat, kase ef yo' bile er crow-fedder wid pearlash an' sof'-soap,
yo' kin cut um all ter smidgins (bits), but yo' kyarn't bleach um
w'ite. Brimstun kyarn't do dat ! "

Aunt Mymee's adult friends made haste to compliment her
story as soon as she had finished, but Tow Head, contrary
to custom, had nothing to say. She was secretly distressed
at the suffering of the poor crows, having a very vivid reali-
sation of it owing to an experience of her own.

Once she had followed Granny into the " smoke-house," and
looked with great interest at the many rows of hams, shoulders,
and " sides " hanging from the rafters. While Granny was
making a great pile of corn cobs in the middle of the earthen
floor, Tow Head hid behind a barrel in a corner, and waited
for Granny to search for her. Granny did nothing of the
kind ; she poured a shovelful of coals on her cobs, and went
off after closing the heavy door behind her, and " reckoning
dat chile gone ter de house." Tow Head never forgot the

awful smoking she received before her cries brought rescue ; therefore she could not enjoy a vision of the strangling, smarting crows.

" Aunt Mymee," she said, by way of changing the subject, " why didn't you tell us, before you began the crow story, what is your favourite food ? "

"Wusser-meat," [1] answered Aunt Mymee, without a moment's hesitation.

" What is it made of, Aunt Mymee ?   What is a wusser ? "

" He's a heap o' t'ings," said Aunt Mymee, laughing. " He's livers an' lights an' kidneys an' hahts—all de pluck— biled down clost an' chopped fine, an' den cooled an' sliced up lak haid-cheese.   Oh ! hit mek my mouf dribble now."

" 'Tain' wusser, hit wassa, an' hit mus' hab dried churries in um," said Big Angy.

" Dried cherries !   How can you get the stones out ? "

" Don't take um out, missey.   Git de wild churry, de brack churry, an' pound um fine, an' putt dat wid de pluck—dat wassa, sho nuff."

Aunt Mymee privately thought it a pity to spoil so excellent a viand as wusser-meat by the addition of the bitter dust of wild cherries, but she did not so express herself ; what she said was, that she did not often eat wild cherries, that she had known of people who ate them falling at once into a deep sleep, especially if they were under the tree, and waking up to find that they had been " tricked " (conjured) by some unknown agency ; and, of course, if you did not know how you were tricked, nor who did it, you never could get free.

" Dat so ! dat so ! " exclaimed Big Angy, eagerly.   " Dat wut happen wid Lil Dove.   Me mammy tole me dat, long time back."

Everybody at this was clamorous for the story of Little Dove.

[1] *Wusser*, from the German *wurst*, or sausage.

" Hit mo de tale ob Lil Dove's son," amended Angy.

That would do just as well, everybody thought and said ; so, after Aunt Mary had handed round generous lumps of prawleens, Big Angy told this :—

In the old time there was a young maiden called Little Dove. She was the most beautiful maiden in all the land and had many lovers, but she cared for none of them, and refused to go with them or accept their presents, or listen to their music. She was an only daughter. Her father loved her very much and would not urge her to marry. The other girls were displeased at this. They wished her to marry ; for so long as she remained single the young men would look at no one else ; they felt a great hatred and jealousy of her, but this they kept secret and were careful to praise her openly and seem to be her friends. They did not tell their real thoughts at all to the old people, though they had no scruples about admitting them to one another.

One day all the girls went out to gather the little black cherries. The birds had been before them and they found but few. They scattered into companies of small numbers to hunt more trees. Little Dove felt hurt that no one asked her to go along as a companion, and wandered off alone.

After a little search, she saw a fine tree growing at the edge of a very deep ravine cut into the soft soil by a feeble little stream. She set down her basket and tried to shake the glistening cherries from the branches. The tree was so strong and firmly rooted she could not shake it enough to bring down any fruit. She stood off and looked at it as she rested from her labours. Those cherries were the finest she had ever seen. Alas ! they were all growing well out of reach instead of some being on the drooping lower limbs. She felt that she must have them. Again and again she strove to shake the tree. She could not. She flung sticks among the branches. Not one cherry fell. She thought she would go away and find another tree, but a great longing for the fruit of that particular one constrained her, and as often as her reluctant feet turned away they turned back again. She tried to climb the tree, but the trunk was as smooth as ice. She sat down and wept childish tears of disappointment and vexation. So absorbed was she that she failed to observe that a young man in all the bravery of a warrior's apparel was coming up the steep, high bank of the little stream. He approached and called her by her name. She looked up in surprise. She did not know the stranger. She saw that he was handsome and very well dressed. His cheeks and the feathers in his scalp-lock were painted red. His leggings and shirt were whitened doeskin, his moccasins and blanket were embroidered with porcupine-quills.

" Why do you weep ? " he asked, and his voice was pleasant.

She hung her head, ashamed to answer, but at last his look compelled her. She told him her wish with regard to the cherries. At once he set his foot against the tree and the fruit fell about them in showers. She forgot the warrior, she forgot everything in her eagerness to possess that which she had craved ; she gathered it hurriedly, she ate of it hungrily. Then a rushing sound came in her ears. Frightened, she looked up from the ground where she sat and saw the warrior coming towards her with his arms oustretched. She fell forward. She knew no more.

When the new moon that shone the night before the cherry-picking was old, she went home to her father. She had been searched for. She had been mourned as dead. At first she was joyfully received, but when she affirmed she had been gone but a few hours, the faces of the old people grew grave, the young people became scornful. Her father withdrew into a dark corner, her brothers went away by themselves. She had no mother to reproach her else she might have heard bitter things.

When an old woman told her how long she had been gone,
when she perceived what all thought of her, she begged that
they would go with her to the tree and see if they could not
help her to unravel the mystery. Some from curiosity or pity
went. They found her basket, which she had not thought to
take back to the village, all broken and weather-stained. They
found the tree that grew on the high bank above the little
stream. Alas ! it was an elm, not a cherry-tree. Surely it
could never have showered cherries into the basket or on the
ground beneath its branches.

Little Dove wept very sorely when her former friends went
away in silence and left her there.

After that life was very sad. Her father and brothers
loved her no more. " To go out and gather cherries " became
a byword and an insult in the village. When she was ill no
one was concerned. Even her old lovers forgot their former
words and feelings, and avenged their slights with cruel jests.
This was more than she could bear, so she went away from
them all and built her a home under that fatal elm tree.
Daily she looked along the ravine, leaving none of its bramble-
covered nooks and fissure unexplored.

"Without doubt he is a great magician," she told herself.
" He may come again, and surely, if asked, would have pity on
a poor girl and make all things pleasant for her again with her
people."

But he never came.

After awhile, a friendless old woman, whose relations were
tired of her, came begging to her door.

" Let me in, Little Dove," she entreated. " I can fish for
you, I can snare birds and squirrels for you. Let me in."

Little Dove let her in, not for the sake of the fish or birds, for
she could catch those very easily herself, but out of com-
passion.

Then she was not so lonely. She told her story over and

over, leaving out nothing, and the old woman listened, nodding her head and saying always—

"I know, I know. Have courage. Some day all will come right. The sorcerer will come again—he always comes more than once to those he comes to at all—then this people will be afraid and ashamed."

This comforted Little Dove somewhat.

Then the bitter winter weather came and they never saw the village people even from afar. No one went by crying—

"Where are the cherries?"

When the winter was past and the cherry-trees bloomed again, there was a bark cradle swinging from a branch of the elm tree—a low branch that suddenly was perceived by two women. That cradle was the elm tree's only blossom.

When the old woman first saw the boy that swung in the cradle, she held him up to the light. "Now," she cried, "the secret magic is revealed."

From the child's crown grew a tuft of vermillion hair, shining like a coal amid the blackness of the other locks.

When Little Dove saw it she was not so much ashamed; when the old woman had been over to the village and told the wonder and returned with many visitors, she was not ashamed at all; she began to be proud.

The visitors invited her to go back to the village with them, but she would not.

"This place will do," she said. "We lack for nothing."

Then they entreated her, at the same time offering many gifts. (They had talked together, privately, and said, "This is the child of a great father. We know the father's name, though we do not say it. Doubtless the son will grow up to be a very wonderful sorcerer. It would be a bad thing to have his ill-will. We must get the good-will of his mother now, then he will be for and not against us after a while.")

She answered them, pleasantly, but would not go from her

tepee,[1] so, finally, all but the old woman went away. They went away, but, now and then, as they moved about, they returned to the tepee[1] under the elm to watch the boy's increasing stature and intelligence.

Never was there a boy like that one. He was soon in appearance and intellect a man. He asked his mother many questions. One day he asked about his father.

She told him the story she had told to others so often.

When she had finished he put his hand to the long red lock. " I will find my father," he said, and the heart of the mother was both sorry and glad when she heard him say it.

Next day he went away. He wandered far, he wandered long, but he did not find his father. He went home to his mother and brooded in silence. One day he lay in the shade of the old tree and dreamed a dream. He awoke and shouted as if he were going into battle. " This is the road," he cried to his mother, and began to climb the tree. He went up very fast ; on the straight trunk which had been so smooth once, but was rough enough then ; on the great limbs ; on the small limbs ; out of sight among the leaves.

The mother called and called.

At first he answered, then he made no answer. He did not come down that day, though she waited and watched under the tree. He did not come down the next, nor the next, nor for three winters.

His mother feared she had lost him, but one morning she looked out and, behold ! the tree was black and shining with ripe cherries.

" He is coming," she said, and sat down on the ground to wait.

In a few moments he did come, walking and sliding down the tree.

He had made a great journey. At the top of the tree, when

[1] *Tepee*, wigwam.

he went up, was a cloud, and through the cloud was a long passage-way like the one a spider weaves between rock and bush. He went through the passage, on and on, till he thought he should never come to the end, seeing nothing in the dim light, until finally he emerged into a beautiful land of forests and streams where the woodpeckers, thick as a flight of locusts, were disporting themselves. They greeted him in his own language and conducted him to their chief. The chief addressed him as his son and talked to him earnestly, instructing him in all things he could need to know.

"I sent you the dream that brought you here," said the father to the son. "I wished to make you wiser than the men who live altogether on the ground."

So the son stayed in the high habitation of the father, learning of peace and war and all that pertained to success in each. One thing only that the father knew he would not teach the son (whom he named "Redfeather) : he would not teach him how to assume the form of a bird. "Not yet, my son," he said. "Not until you come again."

When Redfeather seemed well enough instructed, his father conducted him as far as the tree-top and there took leave of him.

"Go to your mother's people," he said, at parting, "and instruct them as I have instructed you. Put them above their enemies, make them so that their young men shall, in future, know as much as the old ones do now, and that the old ones shall have wisdom beyond measurement. When this has been accomplished you may take your choice, either to stay with them or lead your mother up here."

After saying this the father went back, and Redfeather descended the tree.

When he had finished relating all that had befallen him, Redfeather wished to set out immediately to find his people, who had moved a long way off, but his mother objected. She had not forgotten those last unhappy days she spent among

5

them, therefore she did not wish to rejoin them nor have her son with them.

When Redfeather found his arguments went for nought, he left her under the tree.

" Here you will find me on your return," she told him, for she had no faith in those people.

He set out buoyant of heart. He found the people, he taught them, he led them to battle, he helped them to conquer their enemies, he let them keep all the spoil, he showed them pleasant places in which to dwell.

At first they were thankful, then they were proud, then they were jealous, then they plotted against him.

He found out all these things. He called them together and revealed his knowledge. He renounced them. The wife he married he sent back to her father. He left all behind and returned to his mother. He found her sitting lonely under the elm tree, which was again black with cherries.

" Come up ! " a voice called.

"I could not climb the tree when I was young, how can I now that I am old ? " said Little Dove, weeping bitterly. " Go, my son, without me."

Redfeather took her hand. " Come up," he said, echoing the voice.

He started, drawing her after him.

She found she could go easily ; so they went, the son first, the mother after ; up the trunk, the limbs, the light branches, through the thick leaves.

Some who had pursued Redfeather saw a cloud receive the two. With them went all the good-luck of Little's Dove's people.

" Sarve um right, too ! " said Granny, emphatically. " De proud stummick dat spew out de milk in de mawnin' am boun' ter stay hitse'f on crik-watteh (creek-water) 'fo' de day am done. Dat de sollum fack, hit sholy am."

"Troof dar, Aunt Jinny ; troof dar, Miss Boogarry," echoed the others.

"I wish," said Tow Head, thoughtfully, "that I knew if Redfeather's father ever taught him how to change himself into a bird. Do you think he did, Mrs. Boogarry ?"

"Me an' Redfeather ain' kip sikrits at un nurr" (kept secrets together) Big Angy made answer so grimly that the little girl ventured no more questions. Her little tongue was stilled, though her brain was not. She pondered over Redfeather and his probable career in his father's mansions for a long, long time, paying no heed to the neighbourhood gossip her friends were bandying about. After awhile it seemed to her that she was rocked on a cloud herself, and voices very far away began to sing, not in invitation, but this bill-of-fare, of which she certainly did not partake :—

> "Oh ! chicken-pie an' pepper, oh !
> Chicken-pie is good, I know ;
> So is watteh-million, too,
> So is rabbit in er stew,
> So is dumplin's biled with squab,
> So is cawn biled on de cob,
> So is chine an' turkey-breast,
> So is aigs des fum de nest."

IV.

MORE ABOUT WOODPECKER.

IT was a bright afternoon, but Granny's aspect was exceedingly gloomy. As she left the "calf-lot," where she had been prescribing for a young bovine too soon acquainted with the ills that flesh is heir to, she saw a sight that froze her very blood.

A lane ran between the "calf-lot" and the enclosure where the cabins were, and in that lane stood Tow Head flinging corn-cobs with all her little might at a small, dark bird, which was busily examining the rails of the old worm-fence and the bark of an ancient tree that lounged against them.

"Stop dat! Stop, dis minnit!" shrieked Granny, hastily slipping the bars of the calf-lot in place, and making a dash at the offender. "D'yo' wanter git the whole passel ob us cunjered?"

Tow Head paused in dismay, and looked about for the conjuror.

"W-where is he, Granny?" she asked, faintly.

"On de top de fence. Dar, on de ridah" (rider, top rail), mumbled Granny, nodding towards the top rail of the worm-fence, and then hurrying the little girl through the "big gate" of the less primitive boundary on the opposite side of the lane.

"You're pinching my shoulder," whimpered Tow Head, vainly striving to wriggle out of Granny's iron grasp.

"Nemmine! nemmine!" (never mind!) panted Granny. "Des lemme git yo' in out o' sight."

Tow Head was appalled. Never had she seen Granny's eyes gleam like that since the day she and some of Aunt Mymee's juvenile descendants had tried to convert the big yellow tom-cat into an opossum by trimming the hair off his tail with the sheep-shears. "Many a time and oft" had she had reason to thank her lucky stars that she was not "a nut-brown mayde," and in consequence liable to discipline from the old woman's staff. That wretched little bird seemed to have obliterated the colour line. Ordinarily, the little pickle quailed when she found herself marched towards "The House," but on this occasion, when she was unceremoniously ushered into the cabin and seated in the tallest chair, she felt like a criminal about to receive a life-sentence.

Granny sat down opposite her, with folded arms and a face as expressionless as a mummy's.

Tow Head looked awestruck, looked indignant, defiant, then gave way and began to cry.

"The Bible says you shalt not make yourself a graven image, I heard 'em say it in Sunday School," she sniffled.

"Uh! huh!" exclaimed Granny, in sudden fury, "ole Mymee's bin a-callin' me er gravum image ergin, hez she? An' yo' ter say dat yo' pick up dat meanness in de Sunday skule! Ise 'shame at yo', dat I is!"

"I did hear it in Sunday School," insisted Tow Head, recovering courage, now that she saw she would have Aunt Mymee as a partner in any "fuss."

"Oh, yes! oh, yes!—well, suz! des lemme tell yo' dat yo' betteh git dat lil ole niggah ter putt fo'th huh strenk a-takin' off de tricks dat de woodpeckeh yo' bin flingin' at am gwine ter putt on de fam'bly, stiddier a-settin' Miss Agnes' chilluns ter sass dey Granny."

"Granny, that wasn't a woodpecker. That little bird didn't have a red head."

"Hit b'long in de fam'bly o' de peckerwoods des de same,

an' I lay dat ef hit don't 'scuse yo' on de grounds ob natchel foolishness hit gwine ter raise er mighty ruction w'en hit tell Ole Man Woodpeckeh."

" Who is he, Granny ? " asked the little girl, forgetting her peril, and intent only on hearing a story. " Is he the father of Redfeather, Big Angy was telling about ? "

"Des 'bout de same, des 'bout de same."

" Tell about him, Granny ; tell all about him."

Granny deliberated, fixing her eyes meanwhile on a flaw in the chinking of the wall behind Tow Head.

Tow Head meekly looked at the hole in Granny's boot.

Finally, Granny filled and lighted her pipe, and the little girl heaved a sigh of relief.

" Yo' betteh be a sivin' " (sighing), said Granny, but her tone was not one of commendation. " Dat's right. Ise gwine ter tell yo' one tale dat's gwine ter mek dat plain. Gin'ly, I tell tales unter good chilluns, but dis I gwine ter tell soster keep yo' fum fetchin' de whole ob creation down 'bout our yeahs. Dat's right, hang yo' haid down, but," and Granny softened, " come git in my lap, kase Ise got de misery in my breas', and kyarn't tork (talk) lak I wuz hollerin' thu de big dinneh horn. Dat's de jump ! Now, honey, lemme tell yo', all de woodpeckehs dat e'er comed outen er aig is—*cun-jer-ers !* "

" Oh, Granny ! "

" Yessir ! Lemme tull yo' wut happen wunst, an' I boun' yo' gwine ter lef dem budhs 'lone foh de res' o' yo' natchel life :—

" Wunst, in de ole times, dey wuz er mighty peart (pert, lively, or smart) an' biggetty-feelin' lil boy. He tuck arter de rest ob de fam'bly in dat, to be shoh, kase dey wuz all un um peart, but he wuz de peartes' in de lot, an' dat am sholy sayin' heap. Well ! dis hyeah boy wut I gwine ter tell 'bout, he wuz des up an 'a-comin' all de time. He sot traps an cotch de cotton-tails an' pa'tridges, he dug out de gophers,¹ he head

¹ *Gopher*, a kind of marmot.

off de moles, he steal de budh aigs, he shoot de squir'ls, he tree de 'coons, he drownd out de woodchucks.¹ He des whirl in an' get de whole ob creation down 'pon 'im ; but de day wuz a-comin' w'en all de critturs feel dey cotch up wid' im'. One day he up wid er rock an' bust de laig ob er lil peckerwood dat he see a-knockin' at de do' (door) ob Misteh Wuhm's (Worm's) house.

" Dat sottle de bizniz for dat boy.

" Woodpeckeh fetch one squall an' go hipplety, hopplety home. He fine he pa an' say—

" ' Looky hyeah at my laig ! '

" Old Woodpeckeh look, look long time an' say nuttin.

" Den he cuss.

" Den he ax, ' *Who—done—dat?* '

" ' Dat boy down in de holler.'

" ' Wut he done dat foh ? '

" ' Foh nuttin. I ain't tetch 'im. I ain't ez much ez sen' (send) my shadder 'cross 'im.'

" ' Nemmine ! nemmine ! des wait, my child, twell yo' daddy mek de 'quaintance ob dat boy.'

" ' Fix my laig fust, daddy.'

" ' Dat wut I gwine ter do, my son.'

" Den Ole Woodpeckeh fix that laig up good ez new."

" How did he do it, Granny ? "

" He done hit de way dat suit 'im, dat all I knows. I wuzzen' dar at de time. Howsomedevvah he done hit hit wuz er mighty good job."

" DEN OLD WOODPECKEH FIX DAT LAIG UP GOOD."

" I didn't know birds were doctors."

" Dey's two free tings yo' ain't larn yit," said Granny, with a fine irony that was altogether wasted on her auditor, " an'

¹ *Woodchuck*, also a variety of marmot.

one un um is de pint Ise aimin' at. De peckerwoods ain't no
shoh 'nuff buhds, dey's cunjerers dat kin be buhds ur dey kin
be men, an' de boss un um (of them) all, Ole Woodpeckeh, he
kin look lak de finest kine ob er Injun-chief, ceppin dat he
don't hafter paint red, he des grow dataways."

Here Granny paused and reflected a long time, presumably
on the characteristics and abilities of Woodpecker.

" Did Woodpecker ask the little boy's mamma to punish
him ?" asked Tow Head, after various ineffectual efforts to
attract Granny's attention without addressing her directly.

"Him? huh !" ejaculated Granny
with fine scorn. " He don't ax
nobody ter chew he vittles foh 'im.
W'en he git de laig fix he flewed off
inter de big woods. He fly roun'
dar twell he pick out de bigges'
tree in de kyounty (county), an'
out o' de biggest last yeah's limb,
up todes (towards) de top, he pick
de kine o' maggit dat he want.
Wut kine wuz dat prezackry I
dunno. His wuz de right kine foh

WOODPECKEH'S TREE.

he bizniz, I boun' yo' for dat.

" Well ! he git dat wuhm an' he watch round twell dat boy
wuz soun' er sleep in his trunnle-baid. Den he lay dat wuhm
down, keerful, on de winder-sill, an' he fly in de room an' chahm
dat boy so he sleep lak de daid out in de grabe-yahd. Dat
done, he bore lil hole in he haid, an' ee git de maggit offen de
winder-sill 'an' he putt hit in de lil hole, and kiver hit up an'
mek de place well an' soun'."

" Didn't the little boy ever wake up again ? " asked Tow
Head, in an awestruck whisper.

"Cose (of course) he wake up in de mawnin,' but I lay he
wish he don't. Dat boy bin a-fidgettin' an' a-flouncin' roun'

an' a-stirrin' up foolishness dat done kip he pa a-whoppin' ob 'im wid de trunkstrap study (steadily), e'er sence. Mo'n dat, he ain't de onlest (only) one dat got de maggit in he haid. Heap o' folks got um, an' all fum pesterin' de peckerwoods."

Tow Head felt the crown of her head with a thoughtful air.

" Does a trunk-strap hurt worse than a lady's hand or slipper ? " she asked, seriously.

" Heap wuss," answered Granny, emphatically.

Tow Head's deepening melancholy was touching to behold.

"I reckon yo' safe dis time," said Granny, observing it, " kase yo's young an' ain't had no speunce (experience). Ef yo' promiss dat yo' ain't gwine ter do so no mo', I 'low I kin beg yo' off wid Ole Woodpeckeh."

Tow Head promised with all earnestness.

" G'long in de house, now, an' if yo' mek out ter 'have (behave) yo'se'f twell arter suppeh, mebbe I git Aunt Mary ter tell dat putty tale 'bout de fuss 'twixt Old Woodpeckeh an' Blue Jay."

This statement so cheered Tow Head that she set out for " The House " in the gayest spirits, singing as she went a little song she had learned from Aunt Mymee. She did not finish it, however, for at the door the auntie caught her up in great excitement, informing her that, " I done hunt yo' evverwhurs 'cept in my own mouf," and adding that the new minister was in the parlour, and wished to see all the children. Immediately thereafter, Tow Head was whirled about in a perfect cyclone of preparation.

When she came to herself, she was a very starchy, shiny child indeed, with a fiery warmth in her ears and a sudden chill of bashfulness in her soul. She had barely strength to sidle up to the dignified minister's knee and tell, when asked, her name, her age, the length of time she had attended Sunday School, and her impression that there were twelve commandments and

seven or ten apostles.   Growing bolder, she stated to that
worthy man that she could sing.

"What hymns ?"

"Little grains of water, little drops of sand" and "Lord, dis-
miss us" ; but cabin songs, she frankly added, were a great deal
nicer than hymns.

"What are cabin songs, my dear child ?"

To the dismay and everlasting shame of her parents and
grandparents, and to the speechless amazement of that good
ecclesiastic from "Down East," Tow Head piped the little lay
Aunt Mymee had unceremoniously interrupted a few moments
before—

> "Jay-Buhd a-settin' on a hickory lim',
> He looked at me, I winked at him.
> I up wid a rock an' I hit 'im on de shin,
> An' dat's de way I sucked 'im in."

V.

THE "FUSS" BETWEEN WOODPECKER AND BLUE JAY.

Tow HEAD did not make her appearance in the cabin, as she expected, the evening after her interview with the minister, nor for many evenings thereafter. Her relatives were suddenly awakened to the necessity of making her acquainted with the writings of Matthew, Mark, Luke and John. The little maiden, nothing loth, at once set to work to memorise the names of the apostles, and later proved herself a promising member of the Church militant by taking sides with or against every historical character mentioned in the Four Gospels. Jay Bird and Woodpecker were for the time being forgotten, but one night mamma had a headache and grandma a visitor, so away went Tow Head to the cabin again, and immediately bethought her of the long-promised story.

Granny, with an offended air, pleaded timidity. She "wuzn't use ter tell tales 'fo' sech mighty big strangers."

Tow Head argued and urged in vain. Finally, she remembered that it was Aunt Mary, not Granny, that knew about Blue Jay and Woodpecker, so she turned about with a beaming smile and requested the younger woman to "tell a long, long story."

Aunt Mary had her laurels yet to win as a story-teller, and was anxious to make a beginning, so with no more delay than a preface of giggles demanded, she said—

"All I knows am des 'bout de fuss 'twixt Woodpeckeh an' Blue Jay, an' hyeah 'tis, des ez I done hyeah hit w'en I wuz er gal 'bout knee-high ter er hoppergrass. Foh er long time Woodpeckeh am keep hisse'f ter hisse'f an' ain't r'ar¹ round much. He des mine he own bizniz 'tickler clost. Arter w'iles, w'en he don't putt in nowhurs (show himself anywhere), Old Blue Jay, he come fo' (began) ter t'ink dat de whole yearth wuz hizzen. He smack de young squir'ls side o' de jaw, he et up de aigs in de nestes, an' he flirt he tail-fedders in de eyes o' de turr buhds, an' he des ack scannelous evvy-which-aways dat yo' kin name. But he gwine ter git he come-up-ance (punishment), dat he wuz ! an' at de berry time dat he wuzzent 'spectin' nuttin. Dishaways 'twuz come out : Ole Woodpeckeh, he sorter hyeah sumpin an' he sorter rouge (rouse) up outen he dreamin' an' cunjerin' an' he say, ' Wut dis I hyeah ? '

" De chilluns, dey mek arnser back—

" ' Dunno zackry (exactly), kase yo' ain't lef us play wid de nabeh buhds much.'

" (Dat wuz troof too, kase de woodpeckeh fam'bly wuz quality, an' de chilluns wuzzent 'low ter run roun' an' play wid no half-strainers an' trash.) "

" Those little woodpeckers must have been awfully lonesome," said Tow Head, wiggling her foot and looking both conscious and defiant.

" Nemmine 'bout dat ; dey bin mek out ter hyeah (they managed to learn) dat Ole Blue Jay bin a-raisin' heap o' ruction roun' in dem pahts (parts).

" ' Daddy,' dey say, ' Ole Blue Jay, he say dat he am boss ob dis neck ob de woods, an' hit 'pears lak he mean hit mo'n (more than) dat, kase he bin doin' heap o' debbilment de las' w'iles back.'

" Dat mek Ole Woodpeckeh orfle mad.

" ' Boss is he ? ' sez 'e. ' Well ! I gwine ter see 'bout dat.

¹ *R'ar*, to rear up like a horse, or curvet ; to show spirit.

W'en I wants enny debbilment done round dis hyeah nabeh-hood, I lay I kin do hit my own se'f,' sez 'e.

" So he tell Miss Woodpeckeh she mought ez well go roun' a-visitin' an' see ef she kin pick up enny 'ticklers 'bout Blue Jay fum de nabehs, kase dese marters (matters) boun' ter be look inter.

" So Miss Woodpeckeh, she go, an' w'en she git home an' 'gin ter tell all dat she gedder up, Ole Woodpeckeh he dat mad dat he whirl in an' chop down er good-size hick'ry tree wid he bill, kase he boun' ter hit sumpin, an' ef he ain't hit de tree he mought a hit Miss Woodpeckeh.

" Ez he chop, he mummle an' grummle, lak dis hyeah—

" ' Gwine ter run dese woods, is he ? '

" Whack ! whack !

" ' Et up all de buhd-aigs, hez 'e, an' bruck up all dis yeah's nestes ? '

" Whack ! whack !

" ' Stole er hazel nut right outen de fox-squir'l's paw, on'y yistiddy, did he ? '

" Whack ! whack !

" ' Peck de eye clean outen Miss Cat-Buhd's darter's haid, did he ? '

" Whack ! whack !

" ' Dem's fine gwines-on, ain't dey ? '

" Whack !

" ' I 'low I des lub foh 'im ter kip right on (like to have him continue). Oh, yes ! '

" Whack !

" ' Mebbe I betteh ax Misteh Jay ef I kin stay hyeah, ef I 'have (behave) myse'f, an' ax no questions. Oh, yes ! '

" Whack ! whack ! whack !

" An' so, suz ! he kep' a-grittin' he toofs an' a-whackin' de tree an' a-torkin' unter hisse'f, twell de tree come a-crashin' down, —cr-r-r-ack !—snash !—crash !—boom ! ez de trunk fall,—bam !

ez de lim's slap de ground—an' den, squash ! ez de leafy
branches queeveh (quiver) an' sottle down mungs de bustid
undeh-bresh an' vines.

"My ! how dat ole Woodpeckeh did go on ! Some ob de
chips dey wuz flung so high dat dey lit on de moon, an' dey
dar yit, foh all dis hyeah niggeh know.

" W'en de tree kim down, Ole Woodpeckeh he clumb onter
hit an' he sot dar a-breevin hahd (breathing hard), an' a-open-
in' an' a-shettin' he eyes, des ez ef somebody wuz a-fannin' um
open an' shet.

"All de time he doin' dat," continued Aunt Mary ; after a
break in the narrative to give her an opportunity to depict
Woodpecker's mood in expressive pantomime ; " he wuz mekin'
up he mine (mind). W'en he git dat done ter he noshin (to
his notion or mind), he holler at one ob de chilluns dat wuz
a-peekin' round de aige (edge) ob er gum stump.

" ' Tell yo' mammy notter set up foh me dis ebenin','' he say.
' Mebbe hit mought happen dat I come home late,' sez 'e, sorter
wallin' up he eyeball.

" ' All right, daddy,' holler back de young one, den away de
ole man flewed.

" He flewed an' he flewed," continued Aunt Mary, contem-
plating the smoky rafter above her, from one end to the other,
as if on it she could trace the woodpecker's flight, " des lak
chain-lightnin' wuz arter 'im. He flewed an' he flewed twell .
he flewed ter whah de tall cottonwoods bin t'ickest—not ter de
lil cottonwoods down on de san'-bah (sand-bar), but ter de big,
big ones on de bluffs furdest back fum de ribber. W'en he git   /
dar he don't fly fas' enny mo'. He fly lil way, hop lil way, fly
lil way kine o' keerless lak, ez ef he wuz des sorter playin' roun'
an' 'muzin' hisse'f a-hummin' er chune.

" Wut he do dat foh ? Kase he knowed Blue Jay wuzzent
fur off, an' he 'low he s'prise 'im.

" Putty soon arter, he hyeah de young jay-buhds a-squallin', an' he know by dat dat he gwine ter meet up wid dey pa, berry quick. Shoh nuff, arter w'iles, he see Ole Jay come a-sailin' thu de woods an' light on er low-down daid limb. My! he look dat peart an' sassy a-stannin' dar an' a-balluncin' on he lef' laig de w'iles he nibble at er lil straw same ez ef he hab er fine seegyar in he mouf. He stick he haid on one side w'en he see Ole Woodpeckeh, den he wink, des ez peart ez er free-niggeh buck (young man) w'en de yaller gals go by. Den he spit out de straw an' he holler—

"'Hello, ole man!'

"Ole Woodpeckeh choke back de cuss words an' he say, 'Hello,' too, an' try foh ter look 'gree'ble.

"'Git stahve (starve) out up yo' way?' Blue Jay ax, twissen he neck roun' an' a-stirrin' yundehneat he wing foh lil louse.

"'N-not dezackly,' say Ole Woodpeckeh, mos' a-bustin', he so mad.

"'Ef yo' hongry, des stir roun' an' ketch yo'se'f er wuhm out o' my trees,' sez Blue Jay, sez 'e, a-combin' out he tail-fedders wid he bill, an' no mo' a-lookin' todes (towards) Ole Woodpeckeh den ef he wuz er las' yeah's aig-shell.

"''Bleeged, Ise shore,' sez Ole Woodpeckeh, a-whettin' he bill on er limb. 'You's de boss ob dese woods, I spoge (suppose)?'

"At dat, Blue Jay he fetched er sorter cackle. 'Des jedge foh yo'se'f,' sez 'e. '*I* ain't mekkin' no brags,' sez 'e, 'but I 'low nobody in dese hyeah woods am a-denyin' dat I des natchelly gwine ter lam de stuffin' outen 'im, ef he gib me enny sass,' sez 'e.

"'Uh-huh!' sez Woodpeckeh, sez 'e. 'Uh-huh! Ise mighty glad yo' tole me. Ef yo' hatten ter (had not) tole me I mought a cut er shine ur two my own se'f. W'iles I 'bout hit dough, I reckon I mought ez well mek dat bold ter ax yo', did yo' evveh hyeah tell dat *I* wuz ownin' er heap o' proppity roun' in dese hyeah pahts?'

" ' Yes I reckon mebbe I mought a-hyurn (have heard) dat,' sez Blue Jay, 'but, good lan'! ef I hez, I done fegit um. I'm got nurr kine ob fish ter fry sidesen a-loadin' up my 'membunces 'ith urr folks' ole wo'-out (worn out) brags,' sez 'e.

" ' Who braggin'? wut brags yo' torkin' (talking) 'bout?' say Ole Woodpeckeh, breevin' mighty hot an' quick an' a-torkin' way down in he stummick.

" ' Yourn, ef hit come ter dat,' sez Blue Jay, sez 'e, a-stompin' on de limb lak he feel so good dat he gwine ter pat Juba de nex' minnit.

" ' Tek dat, den!' holler Ole Woodpeckeh, a-hittin' 'im er clip dat des nigh split 'im open. Ise Ole Woodpeckeh, I is, an' Ise gwine ter boss dese hyeah woods des ez I allus hab enduin' (during) ob de forty-'lebin yeahs I bin hyeah (here) befo' de debbil tuck ter mekin' blue jays. Yo' hyeah me! Yah! don't yo' cock up yo' laig at me lak dat, yo' sassy trash, yo'! Come on, den! Come on!'

" ' Don't yo' try ter cunjer *me*, yo' ole bag o' shucks,' Blue Jay holler back, ' kase hit kyarn't be did, no hit kyarn't!'

" ' Cunjer nuttin,' sez Ole Woodpeckeh. 'Who gwine ter tek de trouble ter cunjer sitch er low-life, sneakin', ole aigsucker ez yo'? Des lay down an' lemme tromple de lights outen yo'. Hit'll save me time an' you trouble,' sez 'e.

" Den Blue Jay low hit time someun teach dat low-flung red-head mannehs (manners). 'I des wisht,' sez 'e, ' dat dat lil pee-wee buhd 'u'd come 'long an' tek dis triflin' bizniz offen my han's,' sez 'e, 'but ez him an' all de turr buhds is a-tendin' ter dey own marters, study (steadily), I reckon I boun' ter string yo' 'long de ground my own se'f,' sez 'e, an' wid dat he spit on he claw an' he rattle he bill an' he set ter wuhk ; an' dar dey hed hit, up an' down, roun' an' roun', back an' fo'th twell des 'bout sundown. Long 'fo' dat dough, Ole Blue Jay's bref come mighty shawt (short), he haht (heart) ack lak she gwine ter bust thu he ribs an' he tongue feel lak dat ole straw he wuz a-chewin' w'en woodpeckeh fust lit. Sidesen dat, he'd a giner holler log cramful ob aigs (eggs)—ef he'd hed um— foh des one sup o' cole watteh (cold water), but, de laws o' massy ! he ain't git no watteh, wut he git wuz de bes' kine o' er lickin'. Ole Woodpeckeh, he des natchelly lay 'im out— bedout (without) cunjerin, at dat—an' dat breshin' o' he hide done 'im heaps ob good an' last 'im long time, too."

As Aunt Mary finished there was a mighty clapping at the door, as if two broad and vigorous palms were impelled by a

OLE BLUE JAY LAID OUT.

perfect frenzy of applause. She screamed in affected dismay, lifted one shoulder and drooped the other, clapped her hands over her mouth and sank back as if she were faint just as Granny ushered in the visitor.

" Dellaws ! (La !) Misteh Palmer," she simpered, " I kyarn't speak ter yo' yit. Yo' skeered me dat bad, my haht (heart) am des right up in my mouf."

" I wisht yo'd spit hit out an' let me pick hit up," responded the " genterman,": gallantly

" Tee, hee ! " giggled Aunt Mary, turning away her head,

but holding out her hand. "How menny time is yo' say dat, endu'in' ob de las' week, Misteh Palmer ? "

"I ain't say hit none, bekase I ain't see yo' none," answered "Misteh" or as Tow Head was accustomed to say, "Uncle John " Palmer, with elegant deliberation. "Wut I mought a-*thunk* am sumpin different. Dey is times in de cose (course) ob er genterman's persistence (existence) dat he t'oughts foller de lady ob he ch'ice ez de shadder follers de tree. My deah miss, yo' hez hed de 'zervence ob dat befo' yo' eyes dis long time."

Aunt Mary was so overcome by this that she was forced to pull' the kerchief off her neck and stuff a liberal portion of it in her mouth to smother her laughter.

Uncle John rolled his eyes at her, "lak er dyin' calf," as Granny afterwards told Aunt Mymee, grinned slightly, and then sighed deeply as he subsided into a chair.

"Don't yo' sive (sigh) lak dat," expostulated Granny. "Yo'll draw all de fiah out o' de chimbly an' blow lil missey hyeah clean thu de winder."

"Er genterman kyarn't allus keep down he feelin's," said Uncle John, with another tender glance towards the object of his affections, "but I gwine ter be keerful dis ebenin', I sholy is. An' how is de lil missey ? " he asked, turning towards the child and speaking in a more sprightly tone.

Tow Head was well and said so. Of her own accord she added that the baby was well too.

"Uh-huh ! I t'ought dat mole-foot fetch 'im I " exclaimed Uncle John, with satisfaction. "De chile dat am cuttin' toofses am bound ter hab de right fore-foot ob er mole, ur er necklash (necklace) ob elder twigs, ur er brack silk bag wid de dried up breens (brains) ob er rabbit in hit, else he cut um hahd. Ef I'd a had de infamashun sooneh dat he wuz a-cuttin' I c'd a-save dat po' lamb er heap o' suff'rin'."

"De trouble wuz," said Granny, "dat dem shif'less young niggahs dat Mymee 'low ter tote (carry) dat chile, lef 'im look in de lookin' glass. Dat allus mek er baby cut he toofs hahd."

"Troof, too, Aunt Jinny, but de molefoot fix 'im."

"I dunno," grumbled Granny, "w'y Mymee, ef she kin cunjer so big, ain't cunjer de misery out o' dat chile's gums."

"Some kin cunjer 'bout one t'ing, some 'bout nurr," said Uncle John, easily. "Now, Aunt Mymee, she got de name mungs de gyurls dat she am er daid shot at mekkin' de han' o' lub (hand of love—a voodoo charm which insures marital felicity) an' huh lub-powdehs dey go right ter de spot, time an' time ergin, but de man dat mek de bes' Jack (spell or charm) goin', he sets right befo' yo'."

"How yo' mek um?" inquired Aunt Mary, turning around.

"Ef yo' gimme dat lil w'ite luck-stone Adam gib yo', I let yo' hab mine an' tell yo wut's in hit," Uncle John answered.

Aunt Mary demurred.

"I'll t'row in my rabbit-foot, foh boot," added Uncle John.

"W'ich foot?"

"Right fo'-foot. I don't stop at keepin' off bad-luck 'ith de lef' hine-foot, I hones (desire) arter downright good-luck an' so I kerries de fo'-foot foh dat."

"Lemme see um."

The foot and the "Jack," which latter was a small buckskin bag tied with white yarn, were produced from some secret receptacle between Uncle John's heart and his ancient broadcloth vest.

"Wut sort o' Jack's dat?" Aunt Mary asked.

"'Tain't none o' yo' ole cheap snakeweed 'tricks'; hit am kimpoge (composed) o' de best brimstun to de 'mount ob er teaspoonful, an' de same o' alum, 'sides er chunk ob er root ob Conquer-John (Solomon's Seal—*Poligonatum biflorum*), an' er pinch ob salt."

"W'en Wash wuz a libbin', he gin me a Jack wid may-apple root an' red clober in hit."

"Dat," said Uncle John, "wuz good at dem times, but 'tain't

no good ter de *single* pussons—ez I bress de Lawd yo' am at
dis minnit—seein' yo' ain't double up wid *me*."

This last compliment so " fetched de feelin's," of Aunt Mary
that she agreed to exchange fetiches. Accordingly, she produced the luck-stone, a circular white pebble about three-
fourths of an inch in diameter and of the thickness of a silver
dollar.

Uncle John scrutinised it carefully.

" Hit's all right," he said.   " I wuz a-lookin' ter see ef hit
hed enny brack lines ur specks.   Dat kine is pizen bad luck foh
de one dat kerries um, an' some low-flung niggehs is ob de
meanness o' sperit ter parm um off on dey bettehs.   Now, ef
de brack wuz brack *lettehs* dat's diffunt in de respecks o' bein'
turrwise.   I wunst hed er stone, dat I found on de aige (edge) ob
er crik, dat hed er A an' er B an' nurr letteh dat I kyarn't at dis
minnit name, 'pun 'count ob de entitle ob hit a-slippin' my
membry.   Dat stone fotch an' pejuce (produce) de best o' luck,
but, misfortnitly, I drap um out o' my pockit an' tromp on um
w'en I wuz a-sarchin' for ter find um.   W'en I lif' up dis hyeah
stremiky o' mine," continued Uncle John, lifting an extremity
that must have been the despair of shoemakers, " dey wuzzent
much lef' o' dat luck-stone."

This conversation had been carried on in a low tone, as it
was not considered suitable for the child's ears.   Granny, with
the best intentions towards all parties, had endeavoured to hold
her attention by telling a wonderful tale of a " fine hoss-hair
bunnit," once owned by " Miss Agnes," but Tow Head's ears
were as keen as a young fox's, and the only words she missed
were those not intended for her ears.

" I wish I had a luck-stone," she said, walking over to Uncle
John and laying a hand on his knee.

" Des wait twell yo' grow up," said Uncle John, smiling
foolishly, " an' I bound dat yo' git er fine one in de meantimes ;
I gwine ter hab de pledger (pleasure) ter sing yo' er song 'bout

'Peekin' Will de Weaver,' dat am, onless yo' ain't got de pashuns (patience) ter lissen unter er ole squawker lak me."

When was there a time that Tow Head was not all eagerness to hear a story or song? Her enthusiasm moved Uncle John to begin at once. He patted a few strokes by way of prelude, " wished ter gracious he had brought his banjo," threw in an explanation to the effect that Will had clumb on de roof o' de cabin an' wuz a-peekin' down de chimbly," and then burst forth in the following irregular melody :—

" Did yo' evveh see a chimney-sweeper
Half so black as Will de weaver?
Carry him off on de joke,
He'll come no more to stop my smoke.

I built me up a rousing fire,
I built it to my own desire.
Hit's up the chimny de fire went blazin',
Hit's down de chimbley he kim gazin'.
Den de nasty wretched soul
Laid stretched out on de chimbly-pole.

Den thu de room 'ith my foot I kicked 'im.
Den ev'y time I kicked 'im he spoke,
' I'll come no mo' ter stop yo' smoke.'
Den out de do' 'ith my foot I kicked 'im,
An' ez out de do' 'ith my foot I kicked 'im,
Den out de gate my dog did shake 'im,
An' ev'y time he shook 'im he spoke,
' I'll come no mo' ter stop yo' smoke.'

Now he foot in he hand an' he clo'es likewise,
Carry 'im off wid he two brack eyes.
Now, hit's carry 'im off on de joke,
Les' I t'ink ergin I'll mek 'im smoke."

VI.

HOW WOODPECKER MADE A BAT; ALSO SOME OTHER FACTS OF NATURAL HISTORY NOT GENERALLY KNOWN.

WHEN Tow Head hurried into the cabin the next evening, all eagerness to see if Uncle John was present with his banjo, she was greatly disappointed to find that the only "company" was Big Angy. Her greeting had so little warmth in it that Big Angy considered a grunt the only reply necessary, and at once went on with her interrupted conversation.

"Oh-wee (*oui*)," she said, "me know dem woodpeckeh man, well. Him de *rouge-nain*—de *petit homme rouge*. Sartain! Ef I know dat Aunt Mary tell o' heem, I be hyeah las' night. Oh, me know!—*va !*—H-s-s-t ! de tale of de bat, I kin tell hit."

"Dat's good news," said Granny, cheerfully. "Des go right on wid um, Miss Boogary. We is all got owah yeahs (ears) cocked foh hit."

Big Angy went "right on," as nearly as her discursive pre-dilections would allow, but her tales had at the best of times "many a windin' 'bout" that was not "linked sweetness." As her dialect, which was neither French, Indian, nor yet plain Darkey, but contained all three elements capriciously mingled, was like that famous mare that had only two faults—"hard to catch and no account when caught"—it can serve no good purpose to repeat any great amount of it. "Biled down," to quote Granny, the story is this :—

In the old times, when Woodpecker's family was very young, he was once out on the prairie looking for medicine. He was gone a long while. What he sought he was longer in finding than he had expected he should be. When he was successful he still loitered, and was in no hurry to get home. He had with him his magical whistle made from the bone of an eagle's wing, and he would have played strange music on it had he not heard the doctor of the prairie-chickens pounding on his drum. " Something is going on," said Woodpecker, and he hid himself in a thicket of plums and burning-bush (bitter-sweet), hoping he might learn some more magic, for Prairie-Chicken knew a great deal, but as he was no friend of Woodpecker he never imparted to him any secrets. He listened eagerly, but the sound of the drum ceased suddenly, and he heard voices. He looked sharply into the grass and saw a field-mouse, then he glanced into a thick tangle of vines and saw a small, ill-favoured night-hawk. He gave heed to their conversation, at first from idle curiosity, but he soon had a much stronger interest. The two were discussing how they could best contrive to get Woodpecker's family for supper. This they wished not merely because the young ones were fine eating, but because whosoever ate them would have great power in sorcery. They further decided to contrive that the blame should be laid either on Black-Snake or Catamount. After much discussion, they agreed that Black-Snake should bear the punishment of their misdeeds. The first plan was to eat all the little woodpeckers but one, themselves, then invite him to sup at the foot of the tree where the nest was, give him the last one, and hurry away. Even if old Woodpecker did not find him, his slimy track would betray the fact of his visit. This plan was not quite satisfactory ; the wicked ones feared that the feast would make Black-Snake too wise to fall a victim to their wiles, so they concluded it would be safest to feed him with a toad. This settled, the next point was to get old Woodpecker and his wife out of the way. This was easy

enough to manage. They remembered hearing Woodpecker's
wife say it was a time of year that they hid themselves and had
dreams. So all things promised well. Field-Mouse went home.
Night-Hawk went to sleep among the leaves. Woodpecker
quietly flew to his tree. At once he sent the children away,
not, however, before he had plucked a feather from the wing of
each. These feathers he blew into the air, and they came back
to him birds. All but one of these magical birds he put into

WOODPECKER MAKING BIRDS.

the nest lately filled by his children. The one he kept out he
carried down to the river bank and filled with pebbles. " Take
care you are the last bird eaten by Field-Mouse," he commanded. The magical bird promised obedience, and was
dropped into the nest with the others.

That night the hawk and the mouse went to the nest,
Mouse riding on Hawk's back like a witch riding an owl. They

ate all the birds, and enjoyed the feast with wicked delight and triumph. Last of all was eaten the bird fed on pebbles. Then Mouse mounted again, and Hawk endeavoured to fly down from the tree. He could not move, he was pressed flat against the limb on which he sat. When he found what a burden Mouse had become he reproached her bitterly for her greediness.

She was angry, but gave him no answer ; she could not speak, so sick and oppressed she felt from the weight inside of her.

OLE WOODPECKER, MOUSE, AND NIGHT-HAWK.

Hawk became furious, and tried to throw her off, but she clung to him desperately.

They had a long struggle, and during its continuance she kicked holes in his back and her feet slipped into them. When they at length fell to the ground, her weight still held them fast together, so in terror and hatred they fought and wrenched each other as they lay on the earth. The struggle lasted all night. In the morning Mouse threw up the pebbles, but that did her no good. She had grown fast to Night-Hawk, and to this day has continued to be a part of him. This is very terrible for both, but they cannot help it. Now they are called " Bat," as if they

were one. Another thing remember concerning them : so
awful is the memory of that night when they were made one,
and so fearful are they of being filled up with
pebbles again, that they always rest and sleep
head downwards, as any one can bear witness who has ever seen a bat in repose.

When Big Angy had finished she assumed
a severe cast of countenance, and looked into
the fire as if no thought of applause or admiration had ever crossed her mind.

MOUSE HAWK.

" Dat er mighty fine tale," said Granny, emphatically.

" So 'tis, tee-hee !   So 'tis, tee-hee ! hee ! hee ! hee ! "
snickered Aunt Mary.

" That other one," affirmed Tow Head, in a still, small voice,
" was better, and so was Aunt Mary's story about the fight.
Do you think, Mrs. Boogarry, that this Mr. Woodpecker is the
one that lived in the cloud at the top of the tree ? "

" 'E ain't say ter me ef 'e wuz ur ef 'e wuzzent," growled
Angy, without turning her eyes from the fire. " Yo' dat-smaht,
missey, yo' berr g' long an' ax um."

" I would, if I knew where he lived," sighed Tow Head, "but
you see I don't.   Could you show me the way ? " she asked,
suddenly brightening.

Angy gave a short laugh and looked around. " Me do dat
w'en de fros' git out de ground," she said, with a wink at Aunt
Mary and Granny. " Dish not de time de yeah foh huntin'
nuttin 'ceppen rabbit ! "

" Tell me a rabbit story," said Tow Head, promptly.

Big Angy shook her head. " We ain't at de eend o' Woodpeckeh yit," she said, decidedly.

" Let us hurry, then ! " cried the child, impatiently.   " Aunt
Mymee will come for me as soon as she rocks the baby to sleep,
and I do, *do*, DO want to hear a rabbit story.   What else did
Woodpecker do ? "

" Sot er man crezzy (crazy) dot bin my fren' an' kill 'im at de las'," said Big Angy, sententiously.

Tow Head gave the same sort of a delighted shiver as that with which she always greeted the account of little David holding up big Goliath's head.

" Oh ! oh ! " she cried, " do tell it quickly. Never mind the knitting. I'm sure you're working on my mittens, and I don't need them. When I go out of doors I can roll my hand up in my apron, just like Aunt Mymee does. *Don't* stop to count stitches ! "

Big Angy was in no mind to let the stitches go. She counted and re-counted at the scrap of work she had taken from her bosom as she finished her story, until it seemed as if she had counted stitches enough to cover the hand of a giant. When she was through, she took one stitch and then counted all over again with extreme deliberation.

Aunt Mary looked at Tow Head, giggled, and then retired to a corner to meditate on the withering look Granny cast upon her.

" Hit," drawled Angy, " was Jean—Jean Lavallette—that lib in de big *plastered* house in de uppeh bottom. Jean, he bin rich. He papa gin 'im lots o' lan', lots o' money."

" Dat wuz good," commented Granny, removing her pipe from her lips for a moment and stirring in the smoking bowl of it with her little finger ; " but dat all dey wuz (that is all there was) good 'bout Jean, sholy. I knowed 'im. In de p'ints o' fack I laid dat po', mizzible sinneh out. He wuz the leastest putty cawpse dat e'er fill up er coffin, dat I knows."

Angy cared nothing about Jean's lack of beauty as a corpse, she went right on with her story and stated, presumably to the back log, for her gaze never turned from it, that Jean was rich, that he married a beautiful wife, rich also in ponies, cattle, and land. So well off was he that he had no need to work. He became a very idle fellow, he laid on the grass and thought of nothing. Because one cannot always do nothing at all but eat and smoke, in mere wantonness of spirit he took to throwing stones at the birds. He began with the jays and robins, because they hopped about him and seemed to mock his laziness. When he had grown so expert at his wicked pastime of striking the little creatures that his very first throw stunned the one he aimed at, he was no more content to kill robins and jays, he slaughtered indiscriminately. Soon none were left but wood-peckers. "Have care," said his friends to the bold fellow ; "it is the worst of luck to get the ill-will of *le nain rouge*.[1] Some of these woodpeckers about here are real birds, but we know not which feathered skin hides the sorcerer or his children."

At such warnings Jean only laughed, or if he said anything it was to boast loudly that he had killed woodpeckers and would do it again.

Mark the result. After killing woodpeckers it was no time at all until he took to drink. Oh ! not merely to getting drunk at the dances and on holidays, that, to be sure, was to be expected, but he took to keeping the jug always at his right hand, and truly the weeds never had a chance to grow while it was still. Drink, drink, drink he would, from sun-up to sundown, and from starlight to sun-up again, even reaching out for the *eau-de-vie* in his sleep. For the matter of that, he was never quite awake, nor quite asleep, though almost all the time he breathed as if the black dog of the witches were in his throat.

All things went wrong with the farm, in spite of Isabel's hard work and care, and because of this, the bewitched creature would sometimes rouse up and curse her. One day, when she

[1] The red dwarf. The earliest Latin races, Etruscan and Sabine, recognised in the woodpecker " the red dwarf," or red-capped goblin, whom they called *Pequ*, Picus, and Picumnus. Hence from *Pic*, the word *pecker*—*Vide* Preller, *Roman Mythologie.*—C. G. L.

was at work in the field, the baby took a fit and died, with Jean looking on and doing nothing.

Isabel buried the baby and went home to her father.

Then the stock was stolen, the prairie-fire took the fences, the fodder rotted in the fields. He looked about him, one morning, frosty enough to brighten his wits, and found not even the smallest of small pigs was left to him. He was hungry, he went to catch a fish. As he started, he saw a woodpecker running along a tree-trunk. Full of fury, he swore terribly, and flung the empty whiskey-jug directly at it. In an instant, what a change ! The bird was a man, small, fierce, terrible, breathing flame. It flung a dart of lightning through him, it spit flames. into his eyes.[1] He fell insensible from pain and fright, and knew no more until evening, when some neighbours happened to pass along, and found him more dead than alive. For a long time after they had restored his consciousness, he shrieked and raved of the little red man, and many times told all that had happened. Nothing, not even holy water, did him any good. After much suffering he died, and no wonder, for there is no limit to the power of an offended *homme rouge.*

Tow Head was speechless. Aunt Mymee came in with a peremptory command for her " to show herself mejumly (immediately) at de House," and she was not loth to obey. She was really sorry when, in answer to a most flattering invitation, Aunt Mymee agreed to stop a few moments and "top off de ebenin' wid a chune (tune)."

" Don't," entreated Tow Head.

" Des er minnit, honey," said Aunt Mymee, retiring, with the child in her arms, to the corner farthest from the others.

" Now, ladies, mek ready foh de co-is (chorus), an' git yo' moufs in chune."

[1] The Romans were very much afraid of being blinded by the woodpecker. To prevent this they carried as a charm either the root of the red peony, or red coral.--C. G. L.

The "ladies" "chuned up" by laying down their pipes and opening their mouths.

Mymee began—

> "Death-watch tickin' in de wall."

To which they responded with all the strength of their lungs—

> "Hyo! hyo, niggah!"
>
> ".De bigges' tree is boun' ter fall."
>
> "Hyo! hyo, niggah!"
>
> "Ole man count he steers an' crap."
>
> "Hyo! hyo, niggah!"
>
> "Des wait ole man, yo' gwine ter drap."
>
> "Hyo! hyo, niggah!"
>
> "O, genlermens, look out! look out!"
>
> "Hyo! hyo, niggah!"
>
> "De Ole Bad Man, he mighty stout."
>
> "Hyo! hyo, niggah!"
>
> "Yo' git flung down befo' yo' t'ink.'
>
> "Hyo! hyo, niggah!"
>
> "Den, in de pit yo' bile an' swink."
>
> "Hyo! hyo, niggah!"

VII.

WOODPECKER AND GREY WOLF—WOODPECKER, THE HUNTER, AND DOG—HOW REDBIRD CAME BY HIS BRILLIANT PLUMAGE.

THE next evening there was a most delightful reunion in the cabin. Aunt Em'ly was with her friends again, after many days' absence. One of her sons had been "in trouble," owing to his having confused the laws of *meum* and *tuum* one pleasant night, when by chance he stepped into a neighbour's hen-house.

"Des wut I 'spected," Granny had commented, severely, when she heard that the youthful Elisha languished in the "calaboose." "I blames dat up ergin Em'ly, I does so. W'en dat chile wuz er baby, spites o' all I c'd lay offen my tongue (could say), Em'ly use ter cut dat's chile's fingeh nails wid de scissus, stiddier a-bitin' um off. In cose dat wuz bound ter mek 'im er t'ief."

So said they all of them, but they were good to Aunt Em'ly excepting with their tongues. They treated her as if she were in bodily instead of mental distress ; they went into her poor home and helped her with her work ; they gave her of their stores of food and finery ; and, when Lish's short term of imprisonment had expired, and she lifted her abashed head and "showed her face among her friends" once more, she was given the seat of honour, and literally cushioned on down ; for Granny insisted on softening her hard situation as much as might be by the aid of a pillow stuffed with swansdown, and never before

used for any purpose whatsoever save that of ornamentation—
not even the children of " Miss Agnes " had been allowed to
press its sacred plumpness with their little heads.

"Ise feared yo' ain't settin' easy," said Granny, looking at
her guest with great complacency.

Aunt Em'ly, lifted so high in the old wooden rocking-chair
that her feet scarce touched the floor, and seemingly in great
fear lest the mighty and magnificent cushion beneath her
should explode like a bomb-shell, answered with emotion—

" Ise mighty comf uble, Aunt Jinny, mighty comf'uble ; but
Ise oneasy les' I spile dis hyeah piller. Hit's er heap too rich
foh *my* blood."

" Huh ! " exclaimed Granny, with fine scorn, " Ise mighty
ole, and Ise lib er long time an' seen er heap o' pillers in my
day, but I got yit ter see de one dat's too good foh yo' ter set
on, Em'ly."

" Dat's wut I sez."

" Me, too."

" Me, foh nurr."

" Lan' sakes ! " cried Aunt Em'ly, laughing, though the tears were running down
her kind old face, " ef mung han's (among
you all) yo' don't mek out ter spile me, I des
lak ter know who's ter blame, dat's all."

AUNT EM'LY.

"I think you are too good to spoil, Aunt Em'ly," said Tow
Head, adding her mite with all seriousness.

" Yessir ! yessir ! " cried Granny, beaming on the child.
" Des hyeah dat ! Laws ! Aunt Em'ly, dat chile hez des hone
(yearn) foh yo'. Time 'pun time she comed in hyeah an' she
say : ' I wisht Aunt Em'ly'd come.' Hit mos' fotched de teah
ter my eye."

Aunt Em'ly cackled in quite the old-time fashion, and wiped
her eyes on her apron.

" Dat's de bes' chile in de worl'," she cried.

Tow Head was actually embarrassed by this most unusual and unexpected compliment ; but she was not the one to waste her opportunities while she gave her emotions play.

" Tell me a story," she pleaded, instead of returning thanks. " Tell me a rabbit story, Aunt Em'ly. Mrs. Boogarry and all the rest of them keep on telling woodpecker stories, and some of them are funny and some of them scare me."

" Dare now ! I knows un dat ain't gwine ter scare yo', honey, 'bout Grey Wolf an' Old Woodpeckeh. I boun' hit mek yo' laff. Lemme tell yo' dat."

Tow Head had confidence in Aunt Em'ly, and at once agreed to listen to anything she would relate ; so the old woman made one last desperate effort to plant her feet firmly on the floor, and began :—

" One time, w'en Ole Woodpeckeh wuz feelin' dat fat an' sassy dat 'e t'ink one o' he tail-fedders know mo' den er whole passel ob de turr buhds, he strut roun' a-huntin' foh some sort o' debbil*mint* foh 'muse hisse'f wid. He look hyeah an' he look dar, he look hidder an' he look yan (yonder), but he don't see de leastes' mite o' fun, kase w'y, dey wuz wunst er day (they knew) dat 'e des natch'ly lam de peelin' offen Ole Jay Buhd, an' dat skeer de urr buhds so dat dey dassent neighbeh wid 'im no mo', dey des tek up dey heels an' git w'en dey see 'im a-comin'. De mo' dat Ole Woodpeckeh noduss dat de mo' biggetty (arrogant) he bin feel. He feel lak he mo' biggeh den Grey Wolf ur Turkle, ur mos' all dey kinfolks. He des feel lak (as if) Ole Grey Wolf's whole hide ain't mo'n big nuff ter mek 'im er thumbstall. Dat am mos' gin'ly de way, honey, w'en folkses 'gin ter 'mire deyse'fs. De mo' dey 'mire, de mo' dey kin 'mire. Hit's des lak a-larnin' foh ter chaw de 'backy. At the fust, lawsy me ! don't yo' feel mighty peart ! Den yo' feel mighty squawmish in de eenside. Den yo' lay yo'se'f back an' 'low yo' feel mighty mean an' ain't no un gwine ter ketch yo' doin' dat ergin. Ner' day, dough, yo' 'low dat yo' gib hit nurr trial, des foh ter 'vince

7

yo' mine (to convince your mind). Dat ain't so bad ez yistiddy. Nex' day hit mo' betteh yit, an' so hit go 'long twell
yo' a-keepin' at hit study, an' so de 'speunce (experience) go
'long, an' de taste foh de 'backy am up an' a-growin', twell at de
las' yo' ain't satisfy medout um. Yessir, dat de way! 'Backy-
chawin' an' 'mirin' yo'se'f des de same. Yo' got de hand-glass
an' I got de 'backy ; yo' look, 1 chaw ; but hit come ter des de
same, an' boun' ter, now an' ebber an' ebber lastin'ly. Dat wuz
sholy an' suttinly de way wid Ole Woodpeckeh. 'E cock 'e
eye, 'e russle 'e fedders, 'e hole 'e haid on one side, 'e strut w'en
'e walk, an' 'e flop w'en 'e fly. Nemmine, Old Woodpeckeh !
Ole Grey Wolf am a-comin' thu de woods des a-lopin'
(running).

"Ole Grey Wolf, he come 'long, tuhnin' he projects in he
mine, an' he ain't see Ole Woodpeckeh.

"All on de suddint—bim ! Ole Woodpeckeh done hit 'im
er clip des back ob de yeah. 'Well !' sez Ole Grey Wolf, sez
'e, sorter slackin' up, ' de Fall (autumn) hez got hyeah foh sho,
an' I bin dat press foh time dat I ain't noduss de fack twell dat
maple leaf russle down on me des now.'

"Blam !—Ole Woodpeckeh gin 'im nurr clip right on de top
o' de haid, an' honeys, hit wuz er hahd (hard) un !

"Ole Grey Wolf don't stop, but he sorter tuhn he eye up ter
de trees. ' Hit sholy am Fall,' sez 'e, ' kase des now dat mischevyous ole Miss Bushytail bin crack lil nut an' shy de shell
onter me.'

"Grashis ! dat mek Ole Woodpeckeh so mad. He fotched
er squall, suz, dat wuz wuss'n er ghostes' whustle, an' mek de
woods ring ergin. Den he des peck all ober Grey Wolf.

"Grey Wolf trot 'long, he do, des ez gay ez de lil fox in de
grape-season, an' he 'low hit kinder late in de yeah foh skeetuz
(mosquitoes), but he sholy feel um nip wunst ur twiste.

"'Nemmine !' he say, 'dat wuz er skeeter, but nemmine !
I spoge (suppose) we gwine ter git rid ob um mos' enny night

now ; kase w'en de leabes an' de nuts fall free, den Ole Jack Fros' ain't a-settin' in de holler a-smokin' willer-trigs, he's a-packin' up he traps ter go a-trabblin'. Yessir, de fros' gwine ter git hyeah soon an' ketch dem lil skeeter-bugs ' (mosquitoes).

"Oh ! den Ole Woodpeckeh feel mean, I tell yo'. He des dror off, he do, an' he mek cunjerin' rings, he scratch trick-mahks on de ground, he cut signs on de trees, but they don't none un um faze (trouble) Ole Grey Wolf, mine yo'. He des trot erlong thu dem woodses gwine 'bout he bizniz an' bod-derin' 'bout nuttin. One ur two times he grin dat long, slow-comin' grin dat 'e kin grin, an' wunst he look o'er he shouldeh an' laff. Dat all. He ain't mine dem lil cunjerin' gwines-on. He done fegit (forget) mo' tricks den all Woodpeckeh know.

" At de las' Ole Woodpeckeh wuhk hisse'f up so dat he plum crazy a' 'stractid. He fling hisse'f down afront ob Ole Grey Wolf des a-foamin' an' a-bilin'.

"'Kill me !' sez 'e. 'Kill me l I setch er big fool I don't want ter lib no longeh. I ain't fitten foh nuttin but buzzahd-meat. I wanter die an' pe'sh offen de face of de yeath. I hate myse'f so bad dat I des afiah (a-fire) ! '

"'Afiah, is yo'?' sez Ole Grey Wolf, sez 'e, a-grinnin' an' des skusely a-lettin' up in he pace. 'Den I reckon I got ter putt yo' out,' sez 'e.

"Wid dat he up an spit right squar' on Ole Woodpeckeh, an' I lay he *wuz* put out ! He wuz des nigh onter drownded. Honey, dat sassy buhd's *bones* wuz wet t'rough.

" Ole Grey Wolf, he ain't stop dough ; he des rack erlong easy an' mild, an' at de tuhn ob de parf he git plum out o' sight."

"And what became of Woodpecker, Aunt Em'ly ? Did he die ? "

"Oh, no, chile l He ain't ob de dyin' kine. He snuffle an' he sneeze an' he choke an' he gap, an' w'en he git he senses back he strike out foh home. W'en he git dar he hide, and des ez sho ez Ise a-settin' hyeah er libbin' niggeh, he ain't come

out o' dat hole in de tree foh er plum week ! Ole Miss Woodpeckeh, she bin' bleeged to kyar he vittles in ter 'im, ruther
den see 'im styarve hisse'f ter death, kase he dat cut up dat he
des cudn't come out. I reckon he'd a-bin dar yit ef de baby
ain't tuck sick, an' dat baby wuz he fayvo*rite*, so he kim out
ter kyore (cure) hit up."

Big Angy was incensed at this belittling of her hero, and did
not scruple to make her feelings known. In the language of
her father, for there are no "swear-words" in the tongue of

"OLE MISS WOODPECKEH SHE BIN 'BLEEGED TER KYAR HE VITTLES
IN TER 'IM."

her Indian mother, she "cussed" the insulting tale, and then
made haste to relate one which should offset it.

One evening, late, as a hunter and his dog were walking
slowly towards home, they saw before them, in the narrow
path that wound through the underbrush, a very strange little
red man. He seemed to be very feeble, very old, very lame.
He told them, in faint accents, that he was far from home,
weary almost unto death, and ready to perish from long fasting.

The hunter made answer, "If you can reach my lodge you
will be welcome there. I have plenty of food, and a bed of

soft furs for you, but it depends on you to get to them. As you see, I have no horse to place at your disposal."

The little man replied more cheerfully than he had before spoken that he could not walk, that was quite impossible, but, as he was so small, he thought the dog could carry him ; adding that he saw marks on the dog which showed he had been used to carrying a pack strapped on his back.

" That is very true," said the hunter. " When me move our lodge this kind and faithful animal does have a pack strapped

THE HUNTER AND THE LITTLE RED MAN.

on his back. Also my children ride him as if he were a pony, but I will not call on him to carry other burdens unless he is willing. It is one thing to help the family of which he is a part, quite another to be burdened by a stranger—that, too, when he is already weary."

Then said the little man, " All that is true and reasonable, I acknowledge that ; but may I be allowed to speak with the dog myself ? "

The hunter gave permission, so the little red man called the dog close to him, and pleaded very touchingly that he might not be left to die alone in the thicket of hunger and fatigue. "Take me," he begged, piteously, "to the hunter's lodge. I am not heavy when I am at my best, and now I scarce weigh more than a flake of wild cotton."

The dog was an uncommonly good-natured fellow, so, although weary and footsore himself, he was won to allowing the little old man to ride him to the village.

"WITH THAT HE WALKED OFF TO THE OTHER DOGS, WHO RECEIVED HIM WITH SNIFFS AND YELPS OF DERISION."

When they arrived, the little man, as he dismounted, whispered in the dog's ear, "You shall lose nothing by this."

"Oh! that is very well," answered the dog. "You are quite welcome to my assistance. I desire no present." With that he walked off to the other dogs, who received him with sniffs and yelps of derision.

"We met that old man out yonder, too," said they ; "but

we were not fools enough to become his servants. Oh! no, not we. We have enough to do to serve those who feed us."

This mortified the dog, but he was not more mortified than his master. The people of the village were all jeering at the hunter.

"Ah!" said they, "it was you, was it, to whom it was left to bring that wretched cripple among us? We saw him, but he was no relation of ours, not even a friend of our friends. With game growing scarcer all the time, did you do well to bring him to eat your children's meat?"

This made the hunter feel badly, but he did not let his guest know it. He fed the little man, he gave him a place by the fire, he gave him a bed of furs.

The next morning, early, the little man awakened his host and said—

"Owing to your kindness I am quite well again. Now I must be gone. One last favour I ask, will you and your dog walk a short distance with me?"

To this the hunter agreed readily. He was glad that the guest of whom his friends had so low an opinion would soon be gone. He first set before him what food could be found, then called the dog.

When the little old man had eaten, off the three of them went, he leading at a pace with which the hunter and the dog could scarce keep up.

"Stop! stop! Grandfather," cried the hunter, after a little while. "I perceive that you are making a mistake. You are going the way whence we came yesterday. Let us retrace our steps, before we go farther out of your way."

"Come yet a few more steps this way," said the little old man.

So they went on again a long way.

Once again the hunter called out—

"Stop! stop! Grandfather. You are making labour for yourself. The place where we found you is not far from here."

" Come yet a few steps more," urged the little man.

So they went on again until they came to the place where they had met the evening previous.

" Stop! stop! Grandfather," cried the hunter. " We are on the spot where we found you yesterday."

" That is true," said the little man. " It is where I meant to bring you. Now, we will stop and talk a little. You only of all your tribe and relationship have I found worthy of any friendship or consideration. I think better of your dog than I do of your chief or doctor. For this reason I mean to confer benefits on you two that they may not even dream of gaining. I will make of you whatsoever you choose ; I will make of your dog whatsoever he may choose after you are done. You two only befriended me, you two only will I befriend."

So saying, he shot up before them exceedingly tall and terrible. Nevertheless, as they were not of the kind that quails, they looked on him undauntedly.

"Wish !" commanded he who had been the little man, impatiently.

" Oh, great chief, make me the greatest of hunters !" cried the hunter.

" You shall be not only the greatest slayer of beasts, but also the greatest slayer of men," was the answer. " So I say, so shall it be."

Then turned he who had been the little man to the dog.

"What do you choose?" asked he. " Will you be the doctor yourself and turn out that old weed-eater who holds the place ? "

This the dog did not care for. "I have been treated disrespectfully," said he, " by the other animals. Wolves have taunted me for carrying burdens, young dogs have scorned my slowness, beavers have told me my teeth were rotten as last year's briers. Make me strong enough to be terrible to them all."

" Will you be a mountain lion?" asked he who had been little.

The dog joyfully answered he would like that above all things. " Then a lion you are. So I say it, so shall it be," said he who had been the little red man.

After this the man shrank to the size he had been when the hunter and the dog first saw him. Immediately he took affectionate leave of them and ordered them to go home and wait patiently for their heart's desire to come to them.

The hunter and the dog started home, but after taking a few steps they looked back.

No little red man was in sight, but a great woodpecker rose from the grass and flew away.

" This is strange. Where has our friend gone?" began the hunter to his old dog, but he did not finish what he was going to say. He looked into the usually mild and friendly eyes of his companion, they were changed to great yellow moons ; his stature also was greatly increased. Awestruck, the hunter shrank back : at the same moment, with a fierce and terrible cry, the mighty

" A GREAT WOOD-
PECKER ROSE FROM
THE GRASS."

lion—dog no longer—bounded into the thicket and never again was seen by his former master.

The hunter made haste homeward and reached his lodge before the village was astir. He laid down and pretended to sleep late. When he finally rose up, his friends told him his guest was gone, without leave-taking. " Worse than that," they added, " he has stolen your dog, the faithful friend of your children."

The hunter heard them gravely, he said nothing. He thought of his dog's wish and its fulfilment. He made ready his arrows, he tried his bow-cord, he had prepared for him a

quiver of panther skin. When all was done, he started out
to hunt, but before he went he said to the people—

" Lend me many horses. Game is not scarce where I go. I
intend to load all the horses I take with as much as they can
carry."

The people thought he was bewitched by the little red man,
his relations were sorrowful, but he was so persuasive that he
had his way with them. They went along with him and saw
his wonderful success.

After that, he always brought plenty for all when every one
else failed.

When there was a war with enemies, he went to battle and
all fell before him. When the old chief died he took his
place and ruled many years. During all that time he kept
secret the cause of his success, but when he was about to
die he told his sons as a warning to them to invite good fortune
home and not drive it to the lodge of others.

Aunt Em'ly, industriously dabbing her toes against the
floor in a vain endeavour to rock her chair a little, took her
mind off her work long enough to say with fervour.

" Dat am de puttiest ob all de putty tales dat I done hyeah yo'
tell, Miss Boogarry. Hit done tuck all de shine offen dat lil
(little) un dat I muse de chile wid. I 'clar' I is shame dat I tole
tale 'tall' fo' yo'."

" Huh ! " began Tow Head, with a toss of her chin, but her
well-meant protest against Aunt Em'ly's humility was never
allowed utterance. Granny knew by sad and oft-repeated experience the lengths to which her young friend's candour could
be carried ; she knew, too, something of the magnitude of Big
Angy's temper when roused, therefore she hastened to get
command of the conversation herself.

" Dat's er mighty lubly tale yo' tole, Miss Boogarry, so wuz
de one yo' told, Aunt Em'ly, but, lan' o' Goshen ! 'pears lak de
mo' tale dat I hyeah, de mo' dat I hones ('onз) foh ter hyeah.

Ef one ur turr ob yo' folks don't whirl in an' tell nurr tale, I boun' dat I don't get er wink o' sleep dis night, I'll be dat wuhkt up wid a-wishin' an' a-honin'."

"Ise run out," declared Aunt Em'ly.

"No use a-axin' me," giggled Aunt Mary. "I done tole all I knowed in des no time."

"'Tain't my tuhn dis ebenin'," mumbled Aunt Mymee, looking stubborn and puffing smoke till Tow Head, sitting on her knee, appeared in the midst of clouds like a cherub perpetrated by an imitator of the Old Masters.

"I hez ter putt my pennunce (dependence) in yo' ergin, Miss Boogarry."

When Big Angy was in a talkative mood she enjoyed listening to the sound of her own voice too well to coyly withhold it. The mood was on her then, and she at once began as glibly as if she were praising her wares to a customer, on—

HOW THE REDBIRD CAME BY HIS BRILLIANT PLUMAGE.

One time when Woodpecker was far from home and making medicine, a plain bird, with whom he was very little acquainted, came flying to him in great haste and distress.

"Fly home!" cried the plain bird in great excitement. "Fly home!" Your enemies are there before you! They seek to destroy your children! Your wife can do nothing, her threats and entreaties are of no avail!"

When Woodpecker heard these words he did not even stop to thank the bird who sent them, faster than the wind, faster than the lightning he went home.

There he saw a sight most distressing. His wife, wounded and bleeding, was flying about the entrance to their house, and by her desperate efforts just managed to keep Blue Jay and his companion in wickedness, a great snake, from going in to where the children were. This was an awful experience for the poor mother, for she had no magical power, but it was nothing to

Old Woodpecker once he was on the ground. In a moment he drove away his enemies with marks of his displeasure upon them which they would carry for many a day.

When they were out of sight he went in and comforted the children and healed the hurts his wife had received from Blue Jay.

This done, he looked around for the plain bird, but saw him not, and, not knowing the place of his abode, could not seek him.

That was nothing !

Woodpecker made circles and sang songs and spoke incantations, and so summoned the plain bird into his presence.

The plain one flew directly to the presence of Woodpecker, and was so simple that he knew not that he had been summoned by magic. When he arrived he was confused and abashed, and knew not what to say. He wished to go away again, but Woodpecker detained him, made him very welcome, and praised him highly.

" What, benefactor of my family, do you wish as a gift ? " Woodpecker asked.

Plain Bird said he wished for nothing.

Woodpecker insisted that he must receive some gift of his own choosing.

Often Plain Bird refused to ask for anything.

Often Woodpecker insisted on his asking.

Finally the plain one said—

"Oh, mighty conjuror, I am very tired of this dull-coloured coat I wear ! The dust of the earth is not less pleasing to the eye. I should like to have all over me fine red feathers like those on your head."

" It shall be as you wish," declared Woodpecker, pleased that he had compelled a choice of favours.

Then he took Plain Bird to a secret place. Arrived there, he scratched his own wing till a drop of blood came.

" See," said he to Plain Bird, " I shed my blood for you, so strong is my gratitude."

So saying, he took the drop and mixed it with water and a red herb that was medicine. With this mixture he painted Plain Bird. Then he conducted him to a pond, and bade him look at himself.

Plain Bird looked and saw that he was a red bird,[1] glowing, brilliant, beautiful. He thought of his grey little wife, and most humbly entreated that Woodpecker beautify her also.

" Conduct her hither. Something may be done," said Woodpecker.

Redbird flew away and found his wife and brought her to be painted with the blood and medicine of Woodpecker.

Alas ! there was but little of that magical paint left. For this reason she is not so gay as her mate, but still she has bright colour enough to do very well and make her think, as often as she trims her feathers, of the grateful heart and magical skill of old Woodpecker.

The child clapped her hands with delight as Big Angy concluded, and her elders—children as they were of a larger growth—were moved to follow her example.

"Oh ! " exclaimed the little one with a long-drawn breath, " that was be-u-tiful ! That was better than a rabbit story. Couldn't you tell another, Mrs. Boogarry ? "

Mrs. " Boogarry " couldn't, or, what amounted to the same thing, wouldn't. She nipped her pipe-stem with her teeth like a snapping turtle taking hold of a stick, and shook her head without speaking.

"I des now thunk ob one ! " announced Granny, with the surprised and joyful air of one who had come unexpectedly on a long-lost piece of silver.

" Fetch um out, Aunt Jinny, fetch um out dis minnit, les' hit slip yo' membunce afo' yo' knows hit," said Aunt Em'ly,

---

[1] The red-bird or scarlet tanager, a variety of the oriole, is entirely of a brilliant scarlet colour.

slipping off her honourable but uneasy perch, and making herself comfortable on a stool.

Granny, nothing loth, told—

How Blacksnake made Trouble for Woodpecker and Himself.

"One time, w'en Ole Woodpeckeh went a-santerin' home, arter sundown, he hyeah de wussest howdy-do (riot) dat eber wuz in de worl.' He kine o' stiffen hisse'f up w'en de soun' strak 'im an' mend he step.

"Toreckly, he hyeah he ole 'ooman des a-hollerin' an' a-bawlin', an' he putt in he bes' licks an' git home in des no time.

" Dar he see all de neighbehs 'semmle tergedder, some un um a-scolin' an' a-miratin' (admiring) an' a-chatterin' an' a-fussin' roun' Miss Woodpeckeh, an' some un um a-dabbin' an' a-swoopin' at er big brack snake dat wuz a-layin' at de foot ob de tree all budge out an' fit ter bust.

" 'Wut de matteh hyeah ? ' ax Ole Woodpeckeh.

" Ev'body pint at de snake an' shake dey haid mighty sollum.

" Ole Woodpeckeh, he count de chilluns.

" ' Whah de baby ? ' he ax.

" Dey shake dey haid ergin an' pint at de snake some mo'.

" Dat 'nuff foh Ole Woodpeckeh.   He ain't stop ter ax Miss Woodpeckeh ter stop hollerin', he ain't smack de chilluns foh gittin' in de way, he ain't want ter know ob de neighbehs ef de cat got dey tongue, nur nuttin.   He des mek one grab at dat snake— blam ! one eye out a-ready !   Nurr grab !—blam ! turr eye out ! Den he cotch um by de tail an' hole um up an' shake um, an', bress de Lawd ! dat baby-woodpeckeh fall outen he jaw ! "

Here Granny paused, knocked the ashes out of her pipe, blew in the bowl, shut one eye, and pretended to be looking for obstructions in the stem.

" Is that all ? " asked Tow Head, impatiently.

" Hole on, honey, hole on," said Grarny, placidly, the while she hunted for her pocket—a cumbrous affair not sewed in her gown, but dangled between it and her petticoats, and kept from falling to earth by two long strings sewed to its top and passed several times around her waist.

" Your tobacco is not in your large pocket. You know well enough it is in your small pouch at your belt," cried Tow Head, vigorously kicking her heels against Aunt Mymee in her impatience.

"So 'tis, honey, so 'tis," said Granny, regarding Aunt Mymee's vicarious punishment with complacency.

" Is that *all ?* "

" No, honey, Ise yit got de fine-cut dat yo' pa brung me fum town. Dar 'tis, on de shelf, yondah."

" I mean, you hateful old thing, is that all about Wood-pecker's baby ? "

" Shuh ! " exclaimed Granny, beginning to puff at the newly-filled pipe, " is dat tork mannehs ter de ole folks? Dat ain't de way I wuz larnt w'en I wuz young."

Tow Head turned to Aunt Mymee in a fury of impatience, " Do you know ? " she questioned.

" Ef all yo' got on yo' mine," said Aunt Mymee, looking at Granny and speaking with deliberate impressiveness, " am foh ter git dis chile so wuhkt up dat she kyarn't sleep dis night, I reck'n I mought betteh tote huh right up ter de House."

" Ez I wuz a-sayin', honey," said Granny, sweetly, to the child, and taking no notice of Aunt Mymee's remark, " w'en dat triflin' ole pipe o' mine quit a-suckin'—de, baby-woodpeckeh fell outen de jaws oh Bracksnake, but de po' lil crittur wuz done die stone daid. Nemmine ! nemmine, dough ! Wood-peckeh mo'n er match foh dat, an' so I tells you'. W'en he see de baby wuz shoh nuff daid, he go an' he git out de medsum (medicine, or magic) pipe an' he puff an' he suck an' he draw an' he fill dat lil daid woodpeckeh full ob de smoke. W'en dat smoke fill lil woodpeckeh he 'mence ter come ter life.

He stretch he wings fust an' kick one laig, den he flinch he tail
an' dror up bofe laigs, den he shet an' open he bill an' dror
up he claws. Arter dat he gap big an' sneege—a-kwisha ! Dis
done, he wuz well, an' he fly up ter he mammy.

"Den wuz de time dat Ole Woodpeckeh tuhn he 'tention 'pun
Bracksnake ter gib 'im er good sottlemint (settlement). He
kyarn't kill dat villyun out an' out, kase he got cunjerin' sense
in 'im too, but, lan' o' love ! he kin fill 'im wid tricks (spells),
ez full ez de shucks (dried maize leaves) whah de hogs lay is
full ob fleas. He scratch that Bracksnacke down de back, an'
he blow hot on 'im an' dry 'im up lak er last yeah's milk-
weed, den 'e tuhn 'im aloose, an' er fine sight he wuz !

"Sence dat day dat Bracksnake ain't no mo' 'count. He
own folks ain't count kin wid 'im. To be shoh, he cunjer back
he eyesight, ur mo' 'tickler, (or, what is more) he knowed de
weed dat kin do dat, an' he cunjer de weed ter cum unter 'im
an' kyore (cure) 'im, but he ain't got de sense ter cunjer back
he strenk ur he good looks. Fum dat day unter dis he des
wriggle roun' in de grass, he don't climb trees no mo' ur run
fas' 'long de aige (edge) ob de road lak de res' o' he fambly,
an' folkses wen dey see 'im, dey des poke fun at 'im stiddier
(instead of) gittin' skeered. Dey let on, dey do, dat dey s'picion
some triflin' gal done drap 'im offen 'er laig, an' des foh sport
dey calls 'im de gyarteh (garter) snake. Oh, yes ! dat's so, po'
lil wizzle (poor little withered up thing) up t'ing. Ise seen 'im,
menny an' menny's de time, an' so I boun' hez all de res' ob
yo'. 'Tain't but des 'fo' fros' dat I brung one up, a-twustin'
ev'whichaways, on de eend o' my stick, w'en I wuz a-pokin' in
de daid leabes a-searchin' foh warnits (walnuts)."

"I should hate," said Tow Head, uneasily, "to get one of
those things on by mistake. I'm always dropping my garters
and picking them up again. I might pick up a snake, if it
looked just like one. Granny, do you know if they have
buckles on the ends of them ? "

"No, dey don't," said Aunt Mymee, emphatically. "Dar, now, Aunt Jinny, des look wut yo' done! I 'low yo' hafter tell nurr tale ter git de tase (taste) ob dis un outen de chile's mouf."

"Yo' ain't skeered, is yo', honey?"

"N-no," answered the child, doubtfully, "but maybe I will be if you do not tell another story. Sometimes I get scared after I go to bed, when the lights are out and there seems to be such a lot of dark. Those times, the stories you've heard seem to be coming at you if they are not nice."

"Den I gwine ter tell 'bout de pahty (party) dat Ole Wood-peckeh wuz 'tendin' wunst (once attended). De pahty, honey, whah he play on de fiddle up at Perarer-Chickin's house. Mebbe yo' don't keer foh dat tale, do ugh?"

Tow Head did care, and said so, to Aunt Mymee's disgust, so Granny began—

"One time, Ole Perarer-Chicken, he gin er big pahty. All de buhds dey hed er eenvite, clar down ter Cow-buntin' an' clar up ter Ole Woodpeckeh hisse'f. Dem eenvites dey kick up er heap er ter-do-unce (preparation) mungs de buhds. Dey pick de tangles outen dey pin-fedders an' smoove dey quills an' ile dey backs an' breas'es twell dey shine lak er pond in de sun. W'en dey git primp ter dey mine, dey sot out, Ole Woodpeckeh lil arter de res'. Time wuz w'en 'e wouldn't a-gone er step in dat 'rection, but dat wuz 'fo' Ole Perarer-Chicken gun 'im warnin' dat Ole Miss Owl, she 'low she like mighty well ter hab er mess ob young woodpeckehs in 'er pot-pie on de table w'en she git up de suppeh foh de weddin' ob 'er oldes' gal. Ole Woodpeckeh, he wuz much erbleeged foh dat piece o' news, an' he keep one eye out twell arter de weddin'. He ain't ne'er fegit dat good tuhn (turn), an' fum dat day fo'th he pass de time o' day an' ax, 'How am yo' good healt', neighbeh?' w'en dey meet.

"Ez I wuz a-ree-mockin' (remarking), he went ter de pahty. Hit bin hilt out in one o' dem lil open place mungs de woods,

8

an' wuz all green wid grass, an' de grass speckled up wid
berbenyums (verbenas) an' sweet-willyums, an' de likes, an' de
place wuz sorter fence-in wid wild-rose bushes an' de hazel-bresh
dat sorter hug up ergin de plum trees an' saplin's. Hit wuz er
mighty fav'able spot, honey, an' sides de res' dey wuz er lil cl'ar
runnin' crik ganderin' 'crost one cornder.

"So, den ! Dey all got dar, an' dey wuz turr'ble p'lite ter
un nurr an' complymint dey looks, an' ax arter de chilluns.

"Arter w'iles, w'en dey done nibble de grass seeds an' gobble
de groun'-churries an' snap up de bugs an' hoppehgrasses an'
bo' (bore) down in de groun' an' git er wuhm ur two, an' grab
'bout fibe ur six minnuz (minnows) out en de crik, 'corjin' ez
dey tas-tes calls foh, dey all whirl in an ax Ole Perarer-Chicken
foh ter darnce dat darnce ob hissen dat dey hyeah (heard) tell
on so much.

" Now, dat darnce wuz er sorter er cunjerin' darnce, an' e'en
Ole Woodpeckeh des natchelly hone (longed) foh ter see 'im
darnce hit.

" Perarer-Chicken, he ain't nowise sot on showin' off dat
darnce.

" ' I ain't got no moosic,' sez 'e, ' an', in co'se, I kyarn't mek
out medout none. W'en I wuz young,' sez 'e, ' an' not so fat
an' pussy ' (pursy, plump), sez 'e, ' I c'd sing me a little chune ter
darnce by des ez I went erlong, but I kyarn't do dat no mo','
sez 'e, a-shakin' he haid an' a-lookin' sollum. ' Ise gittin' ole
an' tizzicky, now. Ise 'bleege ter 'noledge dat.'

" ' I kin play yo' er chune dat I 'low yo' kin mek out by,' sez
Ole Woodpeckeh, speakin' up mighty quick an' smilin'. ' In
co'se, I ain't no great shakes,' sez 'e, ' but I kin mek out ter
pick er chune an' I'll do hit, rudder'n see all dese hyeah frens
go home dis'pinted,' sez 'e. ' I'm got bofe er fiddle an' er
whustle,' sez 'e.

" ' Le's hab de whustle ! ' sez de comp'ny, speakin' up mighty
f'erce.

"'Yo's mighty kine ter gib ch'ice,' sez Perarer-Chicken. 'Ise sho' I kyarn't darnce ter no whustle.'

" De facks o' de marter am, he don't wanter darnce 'tall, but he don' lak ter 'fuse at he own pahty. 'Sidesen dat, he know dat whustle am dangersome.

"'De fiddle gits hit,' sez de ladies an' gentermens.

"'Ef I mus', I mus', I reckon,' sez Perarer-Chicken, ' but ez yo' 'gree, le's hab de fiddle. De fiddle sorter he'ps out, but de whustle am diffunt.'

" De Lawd know, he don't wanter darnce ter dat whustle, kase hit wuss des er full-size witch foh debbil*mint.* Hit bin mek outen de big eagle wing-bone an' hit des fit ter bust wid cunjurin'. W'en Ole Woodpeckeh blow on hit, he blow all manneh ob chahms right inter de noggins (heads) an' bones ob' de ones dat hyeah 'im blow.

" So dey all know an' dey 'gree on de fiddle, an' dey tork back an' fo'th twell dey all out o' bref, an' den dey sen' Redbuhd arter de fiddle."

" I never saw a redbird that could carry a fiddle, Granny."

" Ef yo' keep yo' eye on um, honey, de charnces am dat yo' will see hit, kase dis hyeah fiddle ain't no biggeh'n de eend j'int ob de ole cat's tail. Hit wuz," said Granny, evidently drawing on her imagination for the child's amusement, " mek outen de liles' gode (gourd) dat e'er growed on de vines. One side wuz hack off an' strung 'cross wid de innards ob er buffler-cricket (buffalo-cricket) foh fiddle-strings, an' ha'r offen er flutterbug (butterfly) foh bowstrings, w'ich de same bow wuz er fishbone.

" Well den !—Quail, Ole Perarer-Chicken's grandarter, whustle de chune dat he wanter darnce by ez well ez she kin twell Ole Woodpeckeh, he cotch um. Den—cr-r-r-eek, s-s-s-quee-ee-k ! squeak ! he draw de bow 'crost de strings an' den de chune, hit come des a-trabblin', an' Ole Perarer-Chicken, he darnce an' he darnce, twell he laigs mos' fit ter drap off, an' dey all mek de gret miration an' gigglin' an' dey

DE BUHDS.

all mought a-bin dar yit a-joyin' deyse'fs ef dey hain't come er
crickle-crackle in de bresh, an' den w'en dey tuhn foh ter look
—ping !— an' dat wuz de fust shot de w'ite man fiah off in dis
paht ob de kyentry.

"De buhds, dey all cut out foh home, liketty-switch (rapidly),
m'dout a-sayin' ' good ebenin',' ur how dey bin 'joy deyse'fs, ur
nuttin, an' hit tuck um long time ter fine out dat de ruction
wuzzent some ob Ole Woodpeckeh's cunjerin' tricks. Lan' o'
Gosha' ! Ole Woodpeckeh, he run wid de bes', wid he fiddle
un'neat' he wing.

"De bow," continued Granny, after a pause which seemed
interminable to her listeners, " he drapped in de bresh some'ers.

" Arter dat, dat same ole gun wuhkt er heap o' mischief, an'
arter w'iles, Ole Woodpeckeh he stop gittin' de credick ob hit.
All de same dough, dey ain't bin sech er mighty menny woodpeckehs kilt. W'en dey wuz, two free w'ite man gotter pay
foh hit. Ef foolin' am did wid er woodpeckeh, de one dat do
hit am de one dat got de bill ter pay, an', genterfolk, cunjerers'
bills am long ones."

" So dey be," said Big Angy, with unction, "an' dat mek I
t'ink 'bout nurr tale."

" Ef yo' please, Miss Boogarry," said Aunt Mymee, " let dat
tale keep de w'iles yo' 'fresh yo'se'f wid Aunt Jinny's pop-cawn
an' honey. I boun' ter kyar dis chile ter baid, else Ole Mistis,
she'll git arter me.—Oh, yes, honey ! Come 'long putty, now"
—this to her reluctant charge—" an' I'll sing yo' er woodpeckeh
song."

The little girl went along " putty," and, as a reward, heard
this touching ballad—

" Woodpeckeh tappin' on de maple bahk.
Miss Wuhm hyeah 'im.—Hahk ! oh, hahk !
Miss Wuhm quiled (coiled) on de parlour flo',
Woodpeckeh bustin' thu de entry do' !
Good-bye, Miss Wuhm, yo' boun' ter git er fall !
Woodpeckeh swallered huh, petticuts an' all ! "

VIII

*HOW WOODPECKER TOOK A BOY TO RAISE AND
WAS DISGUSTED WITH THE JOB. ALSO, HOW
HE SET OUT TO CHARM GRANDFATHER RATTLE-
SNAKE, TOGETHER WITH A HISTORY OF HIS
NECKLACE OF BEARS' CLAWS, AND AN ACCOUNT
OF HIS ATTEMPT TO DESTROY RABBIT'S CUNJER-
BAG.*

IG ANGY had been telling another story of
Woodpecker and boasting of his power,
"des ez ef he wuz huh own kinfolks," as
Aunt Mary privately commented.

Once, she told the company, a band of
people were fleeing from their enemies and,
as they went along in great haste, they
dropped a baby-boy and passed on, not per-
ceiving their loss.

OLE RABBIT. Woodpecker heard the little fellow cry
and, not wishing to see him killed by the enemies of his people
or eaten by wolves or panthers, he carried him home and
brought him up among his own children. He taught the boy
many things and treated him so well that it was a wonder that
he was not perfectly happy, but this he was not. When he found
that he was different from the children of Woodpecker, nothing
would satisfy him but knowing who he was and how he came
to be where he was. After listening to many entreaties, Woodpecker told him all there was to tell, adding—

" Be content here.   I have made a son of you.   Day by day,
as you can understand, I will teach you my wisdom.   Seek not
your own people, as you evidently wish to do ; they are not a
brave people—no mighty warriors are amongst them—they are
not a wise people—their counsellors count for nothing and their
sorcerers are as little children before me.   They are poor, they
are miserable, they are despised by their acquaintances.   Seek
them not."

This was good advice, but the boy, now grown to be a tall
youth, would not heed it ; he was determined to go to his own
kind.

" WOODPECKER TOOK A BOY TO RAISE AND WAS DISGUSTED WITH
THE JOB."

" Then go back to them as you came from them ! " cried
Woodpecker, in a rage.

Immediately the young man shrank to the size of a baby and
never grew any larger, as can be proved, for, after Woodpecker
drove him off, he wandered all over the earth, telling of his
misfortunes and asking vainly for tidings of his people.

Aunt Mymee was tired of Woodpecker, and had made up her
mind to " sottle dat braggin'," so, with a suavity of manner
somewhat at variance with the malice twinkling in her eye, she
said—

" Hit's des pop inter my 'membunce dat in de time pass by, Ise hyurn (heard) er couple ob tales 'bout Ole Woodpeckeh my own se'f."

" Le's hab um," said her friends, quailing, they knew not why.

" De fust am 'bout Ole Woodpeckeh an' how he got he come-uppunce[1] wid Ole Gran'daddy Rattlesnake.   In de ole times, yo' mine, Ole Woodpeckeh, he suttinly hed mo'n he fa'r shear ob truck an' luck, but, suz I foh all dat he ain't out an' out sati'fy wid de gwines-on in de worl'.   Ef yo' tek er long walk, Gord know dat er chunk o' grabble boun' ter wuhk hit way eenside de fines' shoe, an' dat de way Ole Woodpeckeh foun' hit. Thesso I thesso ! (That's so) an' de one blisteh dat de grabble raise mek de feelin's ob de man dat got shoes wuss den de feelin's ob de one dat 'bleege to go bar'foot.   De blisteh on Ole Woodpeckeh heel wuz de 'membunce ob Ole Gran'daddy Rattlesnake an' de big name Ole Gran'daddy got.   All on de suddint he mek up he mine dat 'e gwine ter cunjer Ole Gran'daddy an' den, w'en he got 'im down unner foot, he gwine ter pull out he haht (heart) an' gin it ter he cousin ter kyore up (cure up) er bad cough she got."

" He don't hatter hab Ole Gran'dad foh dat," interrupted Granny.   " Enny rattlesnake haht'll kyore up (heart will cure) de breas'-kimplaint (consumption) ef yo' t'ar hit outen de body an' swaller hit down, p'int fust, w'iles de life am yit in hit."

" Dat fack I ain' 'sputin'," said Aunt Mymee, with a frown, " but 'tain't hyeah nurr dar in dis case.   Ole Woodpeckeh, he hone arter gittin' de haht ob Gran'daddy Rattlesnake an' he ain't gwine ter putt up wid nuttin else, ef he kin he'p hisse'f. Dat am," she corrected herself, " nuttin in de shapes ob er haht, dough, truf ter tell, he honed arter de rattles on Gran'-daddy tail de mos'es."

[1] Equalled or come up to. The formation of verbal nouns in this very peculiar negro dialect distinctly indicates the Red Indian agglutinate combinations.—C. G. L.

"I reck'n, den, he mus' a-bin pester wid misery in de haid (headache)," said Aunt Mary, in a tone of sympathy. "Ef yo' w'ar de rattles ob er rattlesnake in yo' ha'r, yo' ain't ne'er gwine ter hab dat misery."

"Er cabbage-leaf is mos' ez good," amended Aunt Em'ly.

"No, 'tain't," maintained Aunt Mary, stoutly. "Lak-all-wise, de skin ob er rattlesnake wo' round de wais' keep off de rheumatiz an' mek yo' swif' in de foot."

"I kyarn't set hyeah twell mawnin'" (morning), grumbled Aunt Mymee. "Leggo holts (Let go hold) an' lemme tell my tale ter Miss Boogarry. Arter dat, yo' kin brag on rattlesnake grease an' hide foh rheumatiz twell yo' tongues is all wo' ter frazzles,[1] ef yo' am a mine ter.—Miss Boogarry, ez I wuz a-sayin', de rattles wuz de mainest p'int, kase evvy rattle stan' foh er in'my (an enemy) dat Gran'dad kilt, an' dey wuz sech er lot ob um dat yo' kyarn't skusely count um. Dat Ole Gran'daddy chilluns, dey feel stuck-up an' 'bove de neighbehs ef dey hab six ur seben rattles, but dat much ain't count in de crowd on Ole Rattlesnake tail. Ef Ole Woodpeckeh c'd git dem dey'd count ez ef dey wuz *he* in'my (his enemy) made off wid.

"T'inkin' 'bout all dis pester 'im mighty much, so dat 'e don't git no good res', an', ez de cool wedder comed on an' de fros' 'gun ter nip, he git de noshin dat 'e gittin' stiff in de j'ints an' dat 'e des 'bleeged ter hab Old Gran'dad fat foh ter soople um. Sidesen dat, he need de skin ter mek er queeveh (quiver), kase de arrers kep' in dat queeveh fly furder an' kill quickeh den urr arrers. Oh! he des gotter hab (must have) dat sly an' dry ole snake. 'Pun dis 'count 'e don't eat nuttin, an' 'e go 'way 'lone an' t'ink *heap* an' smoke yarb an' drink bitteh watteh.[2]

"Dat all done, 'e set out.

"He go lil way, den Ole Owl come flyin' low an' 'hoo I hoo!'

"'G'long back,' say Owl, 'w'iles yo' kin.'

[1] *Frazzles.* Frayed bits, distorted pieces. *Cf.* German *Fratze.*
[2] An Indian penance or preparation for exertion of magical power.

" Woodpeckeh say, ' 'Scuse me dis time. Tuhnin' back am bad luck.'

" Owl flewed on an' he say, ' boo ! hoo !' dis time.

" Ole Woodpeckeh, he tek er big medsum-pipe an' 'e git some de ashes out o' hit afront ob 'im.   ' Dar now !' sez 'e, 'dat mek all safe.'

" Den 'e go on.

" Bimeby, lil rabbit cut 'cross de road.   He don't look todes Woodpeckeh 'tall, but, all de same, he holler, ' Go back ! '

" Woodpeckeh git down in de road an' scratch crossways ob de rabbit-track an' spit in um, den 'e go on wunst mo'.

" Arter w'iles, er brack wolf jump outen de bresh an' howl lak 'e wuz a-howlin' foh de daid (dead).

" Dat mek Ole Woodpeckeh sweat.   Den sholy he'd a-gorned back ef 'twuzzent too late, but he wuz right inter de Rattlesnake Kyentry.

" Dar in de sottle*mint* he see heap ob Ole Gran'daddy Rattlesnake folks dozin' afo' dey front do's.   Heap un um, too, he see des lettin' on dey dozin' w'iles dey wuz r'aly projeckin' cu'i's (curious) t'ings.   He go on a-parst dem, Ole Woodpeckeh did, an' kep' on a-gwine, twell 'e git ter er high place 'twixt de fawks (forks) ob er crick.   On dat high place wuz er oak tree, de onlest tree dat grow up dar, urr enny urr t'ing too, kase e'en de grass an' weeds wuz all daid an' blowed erway.   Up dar, at de foot ob dat tree, wuz whah Ole Gran'daddy lib.

" Ole Woodpeckeh, he blowed in he whustle, de chahm whustle mek outen eagle-bone, an' dat he do soster (so as to) let Ole Gran'daddy know he a-comin'.   Den he go sucklin' (circling) roun' dat tree, mekin' cunjer-lines dat kin tie down ghostes an' choke debbils.

" Gran'daddy Rattlesnake, he was stretch out on de groun', a-sunnin' hisse'f, an' he ain't go ter de bodderashun ter quile (coil) hisse'f, e'en w'en he hyeah dem awful gwines-on.   He stretch hisse'f lil mo' an' gap wid he mouf.

"Seein' dat, Ole Woodpeckeh, he shoot at Ole Gran'daddy. He shoot tree arrers des ez fas' ez he kin pull de bow-string, an' dem arrers dey wuzzent des common arrers ne'er ; dey wuz chahm, dem arrers wuz.

"De fust two Ole Gran'dad ketch on dem two big toofses o' hissen dat stick up des lak two sickles in de mouf.

"Dem arrers, dey des fall into sawdust.

"De turr one—oh, my ! dat wuz de one dat wukht de sorrer. Ole Gran'daddy swaller um an' den spit um up ergin so f'erce dat hit flewed into Ole Woodpeckeh's eyes, an' putt um ri' spang out !

"Oh, den wuzzent Ole Woodpeckeh in er mighty bad fix !

"Ole Gran'daddy, he r'ar up he haid an' he holler out—

"'Now, Ole Imp'ence, I gwine ter swaller yo' ! Whooh ! Yo' gwine ter be medsum (medicine ; *i.e.*, a charm) foh er long w'iles an' yo' gwine ter fetch me nurr rattle, too.'

"Hit 'u'd all a-tuhned out dataway, too, ef Ole Woodpeckeh ole 'ooman, wut wuz a-skulkin' arter him all de time, ain' whirl in an' hit Ole Gran'daddy sech er lick dat hit mek' er dent in 'e haid dat am dar ter dis day, an' all de chilluns dat he hab sence dat tuck arter 'im too, an' dey got dat se'f same dent, ez I done see myse'f an' yo' done see yo'se'f."

"Troof, too ! I done see um, heaps o' times," commented Aunt Em'ly.

"Dat clip sorter stunded (stunned) Ole Gran'daddy, an' dat gun Miss Woodpeckeh de chance ter git 'er ole man off outen dat kyentry an' home wunst mo'.

"Ole Woodpeckeh, he," continued Aunt Mymee, with a wave of her hand to impose silence on Big Angy, who showed a disposition to interrupt, "soon kyored up dem bline eyes, an' see, des ez good ez (as well as) e'er he done ; 'twuzzen't much ob er job, ne'er, kase Miss Woodpeckeh, she done busted de chahm dat Ole Gran'daddy wuz a-makin' w'en she flewed in 'twix' um an' hit Ole Gran'daddy dat smack. So, all tuhn out berry well ;

but foh all dat, I lay yo' could trabble cl'ar 'crost de Rattlesnake Kyentry an' ne'er ketch Ole Woodpeckeh nur none ob he chilluns ur kinfolks in dar. No, suz ! Ole Woodpeckeh ain't yit fegit de way dem ole bline eyes hurted. Mo'n dat, ef Ole Woodpeckeh hisse'f, ur enny ob de folks, ketch sight ob er rattlesnake, dey des holler an' screech an' cry an' skim round."

Aunt Mymee ceased her recital, and applied herself very seriously to the removal of some obstruction in the neighbourhood of her tympanum, employing for that purpose a cottonwood splinter and a succession of winks and grimaces that lifted every facial muscle out of its lawful position.

Big Angy muttered something that sounded suspiciously like " big lie " ; but Aunt Mymee was a witcher-woman, and not to be openly denounced.

The others laughed and applauded with well-feigned enthusiasm ; but they were between two fires, and anxious to retire to safer ground. Aunt Em'ly rushed to the rescue of her friends with great gallantry.

" Dat sorter 'minds me, I des dunno des how," she said, " ob de tale 'bout how Ole Woodpeckeh git dat putty necklash ob b'ar-claws ; but, arter Aunt Mymee a-holdin' forth so fine, I mos' 'feard ter tell hit."

" Go 'long, Aunt Em'ly, go 'long," said Granny, encouragingly ; "we kyarn't hab too much ob er good t'ing. De mo' I hyeah ob dem good ole tales, de mo' dat I wanter hyeah, an' I boun' dat de res' ob de ladies feels des de same prezack way."

" Dat my feelin's ! " cried Aunt Mary, giggling in anticipation of the amusement her friend was sure to furnish.

Big Angy nodded. Aunt Mymee removed the splinter from her ear, and seemed to nod slightly.

" In de good ole times, w'en all de folks an' beasteses use ter scuffle foh er libbin' des 'bout de same, de beasteses, dey wuz a-merryin' (marrying), right an' lef', all de time, des ez dey tuck er shine (took a fancy), medout a-stickin' ter dey own

kine, ez dey does dese days. Dey merry, merry, merry, de
wolf an' de deer, de squir'l an' de fox, de b'ar an' de folks, de
niggeh an' de 'possum—dar now ! hit 'pear lak de niggeh an'
de 'possum, dey dataway yit 'bout jinedin' (joining) ; but
hit diffunt in de respex dat one git chawed up dese days.
Oh, yes ! in de good time dey all mix up lak de mo'nehs
(mourners) at de camp-meetin'. In dem times, w'en hit been
dishaway, Ole B'ar, he bin a-foolin' round in de aige ob de
sottle*mint*, one day, a-lookin' foh sumpin he could steal for
dinneh, w'en he seed de putties' gal dat he done clap he eye
on sence he wuz bawn. De minnit he see dat gal, he lub 'er
lak er house a-fiah ; he lub 'er mo' hahd den 'er hoss kin kick ;
he lub 'er hahd ez he own se'f kin squeege. W'en he see 'er,
he grin at 'er an' say, ' Come hyeah, putty lil gal, kase I lub
yo' ;' but dat des mek de gal run an' holler, kase de minnit he
grin, dat minnit he show dem big w'ite tushes ob hissen, dat
look lak dey des made ter chaw up 'er whole fambly ter wunst,
let 'lone one lil gal lak dat.

"She holler an' she holler twell huh daddy run out an' look,
an' den run back foh he gun.

"Den Misteh B'ar, he cl'ar out, lak de man wid de yaller
jacket (a small wasp) up he britches-laig, dat hatter spressify
ter de gals dat he done fegit sumpin in he turr coat-pottit dat
he 'bleeged ter hab, an' he mighty sorry, but he kyarn't wait
twell dinneh's on de table.

"Nex' day, dough, he come a-hangin' roun' ergin, an' he
put he paw on he breas', an' he grin, an' he wall up he eye des
lak he plum sick ter show des how big er ijit (idiot) he wuz.

"Dat don't he'p marters none. Lil gal holler. Daddy
come out wid er gun. B'ar skaddle off ter de woods.

"Den de nex' day, de same t'ing all obeh.

"Day arter dat, same ; an' so dat kip up foh er week.

"By dat time de ole daddy wuz des plum 'stractid, kase he
feared Ole B'ar a-layin' off ter eat dat lil gal.

"Ole B'ar, he git desput, an' try er 'splain, but de gal an' 'er daddy dat skeered dat dey won't lissen.

"Ole B'ar, he wait an' he hone, an' he git de simples so mighty bad dat he ain't got no peace ob he life. He des sick foh dat lil gal ; so one day he fling hisse'f down at de foot ob er big tree, an' he t'ink and he t'ink 'bout dat lil gal twell de big teah come in he eye, an' he sniffle and snuff des lak er lil boy arter er lickin'.

"Now, dat tree wut he undeh bin be tree whah Ole Wood-peckeh got he house ; so w'en Ole B'ar sot dar sniffin' an' suckin' he paw, 'twuzzent long twell one ob be chilluns spy 'im. Co'se, arter dey peek at 'im wunst ur twicet, dey gotter run tell dey daddy an' manny dat dey 'spect dey gwine ter hab comp'ny foh supper, kase dey see Misteh B'ar at de foot de tree, an' dey reck'n he gwine ter clamber up soon ez he fetch he bref.

"W'en Ole Woodpeckeh hyeah dat news fum de chilluns he mighty sot up. He ain't 'spectin' Ole B'ar gwine ter clamber up dat high, but he 'low he gwine ter mek mo'n er emp'y money-puss outen dat bizniz. Dis long time he bin a-honin' after b'ar-claws foh mek de finishment ter he necklash. Well den !—at de fust place, he stick he haid outen de do', soster mek ri' shore dat 'twuz Ole B'ar. Den he come a-flutterin' an' a-miratin' down ter whah dat ole lub-sick gump been a-sniffin' an' a-snuffin'.

"'W'y, is dat yo', Misteh B'ar?' sez 'e. 'Is dat yo', sholy? W'y, I 'clar ter de goodniss grashis, dat I dat proud ter see yo' dat I don't know skusely (hardly, scarcely) wut ter do wid my-se'f ! De sight ob yo' am good foh so' (sore) eyes—'tis dat ! '

"Arter dat he come closte, an' ax Ole B'ar ter stay an' tek pot-luck wid um.

"'I dunno des wut we gwine ter hab,' sez 'e. 'Long ez yo' ain't sen' wuhd yo' a-comin', yo' hatter chance hit wid de ballunce ob us ; but I 'low de ole 'ooman 'll toss up sumpin ur nurr dat we kin mek out on. An' arter all,' sez 'e, a-lookin'

sorter slantindickler outen he eyes, ' hit's de wa'm weck'um '
(warm welcome), sez 'e, ' dat putt de good tase in de mouf.'

" W'en he say all dat he know Ole B'ar ain't gwine ter eat
wid 'im. He know dat he kin spend he mannehs an' save he
vittles an' credick at de se'fsame time.

" Ole B'ar, he wuz mighty tickle at de good will ob dat Ole
Woodpeckeh, but he say he ain't fitten foh comp'ny, he feel
so po'ly ; but ef de dinneh-hawn (horn) ain't blow yit, an'
Woodpeckeh got de time ter spar', he'd lak er lil confab wid
'im.

" ' Aw right, den,' sez Woodpeckeh, sez 'e, a-tuhnin' he back
an' a-winkin' ter hisse'f, 'Ise de man foh yo'.'

" Den, medout no mo' howdy-do,
dey go down de woods er ways, an'
B'ar tell de whole tale 'bout de gal.

" Dat tale mos' bust Woodpeckeh.
He 'bleege ter tuhn he haid turr way
twell he git smoove out, den he look
back, mighty sollum, and say—

" ' De trouble am right hyeah, my
kine fr'en'—yo' claws an' yo' tushes
skeer dat gal. Yo' mus' git um off.'

OLE WOODPECKER PULL OUT
DE TUSH.

" B'ar don't lak dat noshun—don't lak hit 'tall ; but Woodpeckeh, he keep on a-torkin' an' a-swagin' (persuading), twell
he say—

" ' Well, I don' lak ter gin um up, but I des mus' hab dat
gal ; so, if yo' sesso, off dey go ! '

" Dat des wut Ole Woodpeckeh want. He cut off de claw ;
he pull out de tush (tusk).

" ' Dar now ! ' say Ole Woodpeckeh ; ' dat mo' lak ! Dat lil
gal boun' ter lub yo' now, she sholy am ! '

" So B'ar go back, an' he mighty nigh git kilt dat time ;
kase w'en de gal see 'im she holler lak er catamount, an' 'er
daddy, dat wuz on de watch foh Ole B'ar, run out wid de gun.

"Ole B'ar, he go back ter Ole Woodpeckeh des a-r'arin' an' a-pitchin'.

"'Wut I done,' sez 'e, 'dat yo' fool me lak dat? Hyeah I is, wid my jaws a-floppin' an' my claws all off, an' de gal am wuss'n befo'!'

"'Nemmine! nemmine!' sez Woodpeckeh; 'des wait, hit'll come right,' sez he. 'Gals is des natchelly shy, lak de quails an' rabbits an' de young deer, dat's all. Des show dat gal dat yo' ain't dangersome, an' den 'track huh 'tention by 'musin' ob 'er, an' de game am yone. I be darncin' at yo' weddin' in des no time. An' dat 'mines me,' sez 'e, 'dat ef yo' kyarn't darnce, now am de time ter l'arn. De gals laks dem dat's light an' gay. Mebbe yo' *kin* darnce, dough?'

"'No,' sez B'ar, sez 'e, 'I kyarn't darnce.'

"'Den yo' gotter l'arn,' sez Woodpeckeh, 'an' Perarer-Chicken de one ter teach yo'. He my fr'en', an' I g'long wid yo' an' ax 'im.'

PERARA-CHICKEN TEACH DAT OLE FOOL B'AR.

"So dey go an' ax Perarar-Chicken, an', arter Woodpeckeh tuck 'im off ter one side an' argyfy some, he 'gree ter de job, an' teach dat ole fool B'ar.

"Bimeby, B'ar t'ink 'e know 'nuff, an' he go ter de place whah lil gal is. He sidle up closte, an' den he darnce!

"Lil gal fetch 'er squall foh daddy, an' out de ole man come an' shoot dat darncin' ijit plum daid, an' mek er baid outen he hide, an' toller (tallow) outen he fat, an' eat up he meat, an' t'row de bone ter de dogs; an' dat de las' o' B'ar. But Ole Woodpeckeh, he am w'arin' er mighty fine necklash o' b'ar-claws yit."

"Dem dat ax he'p in dey co'tin' (their courting), mos' gin'ly gits sarve 'bout dataway," said Granny, sententiously.

"Yo' come mighty nigh a-hittin' de troof dat lick, Aunt

Jinny," said Aunt Mymee ; " dat is, medout de he'p am (helped by) cunjerin' he'p. An' sayin' ' cunjerin',' 'mines me," she continued, looking about her, " is yo' alls e'er hyeah (hear) tell 'bout de time Ole Woodpeckeh laid hisse'f out ter git Ole Rabbit's cunjer-bag ? "

The company had not heard the history; so Aunt Mymee proceeded to enlighten them.

" One time, Ole Woodpeckeh, he git he mine mek up dat Ole Rabbit, he feel heap too biggitty (important), an' de turr crittehs, dey gib 'im lots o' credick foh sma'tness dat he ain't 'zarvin'. Woodpeckeh study an' study 'bout hit twell he feel mos' 'stractid.

" ' How *is* I gwine ter fetch Ole Man Rabbit down ? ' he say ter hisse'f. ' How's I gwine mek de crittehs see dat he ain't de big man dat he sets hisse'f up ter be ? '

" Dat de way he tork, an', suz ! he watch roun' Ole Rabbit's place, night an' day, a-tryin' ter fix 'im. He try foh ter cunjer 'im, but; shoh ! dat don't wuhk.

" At de las', w'en 'e mos' wo' out (worn out) wid a-studyin' an' a-trickin', he mek up he mine dat he gwine ter steal Ole Rabbit's cunjer-bag, dat sholy'd tek de imp'ence out ob Ole Chuffy, kase dat bag, hit des chock-full ob Jacks an' luck-balls an' yarbs an' chahms, let 'lone de roots dat could kill ur kyore (cure) des enny-t'ing an' de big rabbit-foot dat he mammy gun 'im. Oh, yes ! dat wuz er monsus fine bag. Hit wuz full o' dem t'ing I done tole yo', an', 'sides dat, Conquer-John (Solomon's Seal) an' may-apple dat sprout in de dahk (dark) o' de moon an' kin tork in de daid o' de night, an' jimson-buhs (*Stramonium* burs) an' olyantus leabes (alanthus leaves), dat mek de feveh-an'-agev (fever-and-ague) in dem dat smells um, an' de pizon-bags o' snakes an' toad-haids, an' de tongue ob er witch an' de fingeh ob er chile . dat die a-bawnin', an' de slobbeh (spittle) ob er hog an' wolf, an' dem grizzle-blue flowehs dat sprout whah de daid snake lay an' rot. He keep he fine silveh ball dar, too, w'en he home."

9

" Wuz dat de rabbit-foot de lef' hine-foot ob er grabe-yahd rabbit kilt in de dahk o' de moon ? " inquired Aunt Mary, in an awestruck whisper.

" Hit wuz so," answered Aunt Mymee, enjoying the uneasiness of her audience ; " but dat ain' all he got, kase de swamp-witch gun 'im (gave him) de right front-foot, too."

" Wuz de bag er bag ob new linen ? " asked Big Angy.

" Nuh ! " exclaimed Aunt Mymee, scornfully. " Dat's de bag foh er trick.   Dis dyeah cunjer-bag wuz er big bag ob wolf-skin an' hit wuz tan in de crick whah de blizzud flug de sumac-patch.

" W'en Ole Woodpeckeh study 'bout all dem t'ing, hit fah (fairly) sot he mouf a-dribblin'.   Den he mek up he mine he gwine ter neighbeh wid Ole Rabbit, so he git in er good place an' sing er lil fr'en'ly song.   W'en Ole Chuffy tek noduss o' dat, den he fetch 'im er lil passel ob leabes offen de top ob de ash tree, whah Ole Rabbit kyarn't climb.

" Arter dat, he drap in, in de ebenin's, des w'en he hat er mine (mind to).

" One time he drap in w'en dey wuzzent no un 'bout 'cep' des de lil chilluns an' de ole granny dat wuz settin' 'sleep in de chimbly corndeh.   He tork mighty putty ter dem chilluns, an' gin um some clobeh (clover) for gib um strenk (strength) an' some willer-tops foh mek um gay.   W'en dey eat um up, den he fall to an' ax um heap o' queschins.   He ax 'bout dis an' dat an' turr, an' at de las', he say—

" ' Dat er mighty big, strong-lookin' box, yondeh in de corndeh, de one wid de big stone 'pun top o' hit.   Dat des lak one I use ter hab, but I ain' got um now, I sold um.   Mebbe dis heah am de same one.   Lemme see de eenside.   Ef hit my ole un, hit got er mahk in de led (mark in the lid) dat I know, kase I cut hit dar myse'f."

" ' Oh, no ! ' sez dey, 'we dassent ter tech hit.   Dat's daddy's chist.'

"' Wut o' dat ? ' sez Woodpeckeh, sorter limbersome (lightly), lak he wuz a-pokin' fun. 'Ef I look at dat ole box, yo' don't reck'n I gwine ter bo' holes in um wid my eyesight, does yo' ? ' sez 'e, sorter easy an' sorter sassy lak-all-wise.

" De chilluns sorter jubus (dubious). Dey wanter tell, but dey ain't sho' dat daddy won't be mad ef dey does. Arter dey stan' an' grin dry foh er w'iles, de liles' one kyarn't hole in no longeh, an' bust out—

' ' Dat ain't no ole box ! Dat whah Daddy keep de big cunjer-bag an' all dat truck dat go in de big kittle w'en de moon gittin' ole.'

" Dat des de news Ole Woodpeckeh come arter, but he don't git *all* de news he hone foh dat trip, kase Granny, she sorter stretch an' flinch lak she gwine ter wake up, so off he go lak big debbil blow ahine 'im.

" Granny, she wuzzent a-sleepin' lak er rock, she ketch er wuhd ur two, an', w'en she git 'er eye open, she ax wut bin a-gwine on.

" De chilluns, dey feel out o' sorts, an' dey won't tell. Nemmine ! Granny gwine ter ketch um. She see er lil willer-trig (twig) an' er lil teeny-tiny clobeh-stem. Dat all she ax. She fetch out suppch.

" Dey kyarn't eat.

" She look at um long time an' projeck. Sick ? No dem chilluns ain't sick. Cunjer ? No, dey ain't cunjer, kase ef dey wuz, dey'd holler w'en dey go by de big chist. Uh-huh ! dey'd hed sumpin ter eat an' dey 'shame ter tell. Must a-bin Ole Woodpeckeh brung hit, kase de urr neighbehs, dey'd a-stayed twell Granny wuck up. Uh-huh ! dem chilluns is 'feard dey tole sumpin dey otter kep'. Uh-huh ! dey mus' a-tole 'bout de cunjer-bag in de chist. Co'se ! (of course.)

"' *Chilluns !* '

"' W-wassa matteh, G-Granny ? '

"' I wish't Ole Woodpeckeh'd drap in. He ain't bin hyeah

so long dat Ise 'feard dat de fuss yo' mek de las' time he comed hez run 'im off foh good.'

" ' Oh, no, Granny ! He wuz hyeah w'iles yo' wuz a-sleepin'.'

" ' I wish't he stayed, kase I done mek 'im er lil luck-ball foh er present, but, shoh ! he sech er big cunjer-man hisse'f, I don't 'spect he keer foh hit arter all.'

" ' Oh, yes, Granny ! Ole Woodpeckeh des hone arter um. He look at de big chist wut hole de cunjer-bag lak ez ef 'twuz full ob punkin-sass.'

" Now, Granny cotch um ! My suz, she wuz mad ! kase dem chilluns ain't mine dey daddy. She whirl right in an' beat um wid de close-line an' druv um all ter baid (bed).

" W'en Ole Rabbit come home an' hyeah dat gran' tale fum de ole granny he des tickle he yeah wid er straw an' laff. Den he onhitch de silveh luck-ball fum de string dat hilt hit unner he yarm (arm) an' putt dat in de bag in de box 'long o' de res' o' de chahms. Den he go ter baid. De nex' mawnin' he sen' de fambly out a-visitin', an' w'en dey goned clean off, den he sot down an' tork er long time unter dat silveh ball an' tell um wut ter do.

" Dat sottle, he hide.

" Putty soon, 'long come Woodpeckeh, hummin' er lil chune, des foh ter show dat he mighty gaily an' inncint.

" He knock on de do'—' 'Hyo, dar, folkses ! '

" Nobody say nuttin.

" Push de do' open er crack. Peek in. Nobody dar, uh ? Fling de do' wide open. Go in.

" ' Uh-huh ! Uh-huh ! All tuck out somers (gone some-where). Dis hyeah my charnce dat I bin wantin'. Now den, Old Man Chuffy, I gwine ter show yo' dat Ole Woodpeckeh am de biggest man at de hemp-breakin'.'

" Den Ole Woodpeckeh cross de flo'—tippetty, tippetty— lookin' o'er he shouldeh an' jumpin' w'en er leaf fall down fum de tree at de windeh.

" Bimeby, he mo' sassy feelin' an' he try ter git dat big rock offen de chist. No use. He kyarn't do hit. He push an' he pull an' he heave an' he strain, twell de fiah flash outen he eyeball an' de blood hum in he yeahs. Dàr 'tis, yit he kyarn't budge um.

" Den he set back an' cuss—dat wuz w'en he git bref 'nuff.

" 'Shoh ! I gwine ter cut er hole in de side o' dat box an' fetch out de bag dataway ! '

" He cut hole. Hit tek long time, kase dat chist mek outen mighty tough oak.

" Shucks ! W'en 'e retch (reach) in dar, dar nurr box, mo' lil den de fust, ob iun-wood (iron-wood).

" Nemmine ! Cut ergin ! Cut an' cut an' cut an' cut. De lan' sakes, how tough am iun-wood ! .

" W'en he mos' ready ter drap, cut thu. Retch foh de bag —jimminy squinch !—he des ketch a-holt ob er lil hick'ry box !

" Den he cut an' cut an' cut an' mek de hole big 'nuff in de two big box ter git de lil box out.

" He wuz mos' daid w'en 'e git dat wuhk done, but 'e mek out ter git up de strenk ter kyar (carry) dat lil box off ter de deep woods.

" W'en he git dar, lo an' beholes ! he skivveh (discovered) dat de box wuz boun' up wid er hemp rope an' de rope wuz cunjer inter tight knots. Dem knots he don't ontie, he mek out ter cut um. Den 'e git ter de bag an' lif' um out. Hyo ! Dar now ! (There now.)

" Dat—bag—won't—hole—still !

" Hit wiggle an' jounce roun' lak er 'coon. He kyarn't skuse (scarcely) hole um, so he git er big rope an' tie roun' um an' den lash um ter er big tree, an' I des tell yo' dat bag fight an' skuffle twell dat tree skreek an' strain lak 'twuz gittin' pull up.

" Nemmine ! Ole Woodpeckeh t'ink he stop dat. He pile de dry bresh roun' dat bag an' sot um afiah. De fiah buhn high, buhn bright, buhn all red an' yalleh.

"All on de suddent, de fiah go down twell dey des er ball (there was only the ball) un um roun' de bag an' hit—*blue !* De lil tounge lap out fum um too—lick ! lick ! lick ! flap ! flap ! flap ! dem lil tongue go, des lak de whole worl' wuz a-buhnin' up.

"Bimeby, fum de middle ob dat blue ball sumpin say—

"'Woodpeckeh, putt me back ! Woodpeckeh, putt me back !'

"De nex' minnit de silveh luck-ball pop out lak er hick'ry coal an' keep a-jumpin', jumpin', todes Ole Woodpeckeh. Dat skeer Ole Woodpeckeh so turr'ble bad dat he fegit all de spell dat he know.

"'W-w-wut yo' arter ?' he mek out ter mummle ez he back out.

"'Putt me in de lil chist,' say de luck-ball.

"Woodpeckeh tuck 'im up an' putt 'im in de chist, but 'e don't stay, 'e pop out an' mek at 'im ergin.

"'Putt me in de chist,' holler de ball.

"'Ain't I putt yo' in de chist an' mos' buhn myse'f ter def, yo' so hot ?' whimple Woodpeckeh.

"'Putt me in de bag fust, an' den in de chist,' say de luck-ball.

"Woodpeckeh wuz cunjer (a conjuror) his own se'f an' he boun' ter do dat, dough hit buhn 'im ter de bone. He retch inter de blue fiah an' grab out dat red-hot wolf bag an' putt dat red-hot—nuh, blue hot—ball inter hit. Den he tie up de bag ergin wid er string dat wuz des lak buhnin' whiskey-toddy. He hatter tie hit wid cunjer-knots, an' dat wuz slow wuhk. Den he drop dat awful mess inter de chist, an' all dat crowd 'im so dat he ain't got de time ter sing dat song dat kyore up dem buhn ob hissen.

"Den de ball holler out fum be chist—

"'Tie we up des de way dat yo' foun' us.'

"Foh de lan' sake ! He done cut de rope inter smidgins.

"Nemmine ! He hatter git hemp an' twis' nurr rope. Arter dat, he hatter tek de ole rope an' study out how dem knots Ole Rabbit tie in um.

" All dat time dem buhns buhnin' lak de cow-eech an' de tetteh-wuhm an' de run-er-oun' all bile down in one.

" Arter w'iles, he git de knots tie. Den 'e tek dat debbil-box back home.

" ' Men' up dem chist dat yo' chop', say de ball, w'en 'e putt um whah 'e foun' um.

" He go back ter de woods, he git oak, he git iun-wood an' he men' up dem chists an' kyar off de chips.

" ' Den de luck-ball say—

" ' I reck'n yo' got yo' come-uppance (acquaintace), so I let yo' off easy dis time. Des be comf'tible in yo' mine. Dis marter am dat lil dat I ain't gwine ter pester Ole Rabbit wid namin' hit. G'long home, now, an' 'have yo'se'f fum dis out.'

" So Woodpeckeh go home, an' dem buhns wuz lef' so long dat he kyarn't skuse (hardly) cunjer um 'tall. Dey wuz bad long time an' he wuz keep mighty still.

" Arter w'iles, w'en he do git well an' fly fo'th wunst mo', de fustest pusson dat he meet up wid bin Ole Chuffy, an' Ole Chuffy he sorter grin an' flinch de nose an' say—

" ' Hyo ! Neighbeh, whah yo' bin, dis long time ? '

" Woodpeckeh, he git de dry grins an' he kyarn't say nuttin."

Big Angy rose in a fury she dare not express in words and silently took her departure.

Aunt Mymee smiled slightly and hastened the retreating footsteps by elevating her voice and singing—

> " Ez I went obeh de watteh,
> De watteh went obeh me.
> I seen er lil young peckehwood
> A-settin' on er tree.
> I holler out—' Yo' raskil ! '
> He holler back—' Yo' t'ief ! '
> I up wid er crookid stick
> An' knock out all he teef."

IX

SOME TALES IN WHICH BLUE JAY AND HIS
"GWINES-ON" FIGURE CONSPICUOUSLY.

" GRANNY, if you don't tell me a rabbit story, I will not come here any more."

" Oh I go 'long, honey, wid dat kine o' spressifyin'. I'm got er heap betteh tale den any rabbit tale foh yo'. I 'gun ter study 'bout hit in de night, las' night, an' hit rowge (rouse) me up so dat I ain't git er wink ob res' (rest) sence de chickins crow foh midnight. I'm gotter tale 'bout Ole Blue Jay, honey."

" Why, he isn't of much account, is he, Granny ? "

" Des hyeah dat chile !—an' he de one dat go ter Hell a-Friday an' kyar san' (sand) an' de 'count ob all de bad folkses do, an' w'en he tek dat san' an' buil' up de walls ob de Bad Place an' den gin out all de bad news ter de Ole Boy, den he load hisse'f up wid all de lies dat he kin tote an' comes back mungs us I 'Much 'count, huh ?—w'en he git back an' tuhn dem lies aloose, de Lawd know hit mek no eend o' quoilin' (quarrelling) an' fussin' I "

" I don't think that is nice of him, Granny. It is awful to tell things that are not true of people. Why, it isn't even nice to tell what you really know if it's unpleasant. You have said that yourself. Don't you remember when I told some ladies about Cousin Georgie falling head-first into the big apple butter-jar the time he tried to help himself without anybody knowing, that you said to me—

" ' Tell-tale-tit,
Your tongue shall be slit,
And every dog in our town
Shall have a little bit ' ?

Don't you remember that, Granny, and that I was so angry I cried ? "

" Sartin, honey, sartin, but dis hyeah am 'bout er trick play on Ole Blue Jay an' how hit git de folks a-laughin' at 'im. Des lissen wunst, 'bout how de mawkin'-buhd (mocking-bird) sarve 'im :—

" Wunst, in de ole times—de good ole times w'en 'possum-grease an' sweet-tatehs wuz ez plenty ez dooley-bugs an cockle-buhs, an' de roas'in'-yeahs (roasting-ears) comed twicet in de yeah—de (all the) mawkin'-buhds ain't know but des one chune. Hit mought a-tuhn out dat dey don't ne'er know but dat one, but 'tain't tuhn out dataway, an' dis hyeah am de reason ob dat."

" *Do* hurry ! "

" Uh, huh ! so I does, honey.—Ez I wuz a-sayin', 'twz 'long ob Ole Blue Jay, him dat t'ink hisse'f so sma't an' r'aly wuz er plum fool, dat de new chunes kim. Law zee ! heap o' dese hyeah folkses dat am so sot up wid deyse'f am des lak Ole Jay ; some un um's ijits an' some un um's fly-up-de-criks,[1] but dey ain't no diffunce skusely, an' dey all lan' in de mud arter settin' out ter show de res' de comp'ny whah ter walk."

" Dis de way de mawkin'-buhd fust git de ijee dat he lahn some mo' chunes. He bin a-settin' home wid er misery in he back an' er cole in he haid an' er squawmishness in he stum-mick, an' he kyarn't ez much ez sing dat one chune dat he know. He sneege an' he snuffle an' he hawk an' he spit an' he moan an' he groan an' he mope an' he fuss, an' he ain't satify wid nuttin.

" Miss Mawkin'-Budh, she hatter fly roun' an' do de mahkitin (marketing) huh own se'f. One de time she had bin out a-perawdin' eroun' a-huntin' up sumpin dat 'll lay on 'er ole man's

---

[1] Fly-up-the-creek—a kind of small crane or heron.

stummick, she meet up wid Ole Blue Jay. He ain't call ter mine
dat he ain' nurr sot eyes on 'er afo'. She look so spry an' so slim,
dat, at de fust, he mek up he mine dat she er young gal ; den she
squinch huh eye an' look so keen dat he des know she boun'
ter be er widdeh-ooman. He don't ax no queschins dough, he
des say, 'Howdy,' mighty sorf', and ax 'er kyarn't he hab de
satisfaxshun ob kyarn (carrying) home huh truck (vegetables).

" ' Pear lak,' he say, 'hit bin mos' too big er tote foh er slim
young pusson lak yo'se'f. Hit'll be er buhnin' shame ef yo' tote
er load dat'll mek yo' lop-sidey an' spile dat fine fo'm o' yone,'
he say.

" At dat she des laff an' fly off wid de truck.

" W'en she git home, she tell 'er ole man an' he flare up an'
say he gwine ter gib Blue Jay er lickin' foh he imp'ence. Den
he sorter trim up he feddehs an' say he dunno but dat he feel
he strenk a-comin' back some. Dat minnit he 'gun ter mend,
but he wuzzent nigh kyore up yit. He lay off ter git ter mahkit,
nex' mawnin', hisse'f, but be don't git dar yit. He sot out,
'cordin' ter promiss, a-holin' onter daid lim's an' a-leanin' up
'gin tree trunks ez he go, an' a-gruntin' an' a-groanin' lak er pig
w'en hit gwine ter be fallin' wedder, but, arter all dat trouble,
he 'bleeged ter tuhn back an' double up in de corndeh 'gin.

" Miss Mawkin'-Buhd, den she sot out, an' toreckly she fly
back, chirripy-chippyin' an' a-gigglin' fit ter split. She sot down
de vittles, an' den it look lak she des fall down on de groun' she
so tickle 'bout sumpin.

" Dat mek Misteh Mawkin'-Buhd feel mighty frackshis.

" ' Flaxin' roun' a-huntin' vittles seem lak er mighty funny
bizniz foh some folks,' he say, wid he eye harf-shet. 'I ain't
ne'er foun' hit so, but some folks is diffunt.'

" He bin kine o' low down in de valley foh sometime, 'pun 'count
o' de misery in he eensides an' de squawmishniss in he mouf an'
stummick, an' dis hyeah bizniz wid Blue Jay wuz de las' button
off Gabe's coat.

"Miss Mawkin'-Buhd, she ain' say nuttin. She des rock huhse'f backudhs an' forruds an' giggle.

" ' Ef yo' los' yo' sense, yo' ain't los' yo' tongue, too, is yo ? ' sez 'e, an' he say hit dat vigrous dat she know dat she hatter 'splain w'y she feel so snipshus (pert).

" ' Hit's erlong o' dat ole fool ob er Blue Jay,' she say, w'en she ketch 'er bref.

" Dat des wut he s'pishin (suspecting) an' dat wut mek 'im so mad.

" ' I reckin he done mek up he mine dat yo' des ez good ez er widdeh-ooman, ain't he ? ' sez 'e.

" MISS MAWKIN'-BUHD ROCK HUHSE'F BACKUDHS AN' FORRUDS AN' GIGGLE."

"Wid dat she laff ergin twell 'er ole man cuss de whole kit an' bilin' o' blue jays. By dat she know she got ter git 'er ole man outen dat tanter. Wunst he git he dander up right good hit gwine ter hang on lak de eech ur er niggeh's tase (taste, desire for) foh bakin-an'-greens, so she dror down huh face an' look des ez sollumcholly ez de nex' un, an' den she tek on an' call 'im ' honey ' an' ' sugah-lump ' an' heap mo' sorf' name lak dem. W'en she git 'im cheer up some, she tell de tale dat Blue Jay bin tek huh foh er gal, an' w'en he fine she ain't, he so flustrate dat he kyarn't say nuttin.

" Dat sorter pacify Misteh Mawkin'-Buhd, an' he tuhn roun'

an' drap off ter sleep, but de nex' day he git wuhkt up ergin,
an' de nex' an' de nex' de same.   By dat time he git so hot dat
he t'row off all dat misery des lak he ole close, an' he primp up
he feddehs an' he sot out to lay in de truck for de fambly hisse'f,
an' lef Miss Mawkin'-Buhd home ter look arter the chilluns an'
cl'ar up de breckfus-scraps an' sweep.

" He sot out, an' he go 'long a-fumin' an' a-frettin' an' a-cussin'
undeh he bref, but dey ain't ez much ez er squir'l a-showin' hisse'f.   So he go 'long, an' he sorter sottle down, an' de mawnin'
bein' putty, an' him a-feelin' good arter bein' po'ly so long, he
feel so gay he 'gun ter whistle de onles' chune dat he know.
But dat chune ain't las' long.   Des ez he git by de spring an' set
off on er shawt-cut 'cross de fiel's, he hyeah some un ur nurr
a-hollerin'.

" ' Oh, Miss Mawkin'-Buhd !   Oh, Miss Mawkin'-Buhd !
Stay l stay ! stay ! '

" He stop dat whustlin', but he don't stay none.   He des jog
right on.   He gotter big s'pishin who dat ahine 'im, but he don
stop nur pass no wuhds wid 'im.

" Den he hyeah wunst mo'—

" ' Stay ! stay ! stay ! '

" Dat time Ole Jay come a-skimmin' an' a-skippin' up 'long
side.

" ' W'y, Miss Mawkin'-Buhd, is yo' done fegit yo' frens dis
quick ?' sez 'e.

" Well l at dat Misteh Mawkin'-Buhd des lak ter split.   He
know him an' de ole ooman faveh some—dey wuz fust cousins
on dey mammy's side—but in all he bawn days he ain't nurr
'spect ter be tuk foh er ooman-buhd.   He sorter mummle he in
er big hurry an' try ter pass on.

" Jay, he say dat er pity, but he sech er good fren he reck'n ef he
hurry too dey ain't no dejeckshins (objections) ter him gwine 'long.

" Mawkin'-Buhd, he hang down de haid an' don't fetch up er
soun'.

" Dat set Ole Blue Jay up. Fust t'ing dey know, he up an co'te Mawkin'-Buhd des ez sweet ez er niggeh co'tin' er yaller gal wid sweet gum an' 'lasses-candy.

" Mawkin'-Buhd say nuttin, but he listen mighty closte.

" Dat 'courage Blue Jay, an' he say—

" ' Oh ! my deah, sweet Miss Mawkin'-Buhd, my mine foller yo' ez de shadder foller de tree. Oh ! Miss Mawkin'-Buhd, my mine foller yo' ez de big sun-floweh foller de light.'

" Dat de way he go on, an' he say heap mo' I done fegit. Lan' sake ! he des sweetin de fresh ar (air) ez dey go 'long. Bimeby, he git so free dat he 'gin ter baig (beg) an' plead dat Misteh Mawkin'-Buhd run off wid 'im.

" In er sorter mumly v'ice Mawkin'-Buhd 'greed ter dat, but, he say, he boun' ter run home fust and git sumpin dat he 'bleege ter hab.

" HE DES SWEETIN DE FRESH AIR EZ DEY GO 'LONG."

" So dey go back, dough, at de fust, Jay Buhd 'low he kyarn't, kase ef he see Ole Mawkin'-Buhd dey boun' ter be er fuss.

" ' He ain' dar,' sez Misteh Mawkin'-Buhd. ' He out a-walkin'.'

" ' Den I go, my honey-lub ! '

" So dey go back, an' w'en dey git dar, Miss Mawkin'-Buhd, she riz up, she did, an' tole um ' howdy,' an' dat she proud dat Jay Buhd an' huh ole man got ter be frens. De nex' minnit she gwine ter ax Ole Jay ter stay ter dinneh, but he ain't stop foh no eenvite, he des scuttle out o' dem woods lak dey wuz afiah, an' all de time Misteh Mawkin'-buhd holler all dat lub-tork arter 'im.

" Well ! Mawkin'-Buhd git so much 'joymint outen dat w'en he go a-visitin' de urr buhds, dat he tuk up de trick, arter w'iles, ob takin' um all off an' a-mawkin' ob um. In p'int o' fack, dat de way he git de name he go by fix on 'im, 'fo' dat he hab nurr name, de w'iches I done fegit."

Tow Head's applause was wine to Granny's spirit. It stimu-
lated her to the extent of volunteering another story of Blue
Jay's escapades, "kase one tale ain't nuttin w'en yo' come ter
count up de shines o' dat triflin' ole buhd round de young ooman-
buhds."

"Now, lemme tell 'bout dat young Miss Yaller-Buhd. Ez I
wuz say, Ole Jay, he wuz allus de beatenes' buhd 'bout a-runnin'
arter de young folks. Dey's no fool lak de ole fool, de Lawd
know ! an' dar I mek my pint, an' Ole Jay he suttingly wuz de
beatenes' (greatest) fool in de bunch. Dey wuzzent one young
gal-buhd in dat neck ob de woods dat didn't had de charnce
ter fling up 'er haid an' scuttle out o' he way. Dat wuz de
breedin' (cause) ob er heap o' fussmint too ; kase w'en dey th'ow
'im off he tuk out he spite a-whuppin' dey daddies an' all de
res' ob dey men-folks w'en de charnce come 'long. Oh, yes !
he wuz des a-makin' lub an' a-pickin' fusses fum de mawnin'
twell de night, an' de sho-nuff (sure), high-flowed, study
(steady) buhds wuz des plum wo' (worn) out wid he havishness
(behaviour). Dey say, dey do, dat dey hat er good mine ter pay
some gal-buhd ter marry Old Jay an' gin 'im er charnce to sottle
down an' ack lak he sholy got ez much ez er grain ob sense.
Whah de hitch to dat bizniz come in, honey, wuz dat dem
young gal-buhds don't want no ole crow-bait lak dat a-torkin'
sorf' an' a-wallin' up he eye w'iles dey wuz lots ob fat an' sassy
young bacheldeh-buhds des a-hangin' aroun' an' a-watchin' foh
de charnce ter ax um out a-walkin', ur, mebbe, a-flyin', mungs
de tree-tops, whah dey could bill an' coo twell sundown medout
dey mammies a-takin' paht in de sesso (conversation). Shuh !
de gals wid de feddehs des de same ez de gals wid de silk frocks
an' w'ite apuns. Dat's Granny's 'pinjin, honey, an' I 'low dat
dem dat try ter sottle Ole Jay ain't de ones dat gwine to 'spute
hit, mo' speshul, sence de way it tuhn out. Dey kyarn't do
nuttin, none un um, wid dem neighbeh gals, but, nemmine !
Ole Jay, de good time am a-comin' ! Oh, yes !

" ' De good time a-comin', by an' by.
Yo'll git to Jawdin (Jordan), by and by.
Ef de road am rocky, don't yo' cry.
Des keep on a-ploddin' an' don't yo' cry.'

" De good time foh Ole Jay wuz w'en Miss Yaller-Buhd an' huh folks move up fum down nigh Platte Ribbeh. Oh, yes ! dat wuz a big day foh Ole Jay Buhd w'en dey strike dis kyentry, 'deed hit wuz ! He ain't let no grass grow un'neat' he foots w'iles he bin a-settin' up ter Yaller-Buhd. He tote huh akins (acorns) an' 'vite 'er ter de millet-fiel' an' ketch 'er whole fambly er mess o' grubs an' er string o' hoppehgrasses. Dat mek um all grin, kase dat Yaller-Buhd, she bin promiss ter huh elber-cousin (elbow-cousin—distant relative) down whah the fambly kim fum.

" Arter w'iles hit come 'pun Ole Jay dat hit de time o' yeah dat he betteh stop he foolin' an' mek de 'rangemint ter sottle down ter keepin' house. He named dat ter de gal, but, dellaws ! (the Lord !) dat Yaller-Buhd, she sorter primple up 'er feddehs an' fling up' er haid an' hunch up 'er shouldeh an' gin dat ole Daddy Gump no satifackshin 'tall.

" Bimeby, he git desput, an' he sent her wuhd by 'er own lil buddy (brother) dat he gwine ter come arter 'er de Sunday a-follerin', an' she bleeged ter hab 'er close an' 'er dishes ready fuh 'er weddin', ur he ain't a-comin' no mo' ; he plum tuckehed out wi' 'er foolin'.

" De buddy, he grin an' say he gwine ter kyar de wuhd (word), an' he do, mon, an' den dat fambly, from de ole man ter de teentyes' chile in pin-feddehs, dey all holler an' laff twell de woodses ring.

" Ole Jay, he hilt off, des ez he say he gwine ter, an' he ain't see none un um, nur he ain't aim ter (intend to) twell de time he 'pinted. W'en dat come round, he primp up de bes' he kin, an' grease up he feddehs, an' sot out foh Yaller-Buhd's house. Ez he go 'long he look des ez foolish ez er owl dat

bin bile wid de haid on, an' he r'ar his se'f back lak he own er
hunnerd niggehs an' grin lak er bake skunk.

" Ez he go 'long he say ter hisse'f—

"'Ise willin' ter bet er fat 'possum gin er sup o' dishwatteh
dat dat gal bin a-peekin' thu de leabes an' a-watchin' ef I come.
sence de crack ob day dis mawnin'.'

" He come closeter an' sorter shade he eye an' look.

" Don't see no gal a-watchin'.

" Go on furder an' look ergin.

" She ain't dar, suz !

" He look up, he look down, he look sideways.   He ain't seen
none ob de fambly.   Dat sorter check de grins.   Den he git
brash (bold) wunst mo'.

"' Nemmine ! ' he say.   ' Gals, dey's allus sheepish.   She
run an' hide huhse'f an' giggle, dat wut she do.'

" He came closte up.

" All des ez still ez de grabe.

"' Hi ! ' sez 'e, ' dis hyeah am heap to much a'rs (airs) foh er
plain man lak me ! I gwine ter pay 'er up foh dat, an' de res' ob
'er triflin' fambly too, wunst I git 'er tight an' fas'.   I teach um
mannehs on dey wuthless hides, too ! '

" Wid dat he go up an' knock an' knock.

" Arter er mighty long w'iles er sassy fox-squirr'l poke out he
haid fum 'cross de way an' say—

"' Hyo, dar !   Wut yo' arter ?   Ef yo' got er bill 'gin dem
Yaller-Buhds, yo' mighty late 'bout c'lectin',' sez 'e.   ' Ef yo'
got er charge, yo' betteh des putt hit in er gun an' fiah hit off.
Dat de onles' way hit retch (reach) um.'

" Wid dat he feel so sma't dat he des chat-tat-chatteh, lak he
mos' 'stractid wid he own joke.

"' Wut de matteh, hyeah ? ' say Ole Blue Jay, des a-sputtehin'
an' a-stuttehin'.

" 'Dem Yaller-Buhds move back whah dey come fum,' say
Squirr'l, winkin' fust one eye den turr.   'Dey move off, but

dey ain't move by deyse'f. De new son-in-law wuz on hans ter he'p, in co'se. He done all de heft ob de pullin'-out' (most of the moving).

" ' De—*whut*! ' sez Ole Blue Jay, a-lookin' sorter wizzly (shrunk up) an' cole.

" ' De new son-in-law,' sez Squirr'l, a-scratchin' he yeah wid he lef'-han'-hine-foot, but a-lookin' at Ole Jay all de time. ' Miss Yaller-Buhd—yo' know dat gal—she wuz merry one o' dem Bobberlinkum kinfolks ob hern. W'y Ise sholy s'prise, Misteh Jay, dat yo' a'nt hed no eenvite, beein' ez yo' sech er fren ob de fambly,' sez 'e, lookin' mighty sollum. ' I reckin

" OLE JAY, HE DES TUHN HE BACK ON SQUIRR'L AN CUST."

w'y dey don't 'vite yo' ain't no imp'uence, dough. I reckin hit des kase dey t'ink dat er ole chap lak yo' ain't tek no intruss in sech doins.'

" W'en he say dat he wunk.

" Ole Jay, he ain't mek no arnser, he des tuhn he back on Squirr'l an' cust."

" He was a very naughty bird, Granny. If he does that he will surely go to the Bad Place when he dies."

" He go dar a-libbin', honey. Ain't I des tell yo' he go an'
pack san' dar foh he'p buil' up de walls an' keep de po' bilin'
sinnehs in ? Co'se, he don't mine dat, kase he go dar des ez
reg'ler ez Friday come. Yo' ain't ne'er see er jay-buhd a-Friday
in all yo' bawn days, is yo', now ? "

" I can't remember."

" Wut dat yo' kyarn't 'membeh, honey ? " asked Aunt Mary,
who entered the cabin as Tow Head spoke.

" About Blue Jay going to the Bad Place on Fridays, Aunt
Mary."

" Huh I Co'se he go. He de Ole Boy' pet," said Aunt Mary,
for once looking serious ; " but, nemmine ! he git he come-
uppance (settlement) foh all dat. Dar's Miss Wren, now, I boun'
she gin' im er flea in he yeah. Oh, yes ! she mek 'im laff out de
turr side o' he mouf. Miss Wren, she mighty high-strung, an'
hit am er wuhd an' er lick wid huh, an' de lick come fust, ginly.
She de in'my ter de Ole Boy an' all he folks an' frens too.
Wunst she peck 'im in de eye des 'pun 'count ob huh 'ligion,
an' she mos' laid out Ole Jay."

" Tell me about it—tell me *all* about it I Don't skip like
mamma does sometimes when she tells stories."

" 'Tain't me dat skips. Hyeah de tale, honey, but it sorter
triflin' arter wut Granny kin git off :—

" One time, Ole Blue Jay, he wuz a-paradin' thu de woods,
hollerin' sass an' a-peckin' at de young buhds an' a-kickin' up
de bigges' kine ob er fuss ter show off he biggittyness. Den
wuz w'en he git er settin'-down he ain't nowise a-lookin' foh.
Hit wuz dishaways : he wuz a-r'arin' eroun' a-payin' no heed
ter whah he wuz a-gwine, w'en he flewed up—blip I—ergin
sumpin ur nurr, an' he gin er smack wid he bill an' he say—

" ' Git out de way, orkidniss, an' don't stop up de road w'en
yo' bettehs is a-gwine by ! '

" ' Bettehs I ' say er lil fine, f'erce v'ice, an' at de same time he
git er clip un'neat' he wing dat he ain't gwine ter fegit in er

minnit. 'Bettehs, huh? Who dem dat ain't yo' bettehs, Kyentery Jake?'

"Good lan'! wuzzent Ole Jay Buhd mad w'en he hyeah dat sass an' feel dat clip!

"'Des afo' I wipes yo' offen de face ob de yeath, come out o' de shaddehs (shadows) an' lemme see wut sort ob er flea I torkin ter,' he say, soon ez he c'd git he bref.

"He wuz a-seein' den," said Aunt Mary, parenthetically, "but he wuzn't lettin' on, a-puppus to rile Miss Wren, kase she ain't ne'er own up dat she mo' liller den de turr buhds.

"'Come out in de sun, den,' say de lil fine v'ice, 'ef yo' wanter see yo'se'f git de good lickin' dat yo' mammy orter gun yo' dis long w'iles back.'

"At dat dey bofe step out in de bright light, an' Ole Blue Jay 'low dat am de liles' buhd dat he e-er clap eye on.

"'Well! dey ain't no credick ter git outen lickin' yo', yo' po' lil ha'f-er-minnit ob de ooman seck,' he say. 'I reckin I ain't gwine ter kill yo' ef yo' tell yo' name an' whah yo' kim fum.'

"'Ise fum Ole Feginny, I is, an' my name, hit's Miss Wren,' say de lil critteh, ez f'erce ez er catamount, 'an' I ain't tell dat kase Ise 'feard, I tell hit kase I ain't 'shame o' whah I kim fum ur de fambly I 'longs ter. I des kim out hyeah w'en de w'ite folks do—de *quality* w'ite folks dat got heaps o' niggehs an' plundeh ter move.'

"'Uh huh! Uh huh!' say Ole Jay Buhd, a-cockin' up he eye an' a-lookin' lak he know hit all. 'Uh huh! uh huh!—dey hab sech er heap o' plundeh ter move dat dey ain't got no room ter fetch yo' mannehs erlong. Uh huh!—Well! I mighty glad I foun' out w'y yo' ain't got none, I is, fo' er fack.'

"Whoop!.

"Ef dat lil wren ain't got 'er dander up!

"'Wut yo' know 'bout mannehs?' she holler out.

"'Nuttin 'tall, fum wut I see afo' me,' sez Ole Blue Jay, des ez cool ez er cowcumber.

" Hit's de bigges' wunneh dat lil wren ain't bustid she so mad. She r'ared an' she pitched an' she hollered an' she stomped. W'en she git 'er bref, she say—

"'Stop yo' imp'ence, yo' low-down trash ! Ef I ain't squall out ter my ole man dat he come an' trounce de life outen yo', hit's kase I know dat I kin ten' ter dat marter my own se'f. Come hyeah, an' yo'll feel me gittin' dinneh ready foh de buzzuhds ! '

" Wid dat she pitch inter Jay Buhd an', suz ! she gin 'im er sockydolligy (blow) in de eye dat des natchelly shet dat eye. Den, des ez quick ez wink, she play popgun wid turr eye, an' Ole Jay, den he des hatter tuhn tail an' fly inter de woods an' hide hisse'f mungs de t'ick leabes. Ef he ain't done dat, ole Miss Wren, she'd sholy a-kep' 'er promuss an' mek 'im inter buzzehd-meat (a corpse), sho nuff."

The child clapped her hands and laughed, but her mirth was of short duration. She suddenly turned very grave and thoughtful. "Do *you* think Miss Wren was a lady ? " she asked, after long consideration.

" Ain't she say she wuz brung up mungs de quality ? " asked Aunt Mary, winking privately at Granny.

"I don't care what she said ! " exclaimed the child. "She was not a lady. People that slap and bite can never, never grow up to be ladies."

" How yo' fine dat out ? " asked Aunt Mary, with a smile entirely too significant to be pleasant.

The child blushed and wriggled uncomfortably.

"I like Blue Jay better than Miss Wren, anyway," she averred. " He isn't any badder than some other birds."

" Dat's so, honey," said Granny, soothingly. " An' ef yo' am o' mine ter lissen, I tell yo' er tale 'bout de time all de turr buhds hatter gin in ter dat."

" Tell it, you dear, sweet, good old Granny," said Tow Head, caressing the wrinkled brown face of ner friend with both her little hands and heaving a sigh of relief at thought of a stop being made to Aunt Mary's questions.

"Dat's de tale yo' ain' nurr told me," grumbled Aunt Mary, "kase I ain' know ter dis day 'bout Old Daddy Blue gittin' credick nowhurs."

"Ise mighty ole," said Granny, with lofty calmness, "Ise mo'n er hunnerd, an' ef I ain't tole yo' des all de fack dat I gedder up in dat time ahine me, hit kase I ain't yit git de time, Miss Mary Sallee. In co'se, I mought er know mo' ef I bin mo' strong in de haid, but I done de bes' I kin an' I kyarn't po' (pour) hit all out ter wunst."

When Aunt Mary was called by so dignified a title as "Miss Sallee," she knew it was time to apologise.

"I ain't mean no ha'm, Aunt Jinny," she protested, meekly. "In co'se, I know hit tek yo' mighty long time ter tell de ha'f dat yo' know, but dem tales o' yone so fine dat Ise allus on de stretch les' yo' tell some dat I miss."

"Dey ain't no big loss ef yo' do miss um, Aunt Mary," said Granny, mollified by her friend's speech, "dough yo' is suttinly de flattines' lady dat I know in de way dat yo' name um. Lawd! I des wisht I hab er fip (five cent piece) de hunnerd foh de good wuhds yo' gimme, I'd be heap too rich ter wuhk enny mo,' dat I would!"

"If you were rich, Granny, you would move way off into a great house, and then if I came out here I'd cry myself sick instead of hearing pretty stories," cried Tow Head, in vigorous protest against the vanity of riches.

Granny's old laugh crackled like brush fire. "Ef yo' don't cry none twell yo' ole Granny git rich, honey," she said, "dem blue eyes ob yone ain't gwine ter hab de brightness wash out o' um dis side de Jawdin Ribber, dat's shore."

Tow Head thanked her for this renunciation of wealth with a grateful look, but turned the conversation to the procurement of present advantage.

"Do go on with the other story, Granny. Aunt Mymee will come for me as soon as she can leave the baby, and I'll have to go—*immediately*—Mamma said so."

"Hyeah 'tis, chile :—

"In de ole times, Hawk, he wuz de meanes', beatines' t'ing dat go on two laigs. He kilt de buhds, he did, he kyar off de putty lil bunnies, he ketch de chickens, he go ez fur ez ter spy down in de grass an' git a-holt ob Ole Tucky-Hen's young uns."

"That was a shame! The sweet little peep-peep turkies are prettier than anything else in the world. What did he do when he took hold of them? Did he wish to make them cry 'peep, peep?'"

"Wuss den dat, honey, heap wuss. He des tuck um ter he nes', for dem ugly, f'erce young uns ob hissen ter eat, dat wut he did. W'y, all thu de woods an' de grass all de mammies wuz a-cryin' an' a-queechin' foh dey po' lil young ones."

"That's just the way Herod did, but he didn't live long. He was punished for his sins. Was Hawk?"

"Honey, meanness am boun' ter git paid foh at de highes' price goin', des putt dat in yo' pipe and smoke hit, but hole on! lemme tell dis now an' *den* yo' set f'th yo' 'pinyun.

"At de las', Hawk, he git a-holt de bigges' boy ob Ole Blue Jay. Ole Jay, he miss dat chile an' he go a-hollerin' arter 'im evvywhurs. 'Long at de fust, dey wuzzent no one tole 'im wut went o' de chile, kase he wuhkt sech er heap o' debbil*mint* hisse'f (he own bill ain't so mighty clean fum aig-suckin' an' th'oat-cuttin'), but arterwuhds he foun' out. He go a-hollerin' fit ter mek de daid hyeah an' a-lookin' evvywhurs 'cep' in de lookin'-glass, twell bimeby he git way out on de open perarer. Dey wuzzen' one tree dat he hab sp'ile ob nestes in sight. He in'mies wuz all 'way off, an' dar he wuz! He wuz dat tuckehed out dat he squot ri' down flat on de groun' ter res' hisse'f. He wuz dat wo' out dat he ain't pay no 'tenshun

ter nuttin. Bimeby, dough, he rouge up, kase he hyeah heap
o' lil fine soun's. He lif up he yeah an' lissen. De soun' come
mo' plain, hit run 'long de grass lak wile-fiah, 'Wut ail 'im ?
wut ail 'im ?' hit say. He look. See nuttin. Lissen 'gin.
Dar 'twuz ! Den he mek hit out. Hit wuz dem lil brack gnats,
a-hoppin' roun' mungs de blades o' de medder grass.

" ' Wut ail 'im ? Wut ail 'im ?'

" Den de arnser come—

" ' Hawk kilt he fustes-bawn. Hawk kilt he fustes-bawn.'
Hit wuz de grass dat tellt hit.

" ' Who tole yo ? Who tole yo ? ' ax de gnats.

" De win' (wind) tole us. De win' tole us.'

" ' Wut hawk done hit ? Wut hawk done hit ? '

" ' De one wid de nes' in de ole sycamo' tree. De one wid de
nes' in de ole sycamo' tree.'

" ' W'y don't Ole Jay Buhd pay 'im off ? W'y don't Ole Jay
Buhd pay 'im off ? ' ax de gnats.

" ' Kase he 'feard. Kase he 'feard. All de turr buhds 'feard
o' hawk, 'feard o' hawk,' de grass mek arnser wunst mo'.

" Den all de lil bugs an' wuhms down dar mungs de grass
roots tek up de song an' 'gree dat no un kin stan' up 'gin
Hawk. Dey all 'feard, fum fust ter las'. He wuz des de same
ez ole Conqueh-John hisse'f. ' Mo'n dat,' sez dey, ' Ole Jay
Buhd, arter all he ruckshisness, am run plum off. S'pec' he
'feard Hawk eat *him* ef de young meat fall shawt.'

" Dat mek Blue Jay dat mad dat he des riz up a-screamin'—
dey ain't dremp he c'd hyeah, dey tork so fine—an' he flewed
lak he des fresh up in de mawnin'.

" He flewed an' he flewed twell he git ter de ole sycamo' whah
Hawk tuck up he stan'. (He suttinly ain't know twell den dat
Hawk et dat chile.) W'en he git dar Hawk an' he old ooman,
dey bofe gone. Nemmine ! de chilluns at home. He tuck an'
flung um all outen de nes' *an' kilt um daid.*

" ' Bout dat time, hyeah come Hawk a-sailin' home. Ez he

sorter ring round an' sa'nter up, Ole Blue Jay jump right onter he back, an', suz l how he do bite an' claw 'im, on de haid, de wings, de back ! My l he des rode 'im lak er hoss an' bit 'im lak good vittles. Hawk, he ain't kin hit back, kase Jay Buhd right on top ob 'im, an' so hit come ter dat pass dat Ole Jay, he rid 'im plum outen de sottle*mint.* Sidesen dat, he sot er mahk 'pon Hawk, he do, dat stick ter 'im ter dis day. Afo' dat scrimmage, Hawk' feddehs wuz all de same. Dat day dey git all bloody. W'en dat blood dry, hit mek dahk streak an' spot an' dar dey is yit, dey ain't ne'er bresh off.

" W'en Blue Jay git thu wid dat trouncin' he go boggin' (moving slowly or dejectedly) off home whah he lib mungs de cotton-woods. He sorter proud 'bout dat lickin', but, oh l he sorry 'bout de 'casion ob hit. He sot down on er limb wid he tail an' wing a-hangin' an' he ain't say nuttin ter buhd ur debbil, but hit leak out, de tale ob dat lickin' do, kase de win' tell de grass, an' wut de grass know am boun' ter go de rounds. De grass don't keep nuttin back. Den de buhds git de whole tale an', suz, dey mek de miration l Dey ain't *sot* on (do not like) Ole Jay, but, my l he er suckin' turkle-dove 'long o' Hawk."

While Tow Head was trying to make up her mind whether she liked that story or not, Aunt Mymee appeared and gave her a concise invitation, in the name of her parents, to " 'have putty," say her prayers and go to bed.

As a reward for " 'havin' tollible," Aunt Mymee sang her this song, which is supposed to imitate the scream of a jaybird :

" Ez I wuz gwine thu de woods, I met er sassy jay,
                    Jay ! Jay !
I axt 'im wut dey wuz ter eat an' wut dey wuz ter pay,
                    Pay l Pay l
Ez I wuz gwine 'crost de fiel', I met er sassy jay,
                    Jay ! Jay ! Jay !
I axt 'im wut dey wuz ter eat an' wut dey wuz ter pay,
                    Pay ! Pay ! Pay l
Ez I wuz gwine up de hill, &c.,

Jay ! Jay !—Jay ! Jay !
I axt 'im wut dey wuz ter eat, &c.,
Pay ! Pay !—Pay ! Pay !
Ez I wuz gwine down de lane, &c.,
Jay ! Jay !—Jay ! Jay !
I axt 'im, &c.,
Pay ! Pay !—Pay ! Pay ! Pay ! "

X.

"OLE RABBIT AN' DE DAWG HE STOLE"—HOW HE OBTAINED GOPHER'S WINTER SUPPLIES.

ON'T *any*body know any more rabbit stories?"

Tow Head's glance wandered from one to another of the five wise women grouped about the fireplace, fraught with mingled scorn and entreaty.

The wise women, led by Aunt Mary, laughed so exasperatingly, that Tow Head's small stock of patience flared up and went out

THE RABBIT FAMILY.

like the spray of dead leaves clinging to the great log that did double duty as heater and illuminator.

"I'm going to Mamma," she said, rising with a great show of offended dignity. "I'm going immediately," she added, crossing the floor. "I'm not afraid of the dark."

"Co'se not," said Granny. "None o' yo' folks 'feared o' nuttin. In dat dey's diffunt fum Ole Rabbit, wid all he sly trick, he git skeered."

"Who sesso?" growled Big Angy.

" I sesso.   I kin prube dat, too, by de tale ob Ole Chuffy an' .
dat dawg he stole fum de w'ite man.   Wuzzent he skeer w'en
de dawg tuck out arter 'him ? "

" I ain't mine dat tale."

By this time Tow Head was in Granny's lap and the two
friends were sitting cheek pressed against cheek, greatly to
Aunt Mymee's chagrin.

" Hit wuz lak dis," said Granny, pressing the child closer and
half-shutting her eyes.

" In de good ole times, Ole Rabbit wuzzent scrouge (crowded)
none by de neighbehs.   Hit wuz miles ter de corndeh ob enny
urr man's fiel'.

" Arter w'iles Misteh Injun an' he folks, dey sot um up er
sottlemint, but dat ain't nuttin, kase dey wuz allus a-perawdin'
eroun' an' a-ketchin' up dey plundeh an' a-movin'.

" Bimeby, dough, 'long come de w'ite man, a-choppin' down
de trees an' a-diggin' up de yeath.   Den wuz de time all de
crittehs pack up dey go-ter-meetin' close in er piller-case an' git
ready ter staht off, kase dey know Misteh W'ite Man come foh
ter stay, an' he ain't de kine dat want ter sleep free ur fo' (three
or four) in de baid, an' dey ain't, ne-er.   Dat am, all un um 'cept
Ole Chuffy Rabbit an' de Squirr'l fambly sot out ; dem two
'low dey gwine ter tough hit out er w'les longeh.

" Wut pester Ole Chuffy mo' den all de res' wuz dat w'ite
man's dawg.   Hit wuzzent lak dem Injun dawgs dat's scattein'
(running) roun' de kyentry terday, an' in de pot termorrer."

" What kind of a dog was it, Granny—exactly what kind ? "

" Hit," said Granny, reflectively, with a look into space as if
her mind's eye beheld it—" hit wuz er houn'-dawg.   One o' dem
lanky, shahp-nose dawg dat hunt all day an' howl all night.
Hit wuz ez still ez er fox on er tuck (turkey) hunt fum day-
break twell cannel-light, but des wait twell de sun go down an'
de moon come up—oh, Lawd !—' Ah-oo-oo-oo ! Wow, ow, ow !
Ah-oo-oo-oo ; Wow, ow, ow !' hyeah hit go fum mos' sundown

ter mos' sun-up, an' dat wuz de mos' aggervatines' soun' dat de Ole Boy e'er putt in de th'oat ob er libbin' critteh. Hit des 'stractid Ole Rabbit. He flounce roun' in de baid lak er catfish on er hook. He groan an' he grunt an' he tuhn an' he roll, an' he des kyarn't git no good res'. He bin one o' de smoove-torkin' kine gin'ly, but dat houn', hit mek 'im cuss twell Ole Miss Rabbit, she 'bleege ter roll de bed-kivvehs roun' huh yeahs, she dat scannelise.

" ' W'y don't yo' get outen de baid an' tuhn yo' shoe wid de bottom side up an' set yo' bar' foot onto hit ? ' she say. ' Dat mek enny dawg stop he yowlin'.'

" ' Well ! ain' I done it forty-leben ti me ? say Ole Man Rabbit, des a-fumin' an' a snortin'. ' Ain' I bin a-hoppin' in an' out de baid all he lib-long night ? Co'se hit stop um foh er harf er jiff (an instant) an' den hit chune up ergin 'fo' I des kin git de baid wa'm unner me.'

" ' Ah-oo-oo-oo ! Wow, ow, ow ! Ah-oo-oo-oo ! Wow, *ow*, ow ! ' Dat ole houn' fetch er yowl dat fa'r (fairly) mek de man in de moon blink.

RABBIT TEK DAT TOLLER-DIP IN HIS HAN'.

" ' Cuss dat ole dawg ! Cuss 'im I say ! W'y don' dat fool dat own um, stuff er cawn-cob down he frote, ur chop he wuthless kyarkiss inter sassidge-meat ? ' sez Old Rabbit, sez' e. ' I gin up on de sleepin' queschin, dis night,' sez 'e, ' but I lay I ain't 'sturb lak dis in my res' tormorrer,' sez' e.

" Wid dat he bounce out on de flo' an' haul on he britches, an' light er toller-dip, an' he tek dat toller-dip in he han', an' he go pokin roun' mungs de shaddehs lak he a-huntin' foh sumpin.

" Scratch, scratch ! scuffle, scuffle ! he go in de corndehs ob de cubberd.

" Ah-oo-oo-oo ! Wow, ow, ow ! go de houn' outside.

" Scratch, scratch ! scuffle, scuffle !

" Ah-oo-oo-oo ! Wow, ow, ow !

" Scratch, scratch ! scuffle, scuffle !

" Ah-oo-oo-oo ! Wow, ow, O-O-OW !

" An' so dey kip hit up twell ole Miss Rabbit dez ez mad at one ez turr.

" ' Wut *is* yo' doin', Misteh Rabbit ? ' she ax. ' Is yo' run er brier in yo' foot ? Is yo' gittin' fat meat foh hit ? '

" ' No,' sez 'e, mighty shawt ; ' I ain' got no brier in my foot dat I knows on, but I gotter brier in my mine 'bout de size ob er snipe-bill, ef I ain't mistookencd.'

" At dat she let fly er swa'm o' queschins, but he des grin dry and say—

" ' Ax me no queschins an' I tell yo' no lies, Don' bodder me, ole ooman. I ain't feel berry strong in de haid, dis mawnin', an' 1 mought answer queschins wid my fist, ef I gits pestered.'

" Dat shet 'er up, in co'se, dough she ain't satisfy.

" Toreckly, day gun ter brak an' he blow out de cannel an' she sot in ter git brekfus.

" Ez de light git strong, she noduss he step sorter lop-side.

" ' *Is* yo' got er brier in yo' foot ? '

" ' Hit in my mine, ooman.'

" Putty soon she holler out—

" ' Who bin techin' de braid ? Somebody bin a-cuttin' de braid ! I lay I gotter trounce dem greedy chilluns for dat. 'Pear lak I kyarn't set down nuttin, dese days, but dey gotter muss in hit ! I gwine ter cut me er big hick'ry lim', dis mawnin', an' see ef I kyarn't lick some mannehs inter de whole kit an' bilin' un um ! In de meanw'iles o' gittin' dat lim', I gwine to smack de jaws ob de whole crowd.'

" ' No, yo' ain't,' sez Old Rabbit, sez 'e. ' Des lef dem young uns o' mine 'lone. Dey ain't done nuttin. *I* cut dat braid an' I got dat braid an' I ain't gwine ter gin 'er up.'

" Putty soon ole Miss Rabbit sing out ergin—

" ' Who bin cuttin' de bakin (bacon) fat ? ' sez she, ' an

cuttin' it çrookid, too,' sez she. 'I lay I des leaf de breckfus an' set out an' git dat lim', right now,' sez she.

"'No, yo' won't,' sez Ole Rabbit, sez 'e. 'I ain' gwine ter hab de sense w'ale outen dem young uns o' mine. *I* tuck dat fat an' I got dat fat, an' ef I haggle de slice, dat my look out,' sez 'e. 'I paid foh hit, an' I gwine ter cut hit wid de saw ur scissuz, ef I feel lak hit,' sez 'e.

"Wid dat he git up an' walk off, limpetty limp.

"Miss Rabbit ain't see no mo' un 'im twell sundown. Den, he come in lookin' mighty tuckehed out, but des a-grinnin' lak er bak skunk. He sot down, he did, an' et lak he bin holler (weary) cl'ar ter he toes, but he won't say nuttin. W'en he git thu, he sorter stretch hisse'f and say—

"'I gwine ter go ter baid. I gotter heap o' sleep ter mek up, an' I lay no dawg ain' gwine ter 'sturb my res' dis night.'

"An' dey don't. Dey wuzzent er soun', an' Miss Rabbit mek er gret miration at dat in huh mine, but she ain't got nobody ter tork hit unter, twell de nex mawnin', w'en Ole Rabbit git up ez gay an' sassy ez er yeahlin'. Den he hab de big tale ter tell, an' dis wuz wut he tell 'er :—

"W'en he wuz a-foolin' in de cubberd, he git 'im er piece o' braid, an' he tie dat on he foot. Den he cut 'im er slice o' bakin an' he putt dat on top de braid. Den he slip on he shoe an' staht out. Dat he do kase he gwine ter fix 'im some shoe-braid ("shoe-bread") foh ter feed ter dat dawg, kase ef yo' w'ar braid in yo' shoe an' den gin hit unter er dawg, an' he eat hit, dat dawg yone (is yours). He gwine ter foller yo' ter de eends o' de yeath, dat he am ! Ole Chuffy putt de bakin (bacon) on ter gin dat braid er good tase, an' ter fool de folks wut see 'im, kase he gwine ter let on lak he run er brier in he foot an' tuck an' putt on dat bakin foh ter dror out de so'ness an' kip 'im fum a-gittin' de lock-jaw.

"Well ; he tromp roun' twell de w'ite man go ter de fiel', an' den he slip up sorter easy-lak an' he fling dat shoe-braid a-front o' dat ole houn'-dawg. Hit gulf hit down in des one swaller. Yo' know dem houn'-dawgs des allus bin hongry sence de minnit dey wuz bawn, an' yo' kyarn't fill um up no mo'n ef dey got hole in um de same ez er cullendeh.

"De minnit de shoe-braid bin swaller dat ole houn'-dawg des natchelly hone arter Ole Rabbit. He tuck out arter 'im thu de bresh so swif' dat hit sorter skeer Old Chuffy. He wuz des a-studyin' 'bout a-leadin' dat houn' ter de crik an' a-tyin' er rock roun' he neck an' a-drowndin' um, but dis hyeah turr'ble hurry s'prise 'im so dat he des run lak de Ole Boy wuz a-tryin' ter ketch 'im. Hyeah dey had it! Up hill an' down holler, 'crost de fiel' an' round de stump, obeh an' undeh, roun' an' roun', ketch ef yo' kin' an' foller ef you kyarn't! Oh, suz, dat wuz er race!

"No tellin' how hit mought a-come out ef Ole Rabbit hedn' run 'crost er Injun man wid er bow an' arrer.

"De Injun 'gun ter fit de arrer ter de string foh ter shoot dat Chuffy Rabbit, w'en he holler out ez loud ez he c'd holler foh de shawtniss ob her bref—

"'Oh! hole on, Misteh Injun Man, hole on er minit! Ise a-fetchin' yo' er present,' sez 'e—'er mighty nice present,' sez 'e.

"'Wut yo' fetch?' sez de Injun Man, kine o' s'pishis-lak.

"'Hit's er dawg,' sez Ole Rabbit, a-wuhkin' he yeahs an' a-flinchin' he nose kase he hyeah dat dawg a-cracklin' thu de bresh, 'er mighty nice fat dawg, Misteh Injun Man. I hyeah tell dat yo' ole ooman wuz po'ly, an' I was a-brungin' dis hyeah houn'-dawg so's yo' c'd mek er stchew outen 'im,' sez 'e. 'I'd a-fotch um ready cook,' sez 'e, 'but my ole ooman, she des nowhurs 'long o' yone in de mekin' o' stchews,' sez 'e. 'I wuz foh fetchin' er string o' inguns foh seas'nin', an' den I don't know ef yo' lak um wid inguns,' sez 'e.

"DIS HYEAH TURR'BLE HURRY S'PRISE 'IM SO."

"De Injun suttinly wuz tickle wid dat lallygag (humbug) but he don't say much. He des sorter grunt an' look todes de bresh.

"'Dat um! Dat my houn'-dawg a-comin' !' say Ole Rabbit, a-flinchin' mo' an' mo' ez de cracklin' come a-nigheh. 'Yo' betteh shoot um, Misteh Injun, des ez 'e bounce out o' de bresh, kase dat am er mons'us shy dawg, mons'us shy ! Hit won' foller nobody but me, an' I kyarn' go 'long home wid yo' an' tek um kase Ise lame. Las' night I couldn't sleep, my lef'-han'-hine-foot huht me so, an' now I got um tie up in bakin' fat. Shoot um right hyeah, Misteh Injun ! Dat de bes' an' de safes', mon !'

"Des dat minnit out jump de dawg an'—zim !—Misteh Injun des shoot um an' pin um ter de groun'.

"Den Ole Man Rabbit mop de sweat offen he face an' lope off home—leas' dat de tale he tell de fambly, an' ef 'tain't de troof, nobody ain' n'nyin' hit (no one denies it), dese days, an' ez he say ter he ole ooman, hit er good laughin' tale terday, but hit mighty sollumcholly yistiddy, w'en 'twuz gwine on."

"Now, de mos' cu'i's paht (curious part) ob all dis," continued Granny, "am dat sence dat day all de dawgs ack lak dey sholy cunjered. Ef dey enny un um des ez much ez ketch er gimpse ob er rabbit-tail dey des putt out arter hit lak de Ole Boy a-sickin' (driving) um on."

"Dat wuz sholy cunjered braid," said Aunt Em'ly, with conviction, "ur (but) hit don't wuhk dat quick. Yo' hatter w'ar braid in yo' shoe mo' longeh'n dat, urrways."

"Yo' des hatter w'ar de braid twell yo' strenk go inter hit, so's w'en de dawg swaller *hit*, he swaller de tase o' yo'. In co'se, de strenk ob Ole Rabbit go in mighty quick."

"Dat de troof, Aunt Jinny. I tek dat back wut I say ! Lan' ! lan' ! wut don' yo' know ! "

"I dunno dat fine tale o' yone 'bout Rabbit an' de gopheh ez good ez I wanter, Aunt Em'ly. Ef yo' tell hit now, so dat I git de good un um ergin, an' lil missey git de satisfackshin un um too, I reckin I putt in de time a-roas'in' dis hyeah pan ob coffee-beans in de hot ashes."

"Coffee-beans des fit my mouf, dis night, Aunt Jinny. Come in Aunt Em'ly' lap, honey, w'iles I tell yo' dat tale o' Rabbit and Gopheh. Aunt Jinny, dat 'mine (reminds) me—is yo' got enny ob dem lil choke-tatehs dat yo' c'd roas' at de same time yo' foolin' wid de coffee-beans ? "

"Dat I is, an' hyeah dey is ! " cried Granny, dragging a small bag of tubers from among the bandboxes under her bed.

The choke-taters or artichokes, (not the green vegetable rosettes served to "white folks," but the tubers of the great "Jerusalem sunflowers " that come, at Nature's bidding, beside the country road) were buried in the ashes, at a safe distance from the popping coffee-beans, before Aunt Em'ly could give her mind to the tale. Finally, she said—

"'Twuz dishaways, honey' 'bout gittin' de truck Gopheh lay up foh cole weddeh. Ole Rabbit, he putt in de summeh time des lak de worl' wuz hissen ; he wuz a-cuttin' roun' hyeah an' yon, in de bresh an' out ergin, sassin' de boys an' settin' up ter de gals, an' a-perawdin' eroun whahsomedevveh dey wuz enny debbilmint gwine on. He ain't do er lick ob wuhk, he ain't lay by ez much ez er bastet (basket) ob leabes ter mek er sallet (salad), no suh ! an' w'en he ole ooman 'mine 'im o' dat, he des bat he eye lak he 'mos' a-drappin' off ter sleep an' say—

"' Don't pesteh er sma't man dat yo' got de luck ter hab foh yo' ole man wid fool queschins, ole ooman. I got er heap o' folks out a-wuhkin' foh my libbin'. Dey fetch me in de crap w'en de right time come.'

"W'en she git oneasy 'gin an' say she ain't see nobody wuhkin', ceppin' foh deyse'f, an' nobody ain' fetch in nuttin ter de sulleh (cellar), an' de fros' a-comin' on an' de greens 'bout ter gin out, an' whah is dat crap, she wanter know, he des hunch up he shouldehs an' lay back he yeahs an' sing out dat aggravaxin' way he got—

"'Ax me no queschins, I tell yo' no lies. But I know whah dey's good vittles foh er man 'bout my size.'

"Wid dat he go a-skippin' down de lane todes de bresh-patch, whah er passel ob he kinfolks wuz 'semmle ter pass de time axin' one nurr puzzle*mints* (riddles), an' a-tellin' tales an' a-r'arin' an' a-tusslin' an' a-raisin' de Ole Boy gin'ly wid dey laffin' an' gigglemints an' kyarin' on. So he do all de time, an' de days pass by, an' de nights gun ter git sorter cool foh de quiltkivvehs, an' de nuts fall down 'pun de daid grass an' de leabes come a-russlin' 'pun top un um an' de jays holler an' scream lak dey t'ink de sumac-bushes afiah, sho nuff.

"Den de ole ooman ax 'im 'gin—

"'Is dem pussons a-wuhkin' foh yo' yit ? Kase ef dey is,' sez she, 'I reckin dey got de crap mek long 'fo' now, an' I wisht dey git um in de sulleh 'fo' de fros' spile um.'

"He des wink an' grin an' go off a-visitin' he kinfolks, ur kick up he heels mungs de leabes.

"Den de sun look lak er big ball o' fiah an' de a'r wuz full ob smoke fum nowhurs, des ez ef de whole yeath wuz lick up in er turr'ble big perarer-fiah, an' de leabes, dey wuz mos' all down an' de nuts sorter sink in de groun', lak dey good noshin ter plant deyse'fs, an' de weeds in de fence-corndehs an' 'long de aige ob de lane go, 'rittle-rattle, rittle-rattle' in de win,' lak de bones ob er las' Crismus tucky.

"Den de ole ooman, she up an say—

"'De watteh des a-dribblin' outen de corndehs ob my mouf, I a-honin' so arter dem good vittles dem pussons am a-gittin' for yo'. I wisht, Misteh Rabbit, dat yo' tell um ter fetch me er tase, dis blessid day. I kyarn't hole out much longeh, I cross my haht on dat.'

"'Den hole in' (restrain yourself), sez 'e, 'dat am des wut I sot out ter lahn (learn) yo', ole ooman,' sez 'e, a-kickin' up he heels an' a-clippin' down de lane, samer he bin a-doin' all de time.

"Bimeby, Ole Jack Fros', he come ter stay. Hit time ter

git out blankit-kivvehs foh de baid an' flannin-petticuts foh de
chilluns ; hit time foh punkin-sass an' roas' 'possum wid 'coon
gravy ; hit time ter git out de zerves (preserves) an' putt by de
watteh-million ; hit time ter lay by de mint-julip an' git out
de aig-nogg ; time ter lay by de fried chicken an' git out de
pot-pie ; time ter lay by de peach-cobbler an' git out de apple-
dumplin' ; time ter lay by de roas'in'-yeah an' git out de ash-
cake ; time ter lay by de roas' pig an' git out de sassidge an'
chine ; time ter lay by de churry-tart an' git out de mince-pie ;
time ter quit de br'ile buhd an' git out de bake shoat ; time
ter—— "

"Foh de Lawd sake, Aunt Em'ly, stop dat ! Ef yo' go on
dataway, I sholy pe'sh wid hongeh, I shill dat ! I des ready ter
drap spang offen dis hyeah cheer, now ! " cried Aunt Mary.

Aunt Em'ly was greatly gratified by this tribute to her
descriptive powers. She smiled, bridled, and came very near
breaking into an undignified guffaw, but contrived to check
that unworthy manifestation of elation, and continued, with
quiet dignity—

"'Bout dat time hit 'gun ter look ter Ole Man Rabbit
hisse'f dat ef he don't want win'-pie (wind-pie) an' watteh-pud-
din' foh he reg'leh meals, he betteh be a-stirrin' roun'. W'en
he git dat thu he ha'r, he tuck er day ur two foh a-kynsidehin',
an' he w'ar he studyin' cap all de time o' dat time. He study
an' study, but dat ain' hendeh dat w'en he a-santerin' roun' de
fiel's an' lanes he see all dat gwine on. He ain't de one dat
miss nuttin, Ole Rabbit ain't. He ain't lak dem folkses dat
gotter rock deyse'f in de rockin'-cheer wid dey eyes shet w'en
dey a-wuhkin' dey mines (thinking), *dat* he ain't ! *He* SEE,
an' he see wut he gwine ter fetch outen wut he see. All dat
he see mek fat foh Ole Chuffy' ribs, in co'se hit do !

" In de airly mawnin', w'en de fros' wuz w'ite on de stubble
an' de hemp-stalks, an' de sun seem mighty slow 'bout gittin'
'bove de tree tops, he sot out ter look et de young orchahd dat

er mon 'e know sot out, las' yeah. He look long an' he look hahd.

"'Uh-huh!' he say ter dem spin'lin' young trees, 'yo' ain' no 'count foh raisin' apples, fur ez I kin see. I reck'n him dat sot yo' out am mighty dis'p'inted wid yo', but de leabins ob one am de sass ob nurr. Yo' am a-suitin' me mighty well, dis minnit. I ain't keer none foh apples, but I ain't turn up my nose at bahk (bark), ef hit sweet an' good, an' yo' am dat, I boun'. Shoh! I des ez well satify ez ef yo' wuz set out a-puppus ter raise bahk.'

" Wid dat he fall ter wuhk an' git er good big bite o' dat bahk in he mouf. Wooh! p-t-t! s-s-spit!—dat bahk ez bitteh ez duck's gall."

" Duck's gall am good foh de so' (sore) eyes. 'Taint no 'count on trees," interrupted Aunt Mymee.

" Dat so, Aunt Mymee. I ain' 'spute yo' none on dat, but dat stuff on dem trees des ony (just only) *tase* dataway. Hit wuz warnit (walnut) juice dey got on um. Somebody bin a-doctehin' dem trees des ter keep de varmints fum a-gnawin' um. Dat wut Ole Rabbit know too, an' dat wut mek 'im so mad.

" 'Hit's er mighty mean man dat'll go an' dob up er good tree dataway,' sez Ole Rabbit, sez 'e, an' wid dat, he des bust fo'th an' free he mine 'bout de man dat 'u'd do sech er mean, low-down trick. Oh, he des went on! dough dey wuzzent nobody ceppin he own se'f a-lissenin'.

" Bimeby, he git out o' bref an' gin dat up. Hit mighty satifyin' ter de feelins ter 'buse de meanness o' folks, but 'tain't fillin' none ter de stummick. Dat wut Ole Chuffy fine, an' he 'bleege ter look roun' an' ketch up er breckfus somers else. He peek an' he poke an' he don't see nuttin. He go 'long todes de eend ob de orchahd twell he come in sight o' de buck-wheat fiel', but he don't go dar, he know mo'n dat. He des go a-lookin' roun' mungs de lil hills o' fresh dut (dirt) lak he t'ink he los' sump'n dat he gwine ter fine dar."

"Mebbe," interrupted Aunt Mymee, again, "he wuz gwine ter eat some o' dat duht dat wuz flung up by de gophehs. Gopheh-duht mighty good ef yo' got de misery in de stummick, mo' speshul, ef yo' feel squawmish."

Granny elevated her eyebrows, but said nothing. She heartily despised a dirt-eater.

"Uh huh!" said Aunt Em'ly, partly agreeing, "Ise allus hyurn tell dat duht am good foh de watteh-brash an' de likes, but dat wuzzent wut Ole Rabbit up ter. He got de sinkin' in de stummick, to-be-sho, but vittles de dose ter fetch dat up. W'en he wuz at de lil hills, he sniff an' he snuff. Bimeby, he go up ter un un um (of them) an' he tek up lil ob de duht an' feel ef 'twuz wa'm.

"Hit *wuz* wa'm! hit wuz brack duht, kase it wuz mighty new good lan', an' hit wuz ez mealy ez one o' dem tatehs on de h'a'th dar, an'—hit—wuz—*wa'm!*

"'Hi!' sez Ole Rabbit, sez he, 'wut de matteh now? Ole Gopheh, he's a-diggin' he sulleh, deep, diggin' dis late in de season an' dis airly in de mawnin'. Mighty quare, dat am, mighty quare! Wut in de name o' common sense an' wunner, he doin' dat foh? at dis time de yeah, too! I 'low I ain't dat sot (so intent on) arter breckfus dat I ain' got de time ter stop an' eenquieh 'bout hit.'

"Den he up an' go ahine de gopheh-hill—dat des wut dat lil hill wuz, er gopheh-hill at de do' ob Ole Gopheh's house, whah he fling out de duht w'en he dig de sulleh. W'en he go dar, he knock an' he knock, Ole Rabbit do, he knock wunst an' twiste an' den so fas' dat yo' kyarn't count.

"Nobody say nuttin.

"Den he holler out—

"'Hyo dar! hyo!' sez 'e. 'Come ter de do'. 'Tain't no skunk, nur weasel, nur dawg, nur wile cat dat am a-knockin'. Hit's me, Misteh Gopheh, Ole Man Rabbit, a-drappin' in foh er fr'en'ly call.'

"Wid dat Ole Gopheh, he stick he haid out an' say, sorter pleasant an' sorter sheepy—

"''Scuse me, Misteh Rabbit, dat I ain' hyeah yo' at de fust. Ise dat muddle up in my wuhk dat I kyarn' skuse hyeah nuttin. All de same, now dat I do hyeah yo, Ise mighty glad ter see yo', dough I mighty 'shame dat I kyarn't ax you in, but de front entry all clutteh up wid trash so yo' kyarn't git thu.'

"'I des ez lives set out hyeah in de fresh a'r," sez Ole Man Rabbit, 'dat am, ef yo' got de time ter chat. If Ise a-hendrin yo' dough, des say de wuhd an' I tek myse'f off, *dat* quick ! '

"W'en Ole Rab say dat, he yuck (jerked) he hine foot, quicker'n wink.

"'Oh ! yo' ain't hendeh me none,' say Gopheh, spittin' out de duht fum he jaws onter de pile. 'I wuz des fix ter come up wid dis load. Ise proud ter hab yo' hyeah. De sight o' yo' am good foh so'e eyes an' de soun' o' yo' am good foh de weak chist. Yo' fetch so much news w'en yo' come round, hit mighty 'livenin' ter slow, hahd-wuckin' folks, Misteh Rabbit.'

"'Ise er wuckin' mon my own se'f, suh,' sez Ole Rabbit, sez 'e, a-lookin' ez ef he feelin's wuz huht. 'Ise bin a-layin' in er big crap dis yeah—too big, in facks—I ain't got de sulleh room dat I a-needin'. I ain't no diggeh lak yo'se'f; ef I staht a-diggin' now, I ain't gwine ter git dat sulleh done twell nex summeh, an' den wut de use ob er sulleh ? '

"At dat Gopheh, he cock up he yeah an' look lak he hyeah de good news, but he ain't say nuttin much.

"'I git ahine-han's de same way my own se'f,' sez 'e, ' dat w'y I a-diggin' w'en by de good rights I otter be in baid.'

"'I hates mighty bad ter loose dem roots," sez Ole Rab, sorter to hisse'f, ' but I reckin day ain't no hep foh hit. I don't need um an' I ain't got de sulleh room foh um, but lan' ! I hates ter see sech good vittles run ter wase.'

"'Well ! ' sez Ole Gopheh, sez 'e, sorter a-bustin' in on

de remocks (remarks), ' Misteh Rabbit, mebbe I kin kommer-
date yo' some.'

" ' I thot yo' wuz a-namin' dat yo' so crowded dat yo'
a-bildin' mo' sulleh,' sez Old Rabbit, kinder jubous-lak, an'
a-scratchin' he haid lak he a-scratchin' foh news ter come out.

" ' Oh ! ' sez Gopheh, sez 'e, ' I des needs 'bout so much, an'
ef yo' roots so turr'ble fine, I reckin I kin fling out some o' dese
I got an' fill in yone.'

" ' Lemme see dem wut yo' got,' sez Ole Rabbit, a-lookin'
mighty sollum an' slow. ' Mebbe dem des ez
good ez de ones I got,' sez 'e, ' dough, to-be-sho,
dat mighty onlikely, kase I riz dese ob mine my
own se'f, Misteh Gopheh, and, de Lawd know!
I tuck er heap o' trouble. Howsomedevveh,
ef yo'll han' me one ob yone, I kin gin hit er
tas'e, an' den I know how ter 'vise yo'.'

" Soon ez de wudh said, Gopheh, he des
splunge down in de sulleh an' run up ergin wid
er big calamus root in one han' an'er whole
heap o' de tendes' (tenderest) kine o' lil w'ite
shoots in turr.

" Ole Rabbit, he des skuse kin keep fum a-
grabbin' um, he so wuhkt up at de sight o' vittles,
an' all the time he stummick des a-ringin' de
dinneh bell wid bofe han's. He mek out ter hole hisse'f study
dough, an' he tek de calamus an' he tek de shoots an' he
nibble an' tase, nibble an' tase, w'les he shake de haid an'
look way out in de a'r lak de docteh w'en he kyarn't mek
out ef de baby got de measles ur mos' et up wid de fleas.
He keep on lak dat, he do, twell he des nibble de whole
passel out o' sight. Den he gib he haid one las' big shake,
lak he hab heap o' pity foh Gopheh. Den he pick er crum'
ur two outen he whiskehs an' say—

" ' My fren, I ain't de one dat gwine ter 'ceive you, dough

OLE RABBIT
REFLECTS.

de Lawd know ! I hates lak pizon ter huht yo' feelin's an' dis'pint yo' ; dem roots ain't lak de ones I got, no mo' dey ain't.'

At dat Gopheh, he wuz des all struck ob er heap.   He 'spise he winteh truck so dat hit don't seem no mo' 'count den de dry weeds in de fence corndeh.

" Ole Rabbit, he look at 'im mighty kine.

" ' Is yo' got sumpin else ? ' sez 'e, a-smilin' sorter tiahd-lak ' (as if tired).

" ' I'm got er few tatehs an' goobeh-peas an' er gob o'

OLE RABBIT AND MISTEH GOPHEH.

bummle-bee honey,' sez Gopheh, sorter hangin' back wid de wuhds, lak he mos' shame ter let um out.'

" Hyeahin' o' dem t'ings mos' kill Ole Rabbit, but sence he git fill up in de corndehs wid dem w'ite shoots an' calamus, he c'd stan' hit betteh w'en de chat run on vittles, so he look sorter mighty an' toss up he chin an' wuhk he nose an' cl'ar he tho'at, lak de namin' o' dem common vittles mek 'im sorter kintempshis, an' he say—

" ' Uh-huh ! ef yo' satisfy, dat all right, but ef yo' ain't, an'

yo' mine ter tek de trouble, w'en de day git mo' 'long todes noon,
w'en hit mo' mile (warmer), yo' kin fetch in some o' my truck.'

" Seem ter Gopheh lak he dis pe'sh (perish) out, ef he don't
git some o' dat truck, so he up an' say, 'T'anky, t'anky, Nabeh
Rabbit', mighty f'erce (fierce—eagerly), an' he gin ter th'ow out
de truck he got in de sulleh, right off. Den him an' Ole
Rabbit mek de 'greement dat w'en de sulleh all cl'ar out, den
dat Ole Rab gwine ter show 'im de way ter de truck-patch.
Arter dat dey shake de han' pun de bawgin an' Ole Rabbit
'low he 'bleeged ter go 'long home, kase Miss Rabbit, she
gittin' sumpin fine foh dinneh ter sorter sample de goods ' fo '
dey lay um by.

" Wid dat sesso (saying), out he putt, but he ain't go home.
Wut de use, I wanter know ? Dey ain't no pot a-bilin' in he
house dat day. He des tellin' dem owdashus lies ter git Gopheh
all tore up in he mine, an' he done hit too ! Stiddier goin' home,
he go down by de crick ter whah de bank crummle off an' de
watteh wash de roots ob the weeds and briehs out. He lop off
heap o' dem roots, an' he go an' pile um up in er big pile out
in er fiel'. Den he git er gr'a' big lot ob willer-trigs an' one
trash an' nurr, an' he pile dem on too. Den he lope back an'
ax Gopheh will he come 'long, kase now he thu he big dinneh,
he ain't got er libbin' t'ing ter do, ceppin' ter he'p he frens, an'
dat suttingly am er pledger stiddier (a pleasure instead of) er
bodder ter er fr'en'ly man. Den he run on an' say—

"' Hit do me good, too, ter hab de stirrin' roun', kase I des
knows I mek er pig outen myse'f, de dinneh wuz dat good an'
I dat proud dat I raise um myse'f.'

"Dar now ! 'tain't no use ter tell all de speechifyin' dat pass
back an' fo'th 'twixt um. I gwine ter cut dat tale shawt an'
come in 'pun de eend ob it. Ole Rabbit, he tuck an' tuck
Gopheh an' show 'im dat pile o' rubbige an' he sez, sez 'e,
a-smilin' all de time an' a-swellin' out he buzzom—

"' Hyeah 'tis, nabeh ! I done sot him out an' wuhkt hit an'

lay hit by my ownse'f, so I knows des wut yo' a-gittin', but ef
yo' ain't sati'fy wid my sesso, des set down an' try er hunk o'
sumpin.'

"Gopheh, he wuz a-winkin' an' a-blinkin' in de sun twell he
couldn' tell er tateh fum er toadstool, and, sidesen dat, he got
er putty good staht foh er bad cole an' hit gwine ter git wuss,
ef he stay out in de fros', so he say.

"'Nemmine de tasin' des now, my deah Misteh Rabbit, I
tek yo' wuhd foh hit. I 'low yo' know de tase ob Sunday
vittles, ef ennybody do. I des wuhk now an' tase toreckly.'

"Wid dat dey bofe sot ter wuhk, Ole Rabbit a-he'pin'
(helping) lak er fine felleh.

"W'en dey tuck in de fust load, Gopheh, he 'low he tek um
down sulleh hisse'f.

"'All fa'r an' squar',' sez Ole Rabbit, sez 'e, a-tuhnin' he
back an' a-stuffin' he hankercher in he mouf ter keep fum
a-bustin' out a-laffin.

"W'en he sottle down fum dem highstrikes (his excitement),
he tuhn roun' an' say—

"'W'iles yo' down dar, I kin cl'ar up de rubbige out hyeah.'

"Wid dat he grab up er yarmful ob dem nice sweet roots
an' goobehs an' out he git an' hide um in de bresh nigh home.

"Den w'en he git back, he sing out, 'Am yo' ready foh nurr
load, nabeh?'

"Gopheh, he pop out he fool haid and say, 'Yessuh.'

"Den back dey go, in co'se, an' dey kip up dat foolishness
twell sundown, an' den hit too cool foh Gopheh ter stay out
o' do's. He 'low, dough, dat he gwine ter git one mo' load
in de mawin', ef de day tuhn out fine.

"'All ri', des suit yo'se'f, an yo' suit me,' sez Rabbit, an'
wid dat he lope off home an' 'low ter de ole ooman an' de
chilluns dey betteh camp in de brier-patch dat night an' de nex
day, kase de houn's wuz out.

"Dey mo'n willin' ter go w'en dey hyeah dat, an' dey mo'n

THE RABBIT FAMILY.

willin' ter say w'en dey ketch sight ob Gopheh's truck in dar."

" What did Gopher do when he tasted what Rabbit gave him ? " interrupted the child, eagerly.

" Ole Gopheh ?   Huh ! he season he suppeh wid cuss-wuhds, dat night, sholy, but e'en dat don't mek dat ole stuff go down easy an' stay dar.   He set up wid hisse'f mos' all night, an' all de time he wuz a-layin' off ter lam dat ole vilyun ob er Rabbit ter frazzles.   W'y, honey, he dat outdone dat w'en he drap off ter sleep, 'long todes mawnin', he dremp he cut Ole Rabbit's tho'at."

OLE RABBIT AND HIS WIFE.

" Oh, Aunt Emily, did he do it ? "

" Tee-hee ! Not ez Ole Rabbit hyeah tell um. De nex mawnin' hit wuz a-rainin' dat sorter onstudy rain dat flap shuttehs an' fling de daid leabes eroun', an' de nex night hit friz ter stay, so Gopheh don't git out ter do no sottlin'-up.

" Ole Rab, he git back de respec' ob he ole ooman an' brag on hisse'f might'ly 'fo' de chilluns, but I done hyeah tell dat hit wuz er mighty lean gopheh dat comed out en de hill in de aige ob de orchard on de side nex' de buckwheat-fiel', de spring a-follerin'."

The tale of Rabbit's rascality was received with an undue amount of laughter and applause, which, however, was suddenly suppressed by Granny stating emphatically, that when she had " mos' wo' out de marrer-bones cookin' choke-tatehs an' coffee-beans " she did not propose to have them " ruinated" " wiles er passel ob folks gin deyse'fs up ter de haw-haws (laughter)."

This remark was construed as an invitation to partake of light refreshment ; so the " haw-haws " came to an abrupt ending and every one seriously addressed herself to showing her appreciation of Granny's little vegetable roasts. Tow Head, in particular, distinguished herself as a trencher-maid. She never had been able to make up her mind which she preferred, the beans or the artichokes, so she ate impartially of both, without a thought of her mother's hygienic rules and regulations.

" Isn't it strange, Granny," she said, leaning back against her friend with a sigh of satisfaction, " that some people do not know that you must roast coffee-beans till they pop, else they'll be bitter and poisonous and make you very sick ? The new people in the red house on the hill never heard of them till I told them, and then they decided they were a kind of chestnut, and so they ate some raw and were *awful* sick."

Everybody looked serious. Not from sympathy, however. No doubt such ignorant people were " half-strainers " and not fit for association with the " quality " families.

" They did not know artichokes either," pursued Tow Head, " till I 'splained they were the other end of sunflowers, and then the old lady said it was nice that they were good to look at, good to eat, and good to burn when they were dry."

" De seeds mek good ile, an' dat ile mos' ez good foh croup ez goose-grease, dat *I* know," said Aunt Mymee.

" De seeds good foh feed chickin an' mek um fat," added Big Angy.

"Ef yo' putt er row of sun-flowehs 'twixt yo' an' de green

pond, yo' ain' gwine ter hab no fevah-an'-ageh," said Granny.

Aunt Em'ly lifted the little girl from Granny's knee to her own, and began to trot her and sing with a comical inflection that set everybody to laughing and, for the time being, disposed of the sunflower's claims to pre-eminence :—

> " Oh ! de sunfloweh grows an' so do de rose,
> An' pinies fine stan' in er line ;
> But I don't keer at all.
> Dey's des one posy grow foh me,
> Hit don't grow on no big tall tree,
> Hit's backy, backy, backy,
> Back—ee, ba-a-a—KEE."

XI.

FOX TALES.

AUNT MARY had gone to a " ball " at the house of a neighbour ten miles distant from her cabin in a bee-line. She and Uncle John had started off at sundown in the most sociable proximity ; Uncle John, as a matter of fact, bestriding his old claybank mare with great dignity, and Aunt Mary sitting behind him and clasping him closely round the waist as a necessary precaution against the tumbles, sure to follow otherwise, when old Sue affected to see in every stump a bear and in every strip of moonlight a deep-flowing river, and shied or baulked as seemed to suit the occasion.

Granny had professed herself too old for the "foolishness " of balls, and Aunt Em'ly had not been invited, so the two cronies had " made hit up bechux " them to spend a quiet evening together. They were flavouring their reminiscences of the good old times with cold pork-and-cabbage and a modest glass apiece of hot whiskey and water, when Aunt Mymee and Tow Head dropped in for a call.

It required no abnormal keenness of perception to discern that Aunt Mymee was in a very spiteful mood, and that her " ugliness," as Granny called it, was mainly directed towards Aunt Em'ly. In response to a faint invitation, she went to the cupboard and poured from a black bottle, whose existence was supposed to be a secret kept from the child, a generous potation. As she sipped it her temper—not her heart—seemed to expand with its genial warmth. Aunt Em'ly's son had " smacked the jaws " of her favourite grandson, and, although she had very little patience with the small imp herself, she was in a fine fury at the authoress of the smacker's being.

" Ez I come 'long," she said, with an unpleasant smile, " I wuz studyin' 'bout dem ar Fox Injuns dat use ter wuz hyeah, an' dat call in de membunce ob er tale dat I s'pec' lil missey gwine ter lak. Ain' yo' lak de tale 'bout de fox an' de wolf, lil honey ? "

As every one knew, " honey " was always ready for any sort of a story, so Aunt Mymee was at once importuned to tell what was in her " membunce." Nothing loth to begin, with a chuckle that made Aunt Em'ly's soft heart quail, she related—

HCW RED FOX LOST PRAIRIE-WOLF'S DAUGHTER.

" In de ole t'mes, w'en de likely gals wuzzent ez plenty ez dey am in dese times, Ole Perarer-Wolf he hed de gal dat wuz de fines' gal in de kyentry. All de men-crittehs fum fust ter las' dat wuzzent perwide wid podnehs (partner,) wuz des plum 'stractid arter dat yaller wolf-gal. She wuz er sassy critteh, dat gal wuz, an' she grin at all de beasteses, tuhn an' tuhn erbout, lak de gals do down ter dis day, but dey wuz one mighty big des diffunce twix dem time an' now, she hab heap mo' biggeh batch ter pick fum den ef she wuz on hans at dis minnit, an' dat mek er biggitty (proud), an' she fling up de haid an' tuhn up de nose w'en de beaux wanter slack up de co'tin' an' galli-vantin' an' sottle down in de corndeh ter bussin' jaws, an' layin' plan foh keeping house an' ketchin' vittles. No, suh I she ain' wanter sottle down lak 'er mammy.

" Bimeby, huh ole daddy, he riz up. He plum wo' out, he say, wid all de foolishness. He bin kip 'wake o' nights a-lissenin' at de gigglin' an' lallygaggin' (humbugging, chaff) ob er passel ob fools dat wuz a-rockin' deyse'fs in de bes' yarmcheers an' a-w'arin' un um out, an' a-torkin' soft sodder w'en by de bes' rights in de worl' dey orter bin tekin' dey res', an' a-gittin' up dey strenk, ter flax roun' an' yearn dey libbin next dey, all he gwine ter. He des putt he foot down, dat gal gotter mek 'er ch'ice an' sottle down. He done gove in ter 'er traipsin' (tramping) round an' fetchin' home folk ter eat up de vittles an' git wait on by huh mammy, all he gwine ter.

"W'en he say dat, de gal sniff an' pout, but 'tain' no use, an' she know dat, so, arter w'iles, she 'gin ter grin, an' ax 'er daddy an' mammy wut dey lay off ter gin 'er in de way ob close an' kittles. Den she study some who she gwine ter tek.

"Bimeby, she sorter simple (simper) an' drap 'er eye, an' say she sorter kinder t'ink young Misteh Red Fox er mighty propeh man."

"Troof, too," interpolated Aunt Em'ly, delightedly.

"He wuz er sweet torker, dat de troof," continued Aunt Mymee, without looking up ; "de one ain't bawn yit dat kin beat him a-settin' up ter de gals."

"Troof ergin, troof ergin !" exclaimed Aunt Em'ly. "Don't I know dat?—in co'se I does ! Ise one ob de Fox family myse'f."

"So 'twuz gin out," went on Aunt Mymee, evenly, "dat Misteh Red Fox wuz de man, an' all han's lay holt ter git ready foh de big weddin' at Perarer-Wolf's an' de gran' eenfair (infair, feast) de brer o' Red Fox gwine ter gib de young folks de day a-follerin'."

"I boun' yo' dat eenfair wuz fine !" exclaimed Aunt Em'ly, in delightful expectation.

"Dat eenfair don't come off, nur no weddin n-er," said Aunt Mymee, coldly, "an' dis de way o' dat : Misteh Red Fox, he wuz a-settin' wid de fambly an' a-braggin' high on, an' sez 'e—

"'I gwine ter hab er suit o' fine close des lak de w'ite folks has. I done spoke ter de taileh ter mek um, an Ise gwine ter

hab de putties' shiny buttons onter dem close. Ise gwine ter
hab two row down de front ob de coat an' two on de ves' an'
some on de sleebes, and I tole de mon ter putt er button
hyeah——'

" He wuz des 'bout ter retch roun' at de wais ob he coat,
but dat minnit er big flea gin 'im er turrible bite an' he clap
he han' ter de place (fleas is mighty bad in er wolf-house, mo'
speshul in er perarer-wolf's, an' dey so techy 'bout hit yo'
dassent let on dat yo' (you are) bit, an' Red Fox know dat, an'
w'en he grab at de flea he let hit go at de button).

" ' Hyeah, I say ! '—dat mek de button on de knee.

" ' I tole 'im,' sez 'e, ergin, ' ter putt er button—hyeah !'

" He wuz des a-pintin' roun' ter de wais' wunst mo' w'en de
flea tuck 'im in de ribs an' he clap he claw dar, ri' quick.

" ' Hyeah ! ' sez 'e ergin, de nex minnit.

" Ole flea gin 'im er nip on de neck.

" W'en he slap dat, he git er bite in de hip.

" Hit kep up wid de bites an' de ' put er button hyeah's ' twell
Red Fox des wile, an' he scratch mos' evveywhurs. At de las',
dat flea gin 'im er mos' suh-vigrous (savage) bite on de nose, an'
wiles he a-clawin' de place, dat pestehin' critteh git up an' git off.
But, nemmine ! dat ain't lef Red Fox ter j'y hisse'f ; de finishin'
tech bin putt on Ole Perarer-Wolf. *He* bin gittin' madder an'
madder des ri' straight erlong, an' w'en Red Fox 'low he
gwine ter hab er button ' hyeah,' an' clap he claw 'pon de eend
ob he nose, Ole Perarer-Wolf, he des bustid fo'th.

" ' Ki ! ' sez e', ' I done prube (I proved) I wuz in de rights,'
sez 'e, ' w'en I sot hit down dat yo' wuz er plum ijit ' (idiot), sez
'e ; ' I ain't bin nowise sot up (pleased with) wid dis bizniz fum
de staht,' sez 'e, ' but I gin in ter de gal an' huh mammy, but
now I tek my stan',' sez 'e, ' an' all de woman'-folks in de world
ain't gwine ter swage (persuade) me ter hab er mon in my
fambly dat wanter look lak de toadstools a-growin' outen 'im,'
sez 'e. ' Putt er button on yo' nose ef yo' a-mine ter, but yo'

ain't gwine ter kyar hit inter *my* chimbly corndeh,' sez 'e, an'
wid dat he flung open de do' an' druv Red Fox out. He wuz
dat mad, too, dat he won't lissen ter nuttin fum Red Fox, ur
he kinfolks, ur de neighbehs, ur de ole ooman, ur de gal, an'
de nex' week he myar (marry) off dat gal ter de leanes' ole
timbeh-wolf (forest-wolf) dat e'er draw de bref o' life, an' sence
dat he ain't kep no 'quaintence wid no fox somedevveh."

Aunt Em'ly's face had been growing longer and longer as
the recital proceeded. At its close she was almost in tears,
while Granny was thrilled to the very marrow of her bones with
indignation that a tale should be "pintedly" told at, not to, her
favourite guest. The silence might have become embarrassing,
for Tow Head was too sulky for speech because no refreshment
had been offered her, if the fire had not suddenly snapped,
spluttered, and sent a shower of sparks directly at Aunt Em'ly.

"Spit in hit! Quick!" exclaimed Granny.

Aunt Em'ly immediately spat into the fire with great force,
and then went down on her knees and searched the floor to
find out if a little coal had flown with the sparks. When she
discovered none, she thanked the "Good Lawd" fervently.

"Ef de coal had popped hit 'u'd a-bin foh me," said Granny,
musingly. "W'en de hick'ry pop, dat am er call foh de ole an'
fibble ter git ready ter go. Ef hit's de young dat's wanted, hit
show in de widnin'-sheet a-hangin' fum de cannel."

"Dey ain't nuttin gwine ter pop foh yo', dis long time, Aunt
Jinny," said Aunt Em'ly, reassuringly. "Yo' some ole to-be-
sho, but yo' ain't, ter say de wuhd, *fibble*. Now, dem spahks
sholy wuz foh me. I bin a-stavin' off er fuss de whole blessid,
live-long day. Yarly dis mawnin' I milk Old Suke, an' git er
good pigginful too, an' den, ez I go in de do', I step on dat tore
place in my skyurt dat I bin a-layin' off ter men' dis munt back,
an', in co'se, I stummle an' I spill dat milk. I sop up some an'
fling hit on de fiah, so dat fuss pass by. I go ter salt de fry-
tatehs an' I drap salt! In co'se, I fling er pinch dat I gedder

up o'er my lef' shouldeh an' I putt nurr pinch in de fiah,
so dat fuss pass by.   Now de fiah spit at me an' I spit back,
kase de debbil ahine dat, an' now I kyarn't tell whut come
nex'."

"Yo' safe 'nuff, now," said Granny.   "Dey's lots o' luck an'
lots o' trouble in fiah, des ez yo' mine de signs. In de pints
o' dat, dar's maple (maple-wood).   Ef yo' am a-honin' arter
comp'ny, an' t'row de maple on the fiah, 'long come de comp'ny
an' yo' satify ; but ef de hens won't lay an' de butteh run low
an' de poun'-cake et up ter de las' crum', an' some dem triflin'
lil niggehs pile on de maple an' fetch on er whole camp-meetin'
o' kinfolks an' nabehs wid dey chilluns an' huntin'-dawgs, den
yo' mighty much in de noshin ob cuttin' er bunch o' lim's an'
chunin'-up (turning up, *i.e.*, whipping) dem lil niggehs."

" Troof, too, Aunt Jinny.   Dey's de time ter buhn (burn) an'
de time ter hole back fum buhnin' too. I know dat. Dataway I
los' my bes' hog fum my Mose a-flingin' sassafrax-bahk dat Big
Angy gun me ter mek inter tea ter t'in (thin) de richness outen
my blood, kase I wuz des kivveh wid b'iles, an' dey pesteh me,
night an' day—yo' mine how 'twuz—an' I mought a-hed um
yit ef Aunt Mymee ain' tell me ter git er grabble (gravel) foh
each bile an' bile um in milk an' tie um up in er rag an' fling
dat rag 'way off, an' de one dat git dat rag and untie hit gwine
ter git dem bile, an' dat happen sho, an' I git shet un um."

"Where," asked Tow Head, severely, "did Mose throw the
sassafras ? "

" In de fiah, honey, in co'se, dat huccome de bad luck.
Mighty bad luck ter buhn sassifrax.   Hit wuss'n ter buhn ash,
kase, dough ash am cunjerin' wood, de onles' ha'm dat come o'
buhnin' hit am de bad dream dat come fum gettin' de smoke
mix' wid yo' bref."

" Buhnin' mighty dangersome, 'less yo' know zachry how.
Dat gal dat he'p in de kitchen w'en Mary got de fellum on 'er
han' des mos' ruin dis place.   W'y she ackshilly buhn up all de

165

aig-shells ! In co'se, dat stop all de hens fum a-layin'. She buhn braid, too, an' dat mek vittles skace."

" De bes' buhnin' am w'en er chile am bawn wid er veil (caul). Ef yo' buhn dat veil, de chile grow up strong an' de mammy git up soon an' well. Ef yo' let that veil rot, dat mammy gwine ter hab hahd times an' lose dat lil chile."

" Ef yo' buhn dat veil dat chile gwine ter see gostes an' tork wid de daid."

"So ef yo' dry um an' save um."

" Yessir, but yo' kin dry dat veil an' keep um in hid twell dat chile kin walk, den pin dat veil *slack* in huh close an' let huh toddle roun' in de weeds. Ef she lose dat veil unbeknowst, she see de gostes an' de riz-up daid no mo'."

" Gittin' back ter dem foxes, ergin," said Aunt Mymee, cutting across the conversation like a swallow, " hit come in my membunce nurr lil tale—er sorter laughin' tale—'bout de lil foxes an' de lil perarer-chickins. Hit mek mo' betteh tork 'fo' de chillums den gostes an' veils an' de likes."

Granny and Aunt Em'ly accepted the rebuke shamefacedly, and murmured something that might have been either an apology or an invitation to proceed with the "laughing tale," so indistinct was it.

Aunt Mymee chose to consider that it was the latter and drawled out the following—

" One time, er mighty biggetty-feelin' lil fox wuz a-trottin' down de road, w'en he come 'crost er lil perarer-chickin gwine 'long de same way an' a-lookin' mighty soft an' simple.

" ' Howdy ? ' say Fox, a-tryin' ter git up closte.

"'Howdy, yo'se'f? ' say Perarer-chicken, sidlin' off.

" ' How's all yo' folks ? '

"' Des middlin'. How's yone ? '

"' Oh, fine ! '

"' Ise proud to hyeah dat. Wutcher bin a-doin' ob yo'se'f sence las' tateh-plantin' ? '

"'Des a-runnin' roun' an j'yin' myse'f when I wuzzent a-lahnin' (learning) all dat my daddy know.'

"'Sholy, yo' don't set up ter know all dat yo' daddy bin a-ketchin' up sense (finding, since) he wuz tuhn loose on de worl' ! '

"'I does, dough. Ef dey's er slyeh fox in dese hyeah cl'arin's, I 'gree ter pin back he yeahs an' swaller 'im medout grease ur seas'nin'.'

"'De lan' sakes ! '

"'Wutcher bin a-doin' yo' own se'f ? '

"'Nuttin 'ticular,' sez po' lil Perarer-Chicken, a-hangin' down de haid an' a-lookin' ez 'shame ez ef huh tail-feddehs wuz pull out. 'Sence I kim outen de aig I bin dat tuck up wid runnin' up arter mammy an' a-gittin' de bugs an' seeds she p'int out, dat I ain't tuck no time foh lahnin' nuttin 'cept how ter hide ef I see er man wid er gun ur er beastis wid er hongry-lookin' toof a-showin'.'

"Dat las' reemock sorter pleg (plague) dat fox, kase 'e gotter hongry toof he own se'f, but he ain't own up, he des sorter dror hisse'f up an' say—

"'Huh ! des one way ter hide, wut dat ? I mix up de scent, ur I git in de slough, ur I bo' er hole, or—good Lawd ! I cud tell hidin' ways twell plum sundown. Wut yo' one lil way ? '

"'I des git unneat er daid leaf,' whimple out Perarer-Chicken, lookin' des all struck ob er heap wid dat lahnin'. 'In co'se, I sticks out some, but dat ain't nuttin, kase I des de coleh dat de leaf am.'

"'Dat ain't much.'

"'No,' sez Perarer-Chicken, sorter firing up, kase yo' kyarn't allus stan' bein' trompole on an run down ef yo' *is* ony er chicken ; 'no 'tain't much, but hit'll do me twell I kin fly, den I don' need no mo' tricks.'

"Lil fox, he des open he mouf for one mo' brag, w'en, lo an' beholes ! dar come de houn's.

"Chick, she hide. She ketch up er daid leaf an' roll wid um

des lak she wuz a-blowin' er long an git outen de parf an' in mungs de grass an' bresh, but dem houn's, dey ketch a-holt o' Lil Fox, an' ef yo' wanter lahn dem tricks ob hissen yo' hat ter go ax um ob he bresh dat am stickin' 'bove de chimly-piece ob de man dat owns dem houn's. Sartin sho, de bresh am all de hounds lef ob 'im." [1]

Aunt Em'ly was too low-spirited to utter a single word.

Granny was ostentatiously busy with a turkey-quill, dropped from the hearth-wing. Consequently, comments in her case were impossible.

Only Tow Head was left to hurl the discus of the critic, and this she did promptly, but with an obliquity pardonable only on account of her youthful inexperience.

" I hate a story that kills somebody," she said, " and I know just how Foxie's 'lations felt, for some hunters came by here, you know, a long time ago, and their dogs killed my kitten. I cried *awfully*, and I heard Grandma say to Mamma that I seemed to feel that I had lost a 'lation. I didn't *really*, for I have so many 'lations and only had just that one sweet kitty, but I can tell how Foxie's mamma felt. Aunt Mymee, you promised to trick those dogs and you didn't do it."

" I did, too," protested Aunt Mymee. " I gun evveh las' one un um de mange. Ter dis day dey ain't er clean dawg in de crowd. I laid er whole row ob crossed sticks in de road whah dem dawgs boun' ter go by, an' I sprunkle dem sticks wid Oby powdeh dat wuz fotch me fum 'way down Souf. Dat mek um slow an' lame an' spile dey scent, kase dey git hit on de nose too. Arter dat I th'ow lil on dey backs an' dat mek um spotty lak a snake. Shoh ! I lay turr'ble trick on um, on dat am mos'ly foh folkses."

[1] The reader will recognise in this story one of Æsop's fables. It is very remarkable that these tales, probably learned from Canadian French Catholic priests or missionaries, have become well known to the Indians, and, having been adapted to their mythology, are literally believed to have taken place. *Vide* " The Algonkin Legends of New England " for further illustration of this.

"Wut trick?" asked Granny, leaning forward eagerly and dropping her quill unheeded on the glowing hearth.

"Des one o' dem Oby pison," said Aunt Mymee, coolly. "You kyarn' git all de greegins (ingredients) foh hit hyeah, so I don't mek no bones ter tell yo' dat hit am er powdeh mek outen de same hef' ob snails an' lizuhds an' crickits an' scorpums dry down an' beat fine. Huh ! ef yo' git dat on er man's haid, he ha'r all gwine ter fall off an' he eye git dim an' he vittle lose dey good tase an' he gwine ter hyeah de soun' o' crickits an' frogs an' de likes in his yeahs, an' he gwine ter be slow lak de snail an' spotty lak de snake an' he be dumb (stupid) lak de lizuhd, an' he gwine ter be ez full ob misery ez er Injun am ob lice. Dat so, an' he meat gwine ter swivel on' he bones gwine ter crack an' he marrer dry out. Trick, huh ! Wut yo' name dat ? "

"Oh, poor dogs !" cried Tow Head, transferring her sympathies. "Do, dear Aunt Mymee, take that trick off."

Mymee laughed grimly. "De way ter git er trick off," she said slowly, "am ter git er biggeh one fum nurr cunjerer an' putt hit onter de one dat done hit—dat am, ef hit er sprunkle-trick. Wid er bag-trick ur er image-trick, hit am diffunt. Nemmine, dough, dis night. I study up sumpin foh dem dawgs, ef yo' go 'long up ter de House good."

Tow Head, in quite a frenzy of remorse and sympathy, agreed to do anything for the hound's sake, and was led away a willing captive.

Aunt Mymee enlivened the night as she disappeared from view by singing in cheerful tones the following, as Granny said, " owdashus " words, which are supposed to echo the sound of the devil's forge :—

> " Bang-go ! Pang-go !
> Did yo'—ev-veh
> See de—debbil,
> On he—wood an'
> Iun—shub-bil,
> A-t'arin' up de groun' wid he long toe-n-n-n ail ? "

XII.

LUCK-BALLS.

AUNT MYMEE had been in what Granny designated as "a turr'ble takin'," the cause of which was the loss of her most powerful fetich, the luck-ball she had talked to and called by her own name as if it were her double. Her superstitious terrors when she discovered the loss were really pitiable ; her overbearing manner towards the other negroes quite forsook her, her limbs were palsied and her complexion bleached to that awful greyish pallor so much more shocking to the beholder than the lividness of a Caucasian. She had missed the precious ball in the morning, when she was dressing herself, and hastily felt in her bed, expecting to find it there. Not finding it, she snatched off the covers and shook the pillows vigorously. The floor was next scrutinised. No ball could be found. Then Aunt Mymee went wild. Her morning duties were forgotten, she ran hither and thither, looking in all possible and impossible places of concealment and obstinately refusing to state what she had lost. Finally, with a groan of despair, she flung herself down on her cabin floor in a cowering heap and quavered out that she would be better off in her grave, for an enemy had stolen her luck-ball, and her soul as well as her luck was in it.

Her daughter's pickaninnies, in great excitement, spread the news, but scarcely had Granny and Aunt Mary begun to enjoy it when they had "ter laff out o' turr side o' de mouf" ; Tow

169

Head proudly marched to the cabin with an exceedingly dirty little bag in her hand and desired to know if Aunt Mymee's soul was "tied up in that nasty thing ? "

Evidently it was. Aunt Mymee sprang up with a joyful cry and kissed the bag and hugged the finder, then sternly demanded—

" Huccome dat yo' got dat medout me a-knowin' ? "

" Found it by my bed this morning."

" Oh ! honey, w'yn't yo' fetch um ri' off ? "

"I didn't see you. Mamma dressed me this morning."

" Did yo' "—Mymee's voice sank to an anxious whisper— " show dat ball unter 'er ? "

" No," said Tow Head, with great positiveness, " I didn't. She told me, once, when I was telling her about Uncle John's Jack, *never* to say anything more about such wicked idol-ertry, and I promised I wouldn't, and I always keep my promises—if I don't forget. Grandma says that is my best trait."

Aunt Mymee heaved a sigh of relief.

" Dat's er good chile, don't pesteh yo' ma," she said, approvingly, as she began to fumble at the strings wrapped (not tied) round the neck of the dirty bag that had raised such a commotion.[1]

" What are you doing, Aunt Mymee ? "

"Gwine ter gib Lil Mymee er drink. Dat wut she arter, I reck'n, w'en she bust loose. I ain't gun 'er no drink sence er week ergo de day 'fo' yistiddy, an' she boun' ter hab one wunst er week. I wuz dat tuk up wid new-fangle noshins dat I fegit 'er, an', lo an' beholes ! wut does I git foh hit ? "

" Shall I bring you a gourd of water ? "

" No, honey. Lil Mymee, she don' sup watteh," said Aunt Mymee, lifting a dirty little yarn ball out of the dirty little linen

[1] This same incident also occurred almost exactly as here related to my brother—Henry P. Leland—when he was twelve years of age. The old black cook of the family had lost her " cunjerin' bag," when my brother found it. It contained a chicken's breastbone, ashes, and rags.—C. G. L.

bag. "She sup wut Big Angy name *eau-de-vie,* an' dat sholy
am de watteh ob life foh huh, kase ef she don' git un she die."[1]

Aunt Mymee produced a black bottle of Little Mymee's
elixir of life, better known to the general public as whiskey, and
proceeded to moisten, first the ball, then herself therewith ; after
which ceremony she restored the ball to its proper receptacle,
mended the broken string, which had been the cause of its loss,
and made it an ornament to her person by slinging the string
over her left shoulder and under her right so that the ball rested
under her right armpit. She had, beforehand, be it understood,
slipped out of the various waists of her raiment, so that the ball
should lie against her naked body, with no intervening fold of
calico or flannel to absorb its "strenk."

· How that ball was made, what were its components, Tow
Head did not, at that time, know, though she gathered from
the half-whispered gossip of the other aunties that it was the
work of "King" A——, a Voodoo doctor or cunjurer of great
powers and influence.

This A—— was a curious half-barbarian, who never stayed
long in a place, made his entrances secretly and mysteriously in
the night, never confided in any one, never spent money for
anything but whiskey, never lacked for the good things of this
world, and never was reduced to the inconvenience of begging
or stealing, although he was as the lilies of the field "that toil
not, neither do they spin." No cabin refused him shelter and
the best bed and food it could afford. No one knew whence
he came or whither he was going. When four taps were heard
above the latch, some one flew to usher in the guest. "A——'s
dar" was the unspoken conviction. How he came was a matter
of conjecture ; it was generally conceded that he travelled at his
ease on some strange steed of the devil's providing.

As soon as he was settled in his temporary quarters—that is,
had eaten of everything in the larder, drunk generous pota-

[1] This is African, as still practised on the Guinea coast.

THE KING OF THE VOODOOS.

tions of whiskey, and taken possession of the best chair—a messenger was sent out "to pass the word around" that he had arrived.

In the course of the night the answer came in the persons of scores of darkies, some of them from a distance of many miles, who eagerly purchased his remedies, charms and "tricks."

When she was a child Tow Head never once caught sight of him, but in after years she had more than one interview with this "king" of occult "cussedness." When she saw him her disappointment was extreme. There was nothing royal either in his appearance or demeanour. He was, as he is, a black, sweaty, medium-sized negro, half-naked, altogether innocent of soap, and not dispensing the perfume of Araby the blest.[1] His eyes were snaky, his narrow forehead full at the eyebrows but shockingly depressed above. His nose was broad and with a flatness of nostrils emphasized to the perception of the beholder by the high, bony ridge that divided them. His chin was narrow and prominent ; at first glance, it seemed broad by reason of the many baggy folds that surrounded it after the fashion of a dew-lap. He was far from beautiful when his features were in repose, but the time to fully realise that he was a self-chosen disciple of his Satanic Majesty was when he unclosed his great rolling lips in a silent laugh. The yawning cavern thereby disclosed, with its double guard of yellow, broken, "snaggy" teeth set in gums unwholesomely red, and its ugly, wriggling tenant, a serpent-like tongue, were, in themselves, more awe-inspiring than any charm or curse that issued therefrom.

When Tow Head saw him she meekly asked for some talisman to insure good luck to a friend.

" Fetch me," said the ogre, " er ha'r ur two fum de body o' de one dat wants de luck, an' er dollah, an' I mek yo' er luck-ball."

---

[1] Like nearly all the persons described in these chapters, A—— was not quite a negro. His mother was a pure-blood Indian, and the son spoke Indian as naturally as English.—C. G. L.

Tow Head explained that the " ha'r " could not be obtained. The friend was on the other side of the ocean.

" Den fetch de money an' I kin hab red clobeh (clover) stan' in de place o' de ha'r."

Tow Head " fotch " the dollar and then, as she demonstrated that she was something of a witch herself, by repeating the formula she had learned from Aunt Mymee for preparing a " tricken-bag," she was not only furnished the ball but, in addition, was taught how to make it.

This is one way to prepare a " tricken-bag " :—

Take the wing of a jaybird, the jaw of a squirrel, and the fang of a rattle-snake and burn them to ashes on any red-hot metal. Mix the ashes with a pinch of grave-dust—the grave of the old and wicked has most potency in its earth—moisten with the blood of a pig-eating sow ; make into a cake and stick into the cake three feathers of a crowing hen wrapped with hair from the head of the one who wishes an enemy tricked. Put the cake into a little bag of new linen or cat-skin. Cat-skin is better than linen, but it must be torn from the haunch of a living cat. Whatever the bag is, it must be tied with a ravelling from a shroud, named for the enemy and then hidden under his house. It will bring upon him disease, disgrace, and sorrow. If a whip-porwill's wing is used instead of a jay's it will bring death.

" Dat's toll'ble," A—— declared. " Des toll'ble. Thee (three) am er good numbeh, but fo (four) am betteh in de makin' up ob tricks. Good lan' ! ¹ de daid deyse'fs got ter mine de fos (fours) ef yo' mek um plenty nuff. Fo' time fo' time fo' (4 × 4 × 4) am de gret numbeh. De daid an' de debbils gotter mine dat. Des see me mek dis hyeah luck-ball an' kote (quote) um in."

A—— spread his materials, consisting of red clover, dust, tinfoil, white yarn, and white sewing-silk, on a table, called for

---

¹ Good land ! a land ! A common American interjection, not confined to the blacks.

a bottle of whiskey, and, when the last-named necessity of modern "cunjerin" was produced, proceeded to business. He broke off four lengths of yarn, each length measuring about forty-eight inches. These were doubled and re-doubled into skeins of four strands each and spread in a row before him. To each skein was added forty-eight inches of sewing-silk folded as the yarn was.

"Dar now ! " he said, "De silk am ter tie yo' frens unter yo', de yahn am ter tie down all de debbils. Des watch me tie de knots. Hole on dough !—dis fust ! "

The "fust" proceeding was to fill his mouth with whiskey. Then ensued a most surprising gurgling and mumbling, as he tied a knot near the end of the skein nearest him. As it was tightened, he spat about a teaspoonful of tobacco-perfumed saliva and whiskey upon it.

"Dar now ! " he said, "dat's er mighty good knot. Dey ain't no debbil kin git thu dat."

"Stop ! Stop ! You are not dealing fairly with me. You promised that I should hear your incantation, and you mumble so that I cannot distinguish a word."

"Ise a-kotin in (quoting in) de name o' de one de ball am foh. Des wait twell I git thee (three) mo' knots tied in dis hank an' den I kote out loud foh de turrs."

Sure enough, when the mumbling, spitting, and tying had been repeated three times, he laid down the skein, took up the second one, filled his mouth with whiskey, began to tie a knot, and said—

"Gord afo' me, Gord ahine me, Gord be wid me. May dis ball fetch all good luck ter Charles Leland. May hit tie down all debbils, may hit bine down 'is innemies afo' 'im, may hit bring um undeh 'is feet. May hit bring 'im frens in plenty, may hit bring 'im faithful frens, may hit bine um to 'im. May hit bring 'im honeh (honour), may hit bring 'im riches, may hit bring 'im 'is haht's *de*sire. May hit bring 'im success in evveht'ing he hondehtakes, may hit bring 'im happiness. · I ax foh hit in de name ob de Gord."

This he repeated four times, then spat upon the knot, took a fresh drink of whiskey, began on a second knot and repeated the whole performance, exactly as he did also when he tied the third and fourth knots. When this second skein had its four knots tied, he laid it against the first. Before the two had lain several inches apart.

" Now," said he, " ef yo' gotter fair membunce (an' I reck'n yo' has, kase yo' look lak er ooman strong in de haid, er mighty strong ooman in de haid) I 'low dat yo' knows dat chahm off by haht. Dat's yo' look out dough, kase I ain' gwine ter holler hit no mo'. Ise gwine ter say hit sorf (soft) w'iles I ties de fo' knots in dem urr two lil hanks."

When the muttering and spitting at length ceased, and four little skeins with four little knots in each lay side by side, Tow Head asked—

" What is the use of tying all those knots ? "

" Dem knots ! W'y dem knots am in fo's (fours) an' dey tie down all de debbils—debbils is 'fraid o' fo' time fo' time fo'. Likeallwise, de knots bine yo' frens unter yo'. Dey ain't no debbil kin git thu dem knots."

" What is all that other stuff for ? "

" Stuff ! " the "cunjer-man's " tone was indignant. " Des wait twell dat *stuff* git a-wuhkin'. Dat ar piece ob file (foil) rupisent (represents) de brightness ob dat lil spurrit dat gwine ter be in de ball, dat clobeh am in de place ob de ha'r offen de one dat gwine ter own de ball, dat dus' am innemies' dus,' an' hit am ter bline de eyes ob de innemies."

So saying, he drew three of the skeins towards him, twisted them into a little nest and gave them a copious bath of saliva and whiskey.

" It seems to me that conjuring is mostly whiskeying."

' Dey's er heap o' pennunce (dependence to be placed in)

whiskey, sholy, dough in de outlandish kyentry fum whurs dey fetch de niggehs in de fust place, dey tek some sort ob greens an' putt um in er gode (gourd) wid watteh an' set um in de sun twell dey wuhk (work—ferment), an' dat go in de place ob whiskey." [1]

Tow Head would fain have asked other questions, but the "king" waved his hand to enjoin silence. Again he had recourse to the whiskey-bottle, and once more he began to murmur his incantation, pausing only to spit upon the red clover blossoms and the encircling leaves and upon the tinfoil, as he placed them in the little yarn nest and sprinkled them liberally with enemies' dust—a powder that looked as if he had picked it up at a gas-house, although he declared it was dust gathered where the river sand and the clay of the bank met. Suddenly, with a dramatic flourish, he plunged his hand into his bosom and drew forth a ball of white yarn. From this he began to wind the thread about the little woollen nest, all the time keeping up the muttering of the incantation and the attendant punctuation of saliva and whiskey. In a few minutes, he had made a new ball of a little over an inch in diameter. This was a "luck-ball." He held it suspended by a length of yarn and began to talk to it in most caressing tones.

"Promuss dat yo'll be er good ball."

The string began to twirl as if unwinding.

"Dat's right! I know'd yo'd be good."

"You have left out a skein," interrupted Tow Head.

"Dat wuz a-puppus," was the lofty reply. "Now, ef yo' want de good ob dis hyeah ball, yo' ain't gwine ter flusteh me wid queschins."

Tow Head was stricken dumb.

The "king" shut his eyes and proceeded to give an uncanny exhibition of ventriloquism.

[1] Quite true. This is the *pombé* or maize-beer of Africa, used in magic. —C. G. L.

"Now," said he, addressing the ball, as he dangled it between his thumb and finger, "yo' name is Leland, Charles Leland. Ise gwine ter sen' yo' er long way off unter er master, er mighty long way off, 'crost big watteh (the ocean). Go out in de woods an' 'fresh yo'se'f 'fo' yo' staht. Go 'long ! Do yo' hyeah me ? Is yo' gwine ?   Is yo' gwine way off ? Is yo' climbin' ?   Is yo' climbin' high ? "

After each question there was a series of answerings, growing fainter and fainter as the spirit of the ball was supposed to go farther and farther away.

After the last question there was a long pause. Then " Charles Leland " was invited to return. As he was a long way off, the " king " listened attentively to the faint murmur that came in reply, even pressing forward the rim of his ear to catch the faint, far-distant answer.

The answer was evidently what the " king " desired, for he continued to question and receive replies, and each time the question was fainter, and the reply louder. " Is yo' stahted ? Is yo' comin' closter ?   Is yo' gittin' nigh ? Is yo' back ?   Is yo' in de ball ergin ? "

All of " Charles' s " replies were in the affirmative. When he was once more at home, he proclaimed the fact by causing the ball to spin and dance in the most surprising manner. When he finally relapsed into quietude, he had another shower-bath from his summoner's mouth. Then there was nothing more to be done but to wrap the ball in tinfoil and a little silk rag. The only instructions given were to place the ball in a linen bag, attach it to a string of flax or hemp and direct the one for whom it was named to sling the string over the left shoulder and under the right, so that the ball should rest under the right arm. From thence he must be taken once a week and bathed in whiskey, otherwise its strength would die. At any time " he " could be taken out and consulted or confided in. His approval or dis-approval could be felt by the owner, at once, and his help relied on if asked for. Only one warning was given. " Don't tie no knots in he kivvuz (covers)."[1]

Just such a ball was the one Aunt Mymee lost and found. All her acquaintances knew as well as she did what it was to her ; the matter was a theme of gossip all day and inspired Granny and Aunt Em'ly to relate stories of other and more precious luck-balls when evening came on.

Aunt Em'ly's story of Ole Rabbit's silver bubble came first.

" One time, de Debbil's ole ooman, des foh 'muse huhse'f an' pesteh folks, mek de spoht (sport) ob flingin' er silveh blubbeh inter de pond, an' den she gin out dat whoso git um git all de good luck dat am in de worl', an' she mek up er turr'ble speunce (experience, deeds) dat all han's am boun' ter go thu, ef dey git um."

" What experience, Aunt Em'ly ? "

" Des hole on, honey, hole back de hosses an' we git dar bimeby. Hit Ole Chuffy we aim arter now. Dis de way *he* sot out, an' he des natchel honed arter dat ball. He uster go down by de big pond at de aige o' de swamp an' set dar an' study 'bout hit all times o' de day an' night. 'Pear lak he kyarn' git hit offen he mine 'tall ; he tork about hit daytime, he dremp 'bout hit twell he res' bin cl'ar spile. He go on dataway twell he drap off der skin an' bone. He git dat desput dat he lay off ter ax ole Miss Debbil ef she won't please 'um gin 'im dat blubbeh, kase he bin know dat ole ooman sence he wuz knee-high ter er hoppehgrass, an' he he'p 'er out wunst ur twiste w'en Ole Blue Jay kyar tale 'bout 'er ter er ole man. She lak mighty well ter see 'im cut he shines dat mek 'er laff

---

[1] I received this luck-ball in a letter when in Copenhagen. It appeared to be such a mysterious or important object, that an official was specially sent from the post-office with it to the hotel where I was staying, and I received it from him. The reader may find an account of how I myself have seen luck-bags made by witches in Italy, in " Etruscan Roman Relics in Popular Tradition." (London : T. Fisher Unwin. 1873.)—C. G. L.

w'en she git de low-downs fum quoilin' (quarrelling) wid de
Debbil. He know dat, so he go roun' de pond ter de aige ob
de slough—hit wuz in de wanin' ob de moon, *in co'se*, kase dat
am w'en de Debbil an' he folkses am de peartes'. Yessir ! hit
wuz at de wanin' ob de moon, an' de kine (kind) ob er moon dat
comed in new 'way down in de souf-wes', a-rollin' in de sky pun
eend stiddier a-settin' on huh back. Now den, dat wuz er *wet*
moon, hit wuz er moon de Injun kin hang he queeveh o' arrehs
on, kase de watteh gwine ter run out an' dey be no huntin'.
Hit wuz er mighty red moon too, wid sto'ms (storms) a-mum-
blin' in de hot a'r roun' hit. Hit wuz er mighty good night
foh cunjerin' an' a-callin' up de goses an' de booggers (bogies)
an' de laks ob dem, but Ole Bunny, he done fegit dat hit bin
a-rainin' at dinneh-time w'en de sun wuz a-shinin'. Ef he t'ink
o' dat, he know 'tain't no use ter go out an' call up de ole
ooman, kase rain in de sunshine am de sho sign dat de Debbil
bin a-lickin' her.

"Well ! he dat 'stractid 'bout de ball he ain't hed dat in
membunce, so he go ter de ma'sh an' he wait an' he watch, an'
bimeby, he see de smoke rise, 'way out yondeh. Den de
jacky-me-lantuhns (jack-o'-lanterns—will-o'-the-wisps) come
bibbitty-bobbitty by. Den he tek de red clobeh leabes an'
heads dat he fotch a-puppus an' he strow dem on de groun' an'
he set down on um, an' he wait an' he wait.

"Den de brack smoke come nigher an' nigher.

"Den hit stop.

"Den he holler out—

> 'My honey, my love,
>   My turkle-dove,
> Come oveh ! come oveh !'"

"Ez offen ez de smoke stop he holler dat.

"Wut he holler dat foh ?—Kase hit de way ter mek dat ole
'ooman-debbil, come on. All de 'oomans, honey, debbil ur

no debbil, run todes dat kine o' tork. Co'se dey do! All de men-folks kin spressify (express themselves) ter dat.

"Well! at de las', w'en he holler dat twell he mouf wuz ez dry ez er beanpod arter fros', de smoke git closte, den hit paht open in de middle an dar wuz de debbil's ole 'ooman!"

"Was she awfully, *awfully* ugly?"

"Huh! dat she wuzzent! De debbil ain't no fool. He kin

"DAR WUZ DE DEBBIL'S OLE OOMAN."

pick out de good looks de same as de nex' un. She wuz ez putty ez er painter (panther) an' ez sassy ez er yalleh gal (mulatto). She got one fut lak Ole Rabbit dough, an' de urr lak er deer. Huh han's, dey wuz w'ite an' putty, but dey got de claw 'pun de eend lak er pussy-cat's."

"Did she claw Old Rabbit?"

"Nuh, but I ain't 'ny dat (deny that) w'en he see dat ole 'ooman he trimmle lak de leabes. He look an' he sees dat

she bin a-cryin', an' dat mek 'im wish dat he c'd mek he
mannehs (bow) an' cl'ar out.

"'Wut fetch yo' hyeah?' she ax, 'way down deep lak er
buffler-bull. 'Wut fetch yo' hyeah?' sez she, 'hyeah mungs
de daid? Yo' place am mungs de libbin. Go 'way! Git
yo' gone!' sez she.

"Wid dat de smoke shet in wunst mo' an' staht, wimly-
wamly, wimly-wamly, des a trim'lin' 'long, sorter slow, lak de
shadder w'en de win' blow de cannel des de leases' lil mite.

"Den, oh my! Chuffy, he wuz skeert, but he des mek out
ter say—

> 'M-M-M-My h-h-honey, m-m-my l-l-love,
> M—My t-t-turkle-d-d-d-dove!'

"De res' un hit stick in he thote an' he kyarn't fetch hit out,
but, nemmine! dat stop 'er, an' den he git de strenk ter baig
an' plead foh de lil silveh ball.

"She so frackshis, she won't gin 'im nuttin. She say she
done gin 'im 'er own rabbit-fut foh luck, dat one dat 'er
mammy cotch foh 'er, an' dat sholy plenty. Ef he want dat
silveh luck-ball, he des kin wuhk foh hit. Wid dat she go
weevly-wavely off; an' den de jacky-me-lantuhns, dey kim
up an' skeert dat po', lone lil ole Man Rabbit mos' ter deff. He
des clip home, he do, but he ain't got de blubbeh, an' dat mos'
kill 'im. 'Tain't long arter dat twell he *do* git dat blubbeh
dough," continued Aunt Em'ly, smiling on her audience,
encouragingly, " an' dis hyeah dat I gwine to tell yo' am de
whahby he sot ter wuhk.

"He go out in de bresh an' he cut 'im de slimmes' kine ob
er hazel switch, forkin' at de eend, lak dem dar switches dat
de well-diggehs hab w'en dey a-tryin' foh ter fine whah de
watteh am, soster dig de well in de good place. Dat switch he
tuck and tuck home wid him.

"Den he go ter de big woods an' scrabble roun' twell he fine er nut drap offen one dem pignut hick'ry trees. Dat nut he tuck an' tuck home.

" Den he go out ter de fiel' an' he git some hemp, an' he twis' 'im er good stout string, an' he mek er slipknot an' loop in de eend. Den he tuck an' tuck dat string home.

" Den w'en de day git good an' wa'm, he tuck dem t'ings an' he staht out ; but on de way he stop nigh de crik an' cut 'im lil paw-paw (some say ash instead of paw-paw) lim', an' he mek lil hole in dat lil pignut, an' he stick hit on de eend o' dat lil lim'.

" Den he go roun' by de haw trees, dat got de grapevines clamberin' onter um, an' he git er lil daid curleycue (tendril) offen de grapevine, an' he set down an' he buil' er lil fiah outen daid leabes, an' he hole de eend ob de curleycue in de fiah twell hit buhn ri' brack. Dat brack eend he tek an' mahk wid hit dat lil pignut twell hit look foh all de worl' lak er lil pickaninny's haid. He mek lil mahk foh de eyes an' de winkehs an' de nose an' de mouf an' all ; an' w'en he git dat done, he wrop er nice lil rabbit-skin roun' dat paw-paw lim', an' he say, ' Dar now l ain't I got de nice, fine baby l ' an' he cut er pidgin-wing, an' he sing—

> ' Byo baby-buntin',
> Yo' daddy gwine a-huntin'.' [1]

An' he sholy *wuz* gwine a-huntin', kase luck-huntin' am de bigges' kine ob huntin' dey is, ef yo' s'arch up one side ob de yeath an' down de turr.

" W'en he git de baby done, he tuck hit in de one han' an'

---

[1] I think that this is probably the *original* of the Tar Baby, because it corresponds more closely to the making of the magical mannikin as found in European sorcery. Thus in England it is made by putting a " fairy head " (stone, *echinus*) on a tiny body (MS. charms), and in Italy with a distaff. Its object is the same in all, to defeat or act counter to witches and evil spirits, &c.—C. G. L.

de hazel switch in de turr, an' sot out ter hunt er rattlesnake ;
an' bimeby he comed 'cross er big sassy young one, quile up
(coiled up) on er hooraw-nes' (hurrah's nest—an accumulation
of leaves made by wind and water at the edge of a stream), an'
a-takin' er snooze.   Ole Rabbit he crope up, he did, thu de
weeds an briehs, an' w'en he git closte nuff—spang !—he run
dat paw-paw lim' outen de bresh des ez quick ! an' he stick dat
pignut face right at de eye ob Misteh Rattlesnake !   Suz, dat
rowge (roused) up Misteh Rattletail, an' my ! ef he wuzzent de
maddes' !

"'Cuss de impunce ob dat lil sassy niggeh !' sez 'e, and
wid dat—smack !—he hit dat pignut pickaninny de bigges' lick !

" Hit wuz er las'-yeah's pignut, honey, an' de fros' an' de
rain done mek hit mo' sorf den er *dis* yeah's nut, so Misteh
Rattletail done stick he two toofses (he ain' got but des two,
an' dey des a-front de pizon-bag), he done stick um inter dat
ole nut an' dey won't come out.   Dar dey wuz, tight an' fas'.
Den Ole Rabbit he run up, an' he slip dat string wid de slip-
knot roun' Misteh Rattletail' neck twell he mos' choke 'im,
an' he lash 'im fas' ter de paw-paw lim'.   Den he tek a-holt
ob he tail, an'-den don't Ole Chuffy go a-singin' an' a-whustlin'
'long de parf dat lead ter de pond.   W'en he git dar, he fling
in de lim' wid Misteh Rattletail 'pun hit, an' hit stick fas'
at de bottom an' don't come up ; ef hit come up hit sp'ile
de luck, kase dat de p'int, dat yo' th'ow in er libe rattlesnake
by de tail, an' de las' blubbeh dat come up ef de snake lodge,
dat am de silbeh blubbeh, an' yo' boun' ter ketch hit on de
forky switch.

" W'en dat snake stick on de bottom, Ole Chuffy he tek de
switch an' hole hit wid de fawk eend out obeh de pond.   He
watch dez ez keen ez ef he got de eye ob er snake he own se'f.
He watch de blubbehs twell dey come slow an' scatt'in ; den
he haht ri' in he mouf, he dat feahrin dat he miss de right one.

" One come by hitse'f.

" He retch out.

" Hit bus'.

" He mos' fit ter cry.

" One mo' come.

" He retch—quick ! He slip de fawk unneat hit ! He lif' hit up ! He dror hit in ! Hit slip !—O-o-ow !—Hit mos' fal back ! Now he got um ! Hi ! he grab um in de han' ! Dat de silbeh blubbeh, sho nuff ! soun' er (as a) rock an' shinin' lak er chunk ob de moon. Hooray ! Hoo-hoo-hooray !

" HE SLIP DE FAWK UNNEAT HIT! NOW 'E GOT UM !"

" Hit tek Ole Rabbit, arter all,
 Ter beat w'ite folks an' git de ball ! "

The story of the silver ball inspired Granny to relate one she called :—

DE TALE OB DE GOL'EN BALL.

" In de ole, ole times, ole man gwine 'long de big road. Ole man lame, ole man raggeddy, old man mons'us dry, ole man mons'us hongry. See lil cabin down lil lane dat run inter de big road. Po' ole man go up ter de do', knock wid he han" knock wid he stick.

" De do' open, man come out.

" ' Wut yo' want, ole man ? '

" Lemme set down on de bench by de do', an' gimme er gode o' watteh an' er lil hunk o' cawn-pone (maize-bread ; Algonkin, *pān*, bread). Ise ole, Ise lame, Ise dry, Ise hongry, Ise plum wo' out.'

" Man dunno.   He scratch de haid, he roll de eye.

" 'Ooman in de house holler out—

" ' Gib de ole man de butteh-milk outen de crock, an' de wusseh-meat (sausage-meat) outen de pan.'

Man git de beggeh-man de butteh-milk in de crock an' de wusseh-meat in de pan.   He drink de milk, he lick de crock. He eat de meat, he lick de pan.   He grunt, he groan, he stretch hisse'f.

" ' Oh ! gimme er whuff fum yo' pipe,' sez 'e.

" Man scratch de haid, he roll de eye.   He dunno, he say.

" 'Ooman holler out—

" Oh ! tek de backy fum de pouch ; oh ! tek de pipe fum off de jamb an' gib de po' ole man er whuff.'

" Man he do des wut she say.

" Beggeh-man say—

" ' Gimme er fiah-coal.'

" Man git de fiah-coal.

" Beggeh-man light de pipe an' hole de fiah-coal in he han'. Den he smoke an' smoke de backy all erway.   He bat de eye, he grin de mouf, an' lean ergin de cabin wall.

" Fiah-coal buhn dar all de time right in he han'.

" He ain't keer ef hit do buhn.   He bat de eye, he grin de mouf, he lean ergin de cabin wall.

" Man stan' dar in de do' an' watch.

" Bimeby de pickaninny squall.

" Beggeh-man stan' up.

" ' Is dat er mouse I hyeah ? ' sez 'e.

" ' Oh ! dat's my darter, one day ole.'

"'Oh! do huh ha'r shine lak de gole?'

"'Oh, no! a niggeh-chile am she.'

"'Oh! fetch huh hyeah an' lemme see.'

"'Huh mammy won't 'low dat at all.'

"'Oh! fetch huh hyeah ter git ball.'

"Wid dat, de ole beggeh-man he swaller dat fiah-coal an' spit um right up, an' dar twuz!—er lil gole ball wid er yalleh string.

"Den de man fetch lil kinkey-haid, an' de beggeh-man he fling de string roun' 'er neck an' de ball hit fall gin er breas'.

"Den de beggeh-man he up an' git (departed), an' how he go dat man kyarn't tell. He look ter lef', he look ter right, dat beggeh-man clean out o' sight. Den de man tek de chile ter 'er mammy, an' den he run down de lane.

"Look dishaway, look dataway! See nuttin!

"Run ter de big road. Look up de road, look down de road! See nuttin!

"Run back ter de mammy an' de chile.

"'Oh, gimme back dat golen ball! Dat beggeh-man he cunjer, all. He trick dat chile; she boun' ter die.'

"He raise dat chile ter retch de string. Oh! how dat chile done change an' grow. Huh ha'r hit hang 'way down huh back, hit hang ez straight ez cawn-silk too; hit tuhn ez yalleh ez de ball. Huh skin hit tuhn ez w'ite ez milk.

"'Oh, leabe de ball!' de mammy say.

"De man he 'gree unter dat too. He laff an' darnce ter see dat chile. He say, 'Don't nevveh break dat string.'

"De mammy 'gree unter dat too.

"De chile she grow an' grow an' grow.

"De mammy, den, she up an' die.

"Er Oby-'ooman p'izon huh.

"De Oby-'ooman merry 'im (married). She beat de gal, she tell 'm lie; she try ter steal de gol'en ball, an' w'en she fine kyarn't do dat, she slip ahine dat milk-w'ite gal an' cut in she two dat yalleh string.

" Dat ball hit fall inter de grass.

" Dat milk-w'ite gal she tuhn right brack.   Huh ha'r hit
swivel up in kinks, hit tuhn right brack, hit shine no mo'.
De po' brack gal, she gun ter cry.

" De folks run up, dey don't know huh.

" De Oby squall—

" ' Yo' kilt ou' chile ! '

" De folks dey say—

" Yo' sholy did ! '

" De po' brack gal, she cry an' cry.

" Dey tek dat gal, dey tie huh fas'.

" She say, ' I nuvveh kilt no gal !   I wuz dat milk-w'ite gal
yo' hed ! '

" Dey pay no 'tenshun ter dat wuhd.   Dey git de chain, dey
git de rope, dey buil' er gallus-tree up high.

" De po' brack gal, she cry an' cry.

" Huh daddy come.

" She call at 'im—

" ' O, daddy, fine dat gol'en ball, ur yo' see me hang 'pun de
gallus-tree ! '

" De man go by.

" De Oby come.

" ' O, mammy, fine dat gol'en ball, ur yo' see me hang 'pun
de gallus-tree ! '

" Oby go by !

" Huh beau, he come.

" ' Beau, beau, fine dat gol'en ball, ur yo' see me hang 'pun
de gallus-tree ! '

" Beau go by.

" Den all de folks go by, go home, don't hunt de ball.   Dey
spec she die 'pun de gallus-tree.

" Ole beggeh-man, he bline, he lame.   He stop.   He say, ' I
save dat gal.   I save huh fum de gallus-tree.'

" Beggeh-man hole out de gol'en ball.

" She won't die on de gallus-tree.

" He han' 'er back de golen ball, he tell de tale, he show de t'ief.

" Oby, she die 'pun de gallus-tree.

" Beau, he see de milk-w'ite gal, he ketch 'er wais', he try ter buss.

" ' Go 'way, beau, yo' want I die 'pun de gallus-tree.'

" Daddy come up, he say, ' Come home.'

" Milk-w'ite gal, she tuhn de back.

" ' Daddy, I kyarn't. Yo' mek me 'feard de gallus-tree.'

" Beggeh-man change, he putty, now (he had become beautiful), an' oh l he save huh fum de gallus-tree. He tek de gal by huh w'ite han', he lead huh pas' de gallus-tree.

" De folks squall out, ' Come back l come back l an' we pull down de gallus-tree.'

" De man an' gal go on an' on. Dey lose sight ob de gallus-tree.

" De hill, hit open good an' wide. Dey bofe go thu dat big wide crack. Dey done fegit de gallus-tree.

" De hill, hit shet closte up ergin.

" ' Good-bye, good folks an' gallus-tree l ' "

So inspiriting was this finale that everybody began to sing and " jump Jim Crow," a favourite pastime borrowed from the *white* minstrels, so far as the song, but not so far as the " exercise " was concerned.

> " Fust upun de heel tap,
> Den upun de toe.
> Ebry time you tuhn eroun
> You jump Jim Crow.
> My ole mistis told me so
> I'd nebber git ter Heb'n
> Ef I jump Jim Crow.
> Jump Jim Crow—oh,
> Jump Jim Crow.
> I'd nebber git ter Heb'n ef I jump Jim Crow.

XIII.

*HOW THE SKUNK BECAME THE TERROR OF ALL
LIVING CREATURES—A SHORT CHAPTER
FURNISHED BY BIG ANGY.*

SKUNK was Catamount's young brother. He was a disgrace to
the family from the day he was born. He was sneaking, he
was cowardly. He was thievish too, for that matter. He
thought more of getting at a bird's nest and stealing a few half-
rotten eggs than of seeking and overpowering worthy prey.
He gave his strength to catching field-mice and even grasshoppers and locusts. Even gophers and moles despised more than
they feared him. Added to this, he was the most impertinent
and insulting little beast that could be imagined when he was
in a safe place and could call to those whom he wished to
affront from a distance. He even showed disrespect to Grey
Wolf.

This was not to be tolerated, so Grey Wolf called all the
animals together and demanded to know what should be done.

With one voice, the answer came—

" Destroy him. He is of no use whatever."

Now Catamount and Black Wolf said nothing. Catamount
could not excuse and would not condemn his brother. Black
Wolf had plans of his own for the culprit to carry out.

Grey Wolf, thinking that all were agreed, was about to
destroy the miserable skunk, but the contemptible creature flat-
tened himself out at the feet of his master and entreated that

the boon of life might be spared him, no matter if all that adorned and made it pleasant be taken away. So in contempt, rather than kindness, Grey Wolf spared the life of Skunk, but at the same time he shrunk and shrivelled the creature till he was scarcely larger than Gopher. He pared his claws and shortened his teeth. This done, the other animals scornfully departed without taking leave, Catamount going next after Grey Wolf.

Black Wolf had only gone a little way when he turned and went softly back.

" Be of good cheer, little brother," he said to the dismayed Skunk. " Brother Grey Wolf has seen fit to arrange matters so that you shall be in terror of all things breathing. Now, I come to put all things, even Grey Wolf himself in awe of you."

This he promised, not because he loved Skunk, but because it delighted him to thwart the intentions of Grey Wolf.

BLACK WOLF BEHAVES LIKE A SKUNK.

Then Skunk lifted up his head and thanked Black Wolf, and asked—

" What can you do ? My strength is gone, my claws are as grass and my teeth as willow-twigs."

" Watch me," said Black Wolf.

So Skunk watched and saw Black Wolf take an egg from a deserted nest and put in it sweat from his own body, the breath of a buzzard, wind that had passed over the field where the dead still lay after the battle, and a little water from a green pool. When he had stirred these things together, he gave the egg to Skunk and said—

" Wear this, and you shall be the great conqueror. Your strongest antagonists shall turn sickly and feeble before you. Not horns, claws, teeth, sinews, or bulk shall make any difference to you."

So Skunk took the gift with a joyful heart and tried its power on Black Wolf at once.

Black Wolf, sick and howling, fled as fast as he was able from the presence of the ungrateful Skunk he had so terribly endowed.

Then Skunk knew for a certainty that Black Wolf had told him the truth about the gift, so he set out to find his revilers and drive them before him. When he found them, they fled, every one, from least to greatest.

Then Skunk contentedly laid himself down under a tree and went to sleep.

SKUNK.

XIV.

MORE RABBIT TALES.

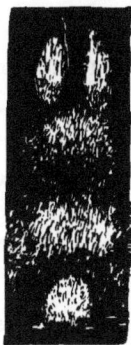

WAS very late when Tow Head and Aunt Mymee made their appearance in the cabin. The little girl had caused the delay. To be quite candid, she and her mother had had certain differences of opinion at the supper-table, and Aunt Mymee had obligingly waited until she recovered from the effect of them.

"Yessum," they heard Aunt Em'ly say as they entered, "hit *wuz* hot an' dry dat yeah, hit sholy wuz. De cawn fiahed w'en 'twuzzen' skusely up ter de fence-tops ; hit wuz laid by 'fo' de summeh wuz out, an' no mo'n harf er crap at de bes', but lan' sakes ! 'twuzzen' so bad but hit mought a-bin wusseh. Hit mought a-bin des lak 'twuz dat time w'en de big watteh-frog git mad at de w'ite folks an' hilt back all de watteh."

"Oh, Aunt Em'ly ! when was that ? " cried the child, throwing herself into the story-teller's arms and beginning to caress the fat black cheek she unintentionally bumped with her hard little head.

"Dat's mannehs, dat am," said Granny, addressing the ceiling. "I wisht Ole Mistis wuz out hyeah ter see some folks settle down in de house ob some yuther folks an' ne'er say 'howdy,' nur nuttin. Dat's de new-fangelums, I reckin . Dey

14   193

done kim in long sence me an' Aunt Mary wuz gals, an' so we specs noduss (notice) dat we don't git. Nemmine, dough, I gwine ter ax Ole Mistis ef dat's wut we gotter look foh fum dis out, kase ef 'tis, I gwineter ax 'er ter lemme go back ter Ole Feginny an' die dar."

Tow Head blushed, hung her head and laughed shame-facedly.

" E-scuse me, Granny," she said. " I was so late that I was afraid all the stories were told, and when I heard Aunt Em'ly just beginning one I was so pleased that I forgot everything else. Don't be angry with me, Granny, I've had *such* a lot of trouble—I'm just like the people Grandpa reads about in the Bible who are *full* of trouble."

A heart ot stone might have been melted by this doleful explanation, and Granny's heart was anything but stony. She accepted the apology, paid for it generously with a fine large gingerbread star, and motioned Aunt Em'ly to proceed.

" Dat time, honey, wuz—dar now I I done fegit de prezack day, but 'twuz in de ole times. Shuck ? wut de use ter tell hit. Hit sech er ole tale an' bin gwine de roun's dat long dat hit a-gittin' all frazzle out."

" *I* don't know it, Aunt Em'ly."

" Den I betteh hed tell um, chile, kase ef yo' see er watteh-dawg, yo' des betteh know de way ter ack."

" I thought 'twas a water-frog."

" Bofe, honey, bofe."

" Des let Aunt Em'ly run dat tale 'cordin' uv huh noshins, honey. Too menny spoons in de cake-dough mek hit fall."

" Very well, but what *is* a water-dog ? "

" Hit des er watteh-dawg. 'Taint no frog, nur no lizuhd, nur no tadpole. Hit des hit ownse'f, an' hit keep de runnin' watteh runnin'. Injun know. Injun lef um 'lone. Ef 'e run up 'gin um, say ' howdy, howdy, uncle,' an' go 'long 'gin. Cullehd man de same t'ing."

" W'ite man come.

" W'ite man see watteh-dawg.

" 'Pooh ! pooh ! kyarn' hab no watteh-dawg a-spilin' de well wut I digs ; kyarn' hab no watteh-dawg a-flouncin' in de spring whah I squinch my thurs (thirst), no suz ! '

" W'ite man tek er big rock, smash po' watteh-dawg—*flat.*

"Den de big frog wut lib unneat de groun' an' own all de springs an' all de streams, git pow'ful mad, kase watteh-dawg de onles' chile o' de on'les' darter wut he hab. So den, he blow de long bref *out*, an' de wattehs, dey all riz an' riz an' riz, an' de w'ite folkses, dey mek de big miration an' dey say—

" 'My ! de watteh mighty high, dis yeah. Dey mus' a-bin heaps ob snow melt 'way up yondeh in de mountains an' de hills an' run down inter de criks an' de big ribbeh ! '

" Ole Frog hyeah dat.

" Nemmine ! he ain't gwine ter 'spute um. He des show de aige o' de ax w'en hit groun', he ain' argyfy 'bout de grine-stun. He fetch de long bref—*in* !

" Now, whah de watteh goned ?

" W'ite folks look dishaway, w'ite folks look dataway. Whah de watteh, w'ite folks ?

" *No—watteh—on—de—whole—face—ob—de—yeath* !

" W'ite folks hunt, w'ite folks dig. W'ite folks fine nuttin. W'ite folks fetch out de hazel lim'. Hazel lim' pint des one way. Pint ter whah de big frog' shouldeh stick outen de groun' lak er big rock. W'ite folks see nuttin. Cuss de hazel lim', cuss de dryness, den go in de meetin'-house an' ax de good Lawd ter gin um rain ; but de rain don' come, kase Ole Frog ten' ter dat. He des hilt up he haid w'en de cloud come an' blow hit back ter T'undeh-Lan'.[1]

" All de cawn dry up, all de grass dry up, de leabes fall offen de trees an' all de beastises run up an' down de yeath des a-hollerin' an' a-bellerin' foh watteh.

---

[1] Thunder-land, which is often described in Red Indian legends.

"W'ite-man kyarn' do nuttin.

"Call on Injun-man. Injun-man kyarn' do nuttin.

"'W'ite-man, W'ite-man, w'y don' yo' lef de dawg erlone ?'

"Call on Niggeh-man. Niggeh-man kyarn' do nuttin.

"'W'ite-man, I ain' got no cha'm ter fetch de watteh back. W'ite-man, W'ite-man, w'y don' yo' lef de dawg erlone ?'

"Call ọn Woodpeckeh. Woodpeckeh kyarn' do nuttin.

"'W'ite-man, W'ite-man, w'y don' yo' lef de dawg erlone ?'

"Call on Rain-Crow. Rain-Crow kyarn' do nuttin.

"'W'ite-man, W'ite-man, w'y don' yo' lef de dawg erlone ?'

"Call on Bracksnake. Bracksnake kyarn' do nuttin.

"'W'ite-man, W'ite-man, w'y don' yo' lef de dawg erlone ?'

"Call on Gran'daddy Rattlesnake. Gran'daddy Rattlesnake kyarn' do nuttin.

"'W'ite-man, W'ite-man, w'y don' yo' lef de dawg erlone ?'

"Call on Crawfish. Crawfish kyarn' do nuttin.

"'W'ite-man, W'ite-man, w'y don' yo' lef de dawg erlone ?'

" All dat time, Ole Rabbit, he a-sleepin some'ers, but 'bout dat minnit, de dryness an' de hotness wek 'im up, an' de fus' t'ing he hyeah am de moanin' an' de groanin' ob de man an' de bawlin' an' de bellerin' an' de growlin' an' de gruntin' an' de squallin' an' de squealin' ob de crittehs.

"'Hi yi, dar!' say he. 'Wassermasser (what's the matter) wid de crittèhs an' de beastises ?'

"Den he fetch er gap dat mos' t'ar 'im open an' den he rub de eye an' scratch de yeah an' set up. Den he stretch hisse'f an' gap some mo' an' look roun'. Dat mek 'im jump l Yes-suh l He jump up an' run roun', a-lookin' an' a-starin'.

"'Ki yi l wut dis ?' he say.

"Den dey wuz de bigges' hollerin'.

"'We all gwine ter pe'sh offen de face ob de yeath, kase W'ite man won' lef de dawg erlone,' say de crittehs.

"'Wut dawg?' ax Rabbit.

"'Watteh-dawg,' sez dey.

"' Wut 'e done ter um ? ' sez 'e.

"' Kill um,' sez dey.

"DEN DEY SHET UP AN' WATCH 'IM, W'ILES 'E LOOK ON DE GROUN' AN WUHK HE MINE."

" Den he slap hisse'f an' cuss.

" Den all de crittehs dey moan an' dey groan, dey bawl an' dey beller, dey squall an' dey squeal.

" ' Shet up ! ' say he, ' an' lemme hyeah my mine wuhk.'

" Den dey shet up an' watch 'im, w'iles 'e look on de groun' an wuhk he mine.

" Bimeby he look up.

" ' Is enny yo' folks see de big frog an' ax 'im, please suh, let de watteh go ?—Shuh ! wut I a-sayin' ? Co'se yo' done dat.'

" Dey all hang de haid. No, dey ain' ax Ole Frog. Dey ain' done nuttin.

" Ole Rabbit, he sniff, he snurl up de nose, he wuhk de whiskehs.

" ' Huh ! ' sez 'e, ' w'en I want er sup o' watteh, I want um. I want um bad,' sez 'e, ' an' mo'n dat, dough I ain't kim ob de wust o' famblies—ef dey's enny ob de harf-strainehs dat am Rabbits, nobody ain' name hit unter me—I ain't dat proud but I ax foh um,' sez 'e, ' an' ax foh um putty, too,' sez 'e.

" ' We ain't 'quaint wid Ole Frog,' says dey, a-lookin' foolish.

" ' Yo' ain't gwine ter git 'quaint wid no watteh, ne'er, at dese rates,' sez 'e, a-th'owin' up he chin an' a-sniffin' mo' an' mo'.

" ' We ain' know whah we kin fine 'im,' sez dey, sorter 'scusin'-lak.

" ' Shucks ! ' sez Rabbit, ' I lay I ain't gwine ter wait twell Ole Frog sens er niggeh on hoss-back wid er eenvite ter drap roun' ter dinneh, w'iles my thote a-pa'chin' erway ter meal-dus'. I gwine ter hunt 'im up de w'iles I got de strenk.'

" Den Rabbit he sot out.

" All de turr crittehs dey foller 'long ahine.

" Rabbit he keep a-goin' an a-goin' up stream—dat am whah de stream uster wuz. Bimeby he come ter de top whah de big spring otter be.

" No spring dar ! Nuttin dar cep er big, green, spotty rock.

"'Hi dar!' sez Rabbit, sez 'e, 'Ebenin', Misteh Frog.'

"Nuttin say nuttin.

"'Frog ain't dar,' say all de crittehs, an' dey gun ter whimple, dey feel so bad.

"'Ebenin', Misteh Frog,' say Ole Rabbit, grinnin' sorter dry an' ginnin' dat ole rock er lil nudge wid he walkin'-cane, 'ebenin', ebenin'.'

"De big rock roll obeh. My! dey wuz er scattimint (scattering) ob de crittehs, dat quick!" exclaimed Aunt Em'ly, illustrating her statement with a snap of her fingers. "Whoo! Yessuh!—an' whyso?—Kase dat spotty, green rock wuz des er piece ob de back ob Ole Frog.

"'Wut yo' war-rr-rr-nt?' sez Ole Frog, sez 'e, an' hit soun' lak de rollin' o' de t'undeh-balls 'crost de sky."

"Floppin'de wings ob de t'undeh-buhds,"[1] corrected Big Angy.

"'Oh, nuttin much!' say Ole Rabbit," continued Aunt Em'ly, smoothly. "'Oh, nuttin much, Misteh Frog,' sez 'e, a-stannin' on one laig an' a-nibblin' de top ob he walkin'-cane sorter keerless. 'I des thunk I'd drap roun' an' ax yo' foh er sup o' watteh,' sez 'e, 'I don' spec er big man lak yo'se'f done noduss lil t'ing lak dat,' sez 'e, 'but de facks ob de matteh am dat dey ain't no watteh a-comin' down todes whah I lib, an' hit am a-gittin' sorter dry down dar—mighty dry, ter tell de troof. 'Deed my gyarden am a-lookin' mighty bad. Hit look mo' lak de las' o' pea-time den de fust o' truck-time,' sez 'e, a-fetchin' er grin, 'an' ef yo'll gimme er sup o' watteh an' den tuhn loose lil mo' an' let 'er run down er past de gyarden, I'll be erbleege ter yo',' sez 'e, 'an' mo'n dat, I'll sen' yo' de fust mess o' truck dat I pick,' sez 'e.

"At dat, Ole Frog, he gin er cr-r-r-o-o-o-oak! dat far heabe up de groun', an' sont de turr crittehs a-runnin' down de holler fit ter split de win', but Ole Rabbit he hole he groun', he do.

"Ole Frog, he roll clean turr side up an' show he des a-bust-

[1] Thunder-bird. The Algonkin spirit of the storm. A great eagle.—C. G. L.

in' wid de watteh he a-holin' back, kase he got he mouf ergin
de deep springs an' a-pluggin' un um up.

"'Wut I a-keerin' foh yo' truck?' sez 'e, an' he v'ice des
boom, 'ain' yo' kilt my gran'son?'

"'No, I ain't,' sez Ole Rabbit, sez 'e. 'I ain' kill nuttin.
Misteh W'ite-man hed de bad luck ter tread on 'im, an' Ise
mighty sorry foh dat, I is so, but lan'! 'tain't so bad arter all.
Des fetch me de pieces un 'im an' I 'low I kin cunjer um libe
ergin.'

"'Don' want none o' yo' cunjerin',' holler out Ole Frog,
a-tuhnin' he haid 'way fum de deep springs soster holler wusser
an' skeer Ole Rabbit bad.

"Dad minnit, de watteh ob de springs bust out an', staht
down dat lone, dry baid ob de stream.

"Seein' dat, Ole Frog gin er nurr cr-r-r-o-o-oak! an' staht
foh ter stop um, but Ole Rabbit, he ain' tek no han' in a-he'pin'
dat out. He ain' bin projeckin' roun' wid de ruff ob he mour
all frizzle inter cracklins an' de sole ob he foot buhn brack fum
tetchin' de groun' an' 'joy hiss'ef 'nuff ter keep hit up study.
No, no, suhs! no, no! De time done come ter stop all dat
triberlashun an' Rabbit de man dat gwine ter do hit. He up
wid he walkin'-cane, he do, an' he job it eenside de jaws ob Ole
Frog an' hole hit dar, an' de cool, cool, watteh, hit run an' hit
run. Hit run hyeah an' dar an' evvywhurs, an' Ole Frog, he
kyarn' git he jaws shet an' stop hit, ne'er.

"Bimeby, de walkin'-cane huht dem big jaws, so Ole Frog
he 'gin ter baig ; den he gin ter plead ; den he 'gin ter promuss, sartin sho, hope he die ef he broke um 'tall, dat he ain't
ne'er gwine ter plug up de deep springs no mo' an' he ain'
gwine ter blow back de clouds an' rain no mo' an' he gwine ter
'have hisse'f all roun'. So Ole Rabbit, he tuck de walkin'-cane
outen Ole Frog' jaws, an' dat walkin'-cane, hit suttinly done
galded dem jaws (made the scars) in de cornders an' dis hyeah tale
kin prube hitse'f in dat, kase dey ain' ter dis day er frog dat ain'

"BIMEBY, DE WALKIN'-CANE HUHT DEM BIG JAWS."

got dem se'fsame mahk in de cornders o' he mouf an' he wuhk
he mouf des lak Ole Frog, he gran'daddy, do w'en he feel dat
walkin'-cane, an' dat trick he sholy do git fum Ole Frog.
Yessuhs! Ole Rabbit he tuck de walkin'-cane outen de jaws,
an' Ole Frog he gin he promuss true, but 'twuz 'bout de big
springs. He ain't mek no promuss 'tall 'bout de lil springs an'
de wells an' de cistuns, so ef yo' see nurr watteh-dawg, foh
Gord' sake lef um 'lone ! " ¹

After nodding an emphatic endorsement of Aunt Em'ly's
statement, Big Angy volunteered to tell another story illustra-
tive of Rabbit's power as a " witcher-man," and at once related
the tale of—

RABBIT AND THE OLD WOMEN.

" One time in the old time, as Rabbit was going along hunting for some fun, he saw some old women heating some large
round stones among the coals of a great fire. They had a great
earthen crock, half-full of water, sitting a little to one side, so,
as he thought this looked like the old-time way of getting ready
to cook something, and as he was hungry, he wished very much
to know what they were going to do. He found himself *very*
hungry and getting every moment more anxious for food, so he
said—

" ' Maybe they are making ready to stew something that I
will like. If I find they are, I will ask for a share. Come ! let
me, at once, put my name in the dinner-pot.'

(" To put one's name in the dinner-pot," is a common form
of the " folk " for " self-invited to a meal.")

" He went towards them, making no sound with his feet, and
warning the grass not to tattle. He had a wish to surprise them.

" Before he could startle them with a call, they mentioned
his name, saying—

¹ This story is a variant from the Algonkin Indian legend of Glooskap and
the Great Frog.—C. G. L.

"'This for you, my Cousin Rabbit! Tee-hee! tee-hee!' laughing as old women do.

"When he heard them he dropped down among the little bushes and grass, and waited to see whether the next words would be friendly or not. They were not, they were far otherwise. It was well for Rabbit that he heard them at the moment he was about to make himself known. The old women were telling each other how, when their husbands and sons came in with Rabbit, whom they were hunting with 'cunjered' arrows, he should be divided, piece by piece, and stewed in the crock with the hot stones. All were to eat of him and thus secure his fleetness, cunning, and 'strength of head.'

"'We shall see!' whispered Rabbit to himself, as he walked out of the brush and up to them, addressing them as he drew near as 'Grandmothers.'

"They knew not what to say, they tried to seem friendly, but returned his greeting with faces turned away. They asked him to sit between them, but this he was wise enough to refuse. He seated himself facing them and looked across, pleasantly. After a silence he said—

"'That would be a good fire to sit in. Those large stones would make a good arm-chair. Have you ever tried it, my dear Grandmothers?'

"They laughed very hard at this, but he kept on talking about it, and finally wagered his body against theirs that he could sit in the fire without burning. After many words, it was agreed that he should go into the fire and sit on the stones.

"If he was burned to death, his roasted body should belong to them ; if he came out unscorched, then they should go into the flames and disport themselves among the glowing rocks and coals. Both parties bound themselves to this agreement by an oath, which could not be broken because it had words of magic in it.

"The old women watched Rabbit go in amongst the flames,

which flared up so high that they could scarcely catch a glimpse of him, but they laughed again, 'Tee-hee! tee-hee!' and talked together.

"'To be sure,' said they, 'roast rabbit is not quite such fine eating as stewed rabbit, but it is sensible to take what is offered, especially in a season when good things are scarce and hunters unlucky, so we will not throw down good and wait for better. Another reason for allowing this fellow to cook himself—it will be a triumph to show the men that we, the old and feeble women, have taken the one they did not find.'

" While they were whispering, Rabbit was sitting in the fire. He seemed quite comfortable, when the wind blew aside the flame and allowed a glimpse of him, and so he was, for his magical breath kept a cool place all around him. Not one hair was singed.

" When he had staid until the sun was going down, and the old women had become impatient and uneasy, he came out of the fire they had kept hot for so long, and bade them look if he were harmed. When they could find neither scorch nor blister, he reminded them of their oath.

" They did not greatly fear.

"' What he can do, we can do,' said they.

" They were mistaken as to their powers. They fell down on the coals and were burnt to ashes—that is, all of them but a few large bones that served very well for drumsticks."[1]

Everybody made a great "miration" over the tale, but nobody knew what anybody said, for Aunt Mary went into such an ecstasy of admiration that she giggled and stamped till, as Granny said, " de whole cabin zooned lak Jedgmint-Day."

" When silence like a poultice came
To heal the blows of sound,"

Aunt Em'ly spoke.

[1] There is an Algonkin (Mic Mac) equivalent for this in the story of the Great Sorcerer and the Porcupines.—C. G. L.

" Dat ain't lak de time w'en Ole Chuff went out foh ter mek de fight ergin de sun."

" Tell dat tale unter me, Aunt Em'ly," cried Aunt Mary, excitedly. " Yo' done tole hit wunst a'ready, but de main p'int I cl'ar fegit."

" Hit wuz lak dis, honey," said Aunt Em'ly, delightedly : " Ole Rabbit, he bin a-stirrin' roun' all de lib-long night, a-tennin' ter some o' dem cungerin' tricks ob hissen, an', w'en de mawnin gun ter break, he wuz plum tuckehd out, an', he lay hisse'f right flat down on de perarer an' tuck er nap dar

" OLE SUN 'E GIT THU 'E TRABBLIN' AN' RUN HIDE."
" CRY ONE GR'A' BIG TEAH ONTER DAT ARRER."

" Bimeby, de sun git putty high an' see Rabbit dar an' des tuhn loose pun 'im, kase ob all de t'ings dat he mek, Sun got de leases' (least) use foh Rabbit, kase Rabbit, one time, he stole Ole Sun's arrehs w'en he back wuz tuhn."

" God made Rabbit, the sun didn't," said Tow Head, severely.

" Dat's so, honey, dat's des de. Bible troof, *now* time, but dat de ole, *ole* time Ise torkin bout, an' den, Ole Sun, he suttin shoh do mek sumpin. 'Tain' *now*, dough, honey, no, suh ! "

" Oh ! Go on, please."

" Ole Sun, he des tuhn loose an' he go fa'r ter fry Ole Rab-

bit, an' dat wek up de ole man arter w'iles, an' he run ter de
shade ter cool he back an' lick he blistehs well.   Den Ole Sun,
he know de fat am in de fiah an' he betteh look out.   Dat
mek 'im hurry an' hit gin de folks er shawt day too, kase Ole
Sun git thu he trabblin' an' run hide.

"Nemmine! nemmine! Ole Rabbit gwine ter fine 'im.

"Arter w'iles, Ole Rabbit do fine 'im too, an' den he 'low he
gwine ter shoot 'im, an' he tuck out dem se'f-same arrehs, Ole
Rabbit did, dat he stole dat time w'en Ole Sun wuz a-settin'
down by de slough a-makin' men-folks.   He tuck dem arrehs
dat wuz 'longin' unter Sun by good rights an' he 'low he gwine
ter kill 'im wid um.

"De fust arreh, he up an' spit on ter mek um fly good.   Den
he let fly.

"Dat arreh flewed inter de ribber.

"Tek nurr one.   Blow on dat foh ter cha'm um.   Blow hahd.

"Dat arreh flewed 'way 'long de sky an' de wins (winds) kyar
um off.

"Tek nurr one, de las' one ob all.   Cry one gr'a' big teah
(tear) onter dat arreh.   Shoh! dat des boun' ter do de wuhk.
So hit do! so hit do!   Hit fly right inter de sun.   Ole Rabbit,
he jump an' he holler, he so gay 'bout hit.[1]

"Hole on, Ole Man Chuffy! hole on wid dat jumpin' an'
hollerin'!   De hot blood a-po'in' down.   Hit fiah, de blood o'
de sun am; hit fiah, Ole Man, a-po'in' down.   Fiah! fiah!
fiah a-po'in' down on de tree-tops, a-po'in' down on de grass.
All de green leabes ob de tree-tops, afiah one minnit; nex'
minnit dey gone!   All de green grass ob the hollers afiah one
minnit nex' minnit all gone!   All de worl' spattehed wid dat
bleedin', all de worl' buhnin', wid crittehs an' all!   Oh, Rabbit!
yo' done so mean! so mean, Ole Rabbit, an' now yo' own coat
a-ketchin' it too!   Run, Ole Rabbit, run an' run!

"He run, he jump in de deep stream.   Deep stream hot.

[1] This incident of the arrows occurs in the *Kalevala.*—C. G. L.

He git on lil ilun (island). Dar he safe, but soun'? Oh, no I he all kivveh wid de sco'ch-mahks ob de fiah an' he kyarn' ne'er cunjer um erway. He got um, he keep um an' so do he kin, fum dat day twell now."

" Are those brown marks *really* scorched places ? "

" Sholy, honey."

" Serves him right, but never mind I Tell how the world— I mean the fire—was put out."

" Rabbit ten' ter dat. W'en he git sottle down an' wuhk he mine some, he know de way am ter cry, ter cry dem cunjerin' teahs, an' dat putt out de fiah."

" He should have cried at once, instead of allowing things to burn up."

" He wuz tuck by s'prise, honey, an' up an' run des lak folks."

" Dat's de way, sholy," assented Aunt Mymee. "Ef he git he breens (brains) a-gwine dat fiah'd a-bin putt right out. W'y de breens ob des er common rabbit am pow'ful e'en w'en de rabbit daid."

" How so, Aunt Mymee, how so ?"

" De eatin' o' rabbit-breens, raw an' hot, gib strenk in de haid ; de rubbin' wid rabbit-breens, dry an' in er brack bag, mek de toofses cut easy e'en arter some un done spile de trick o' de molefoot wid cunjerin'. De toofses bust ri' thu w'en de breens come in de lil brack silk bag an' tek er tuhn at um. Oh, yes ! "

" De breens ob er rat got er heap ob strenk too," said Aunt Mary, visibly elated at having something to tell. " Wunst, I knowed er man dat use ter ketch rats an' pull off dey haids an' suck down dey breens w'iles dey wuz hot wid de life. De life o' de rat-breens go flyin' right inter he breens, so he say, an' gin 'im er heap o' strenk in de haid foh cunjerin'."

" Who sesso ?"

" Ain't I done say he sesso ? "

"Den I ain't a-'nyin' o' nuttin," said Aunt Mymee, decidedly, "but, at de same time, I 'bleege ter say dat I holes fas' ter de breens ob Ole Rabbit."

> "Oh ! Rabbit, he darnce in de bright moonshine.
> He fling up de haid an' he kick up ahine.
> De muel, he graze in de parster nigh,
> He hang down de haid an' he kick mighty high.
> O, Rabbit, Rabbit ! Rabbit, Rabbit !
> La, le, Ole Rabbit ! "

XV.

"BUGS."

Tow HEAD had been very ill. She had slipped away from her guardians, natural and acquired, and had a grand game of snowball with the picaninnies; but, in the end, the way of the small transgressor proved to be hard, her sins found her out in short order, and the name of retributive justice was " Pneumonia." So serious was the case that even Big Angy was in distress, and spent all her spare time in invoking the saints, cursing the doctors, or testing the efficacy of her fetiches. The aunties searched under every doorstone for " tricks," but, it is needless to say, found none. Aunt Mymee would fain have " tricked over " the supposed malign influence, but, as she found nothing, could suspect no one and had no way of finding out what had been done, that was out of the question. If she could have discovered a " tricken-bag," or a rude little representation of the human figure, made of clay, wax, or even snow, and pierced in the breast with a thorn, she could, by burning the evil thing, have relieved the child. As it was, she could do nothing but "hope de doctor ain't *all* fool," and assist in carrying out his orders. When at length the child was convalescent, her patience and skill in ministering to the wants and caprices of the little tyrant were practically limitless. She petted, she soothed, she amused, by turns, so that for years Tow Head looked back on the confinement of the sick-room as a rather pleasant experience—that is, the latter half of it.

" Aunt Mymee," said she, one afternoon, when her tranquillity

15

was restored after indignantly ordering away the panada and
demanding strawberries (which Aunt Mymee, relying on the
shortness of her patient's memory, had promised to pick "in
de mawnin, soon ez I git de time ter scratch de snow offen de
berry-baid)—"Aunt Mymee, the snow should be gone. Do you
know that the musquitoes have come? I hear them buzzing."
"Sholy, honey. I hyeah um my own se'f, *plain.*"
Not for worlds would Aunt Mymee have told her charge
that the buzzing in her ears came from the doctor's quinine
instead of musquitoes.
"They must be awfully thick."
"Dey is so, honey, an' dat 'mines me ob er lil tale dat Aunt
Jinny wuz a-ginnin unter de folks turr night, arter Miss Boogarry tole de tale ob de lightnin'-bugs (fireflies), but I don't
spec yo' keer none. Hit wuz cu'i's—but, shuh! wut yo' a-
keerin' foh Aunt Jinny' tale o' skeeter-bugs, huh?"
"I do care, very much, so tell it, tell it this minute! Hurry!
or I'll put my foot out of bed and take cold."
"Shuh! yo' a-gittin well mighty fas', I kin see dat by de
upshisness yo' 'splay; but hole on, kivveh up dat foot an' I
tell de 'mounts ob de argyfy. Aunt Jinny, she say dat de
lightnin'-bug tale wuz all foolishness (Miss Boogarry ain' hyeah
dat, yo' kin be sho). Dey suttinly wuz er witcher-ooman dat
hab blood-suckin' chilluns, but dat witcher-ooman ain't fall
outen de skies. She bin on de yeath (earth), des lak us folks, an'
den she go unneat (underneath) somers. She stay long time
down dar, an' w'en she come back she des bust thu de groun'
lak dem lil toadstool dat yo' wuz boun' ter eat an' kill yo'se'f wid,
las' summeh, w'en me an' Aunt Jinny tuck yo' thu de woods
unter de gooseberry patch."
"Never mind those old toadstools," cried Tow Head, looking
as haughty as such a thin little girl in such a "skimpy" little
nightgown could. "Go on with the story. Where had the
witch been?"

"Bin a-runnin' wid de Debbil," answered Aunt Mymee, promptly, "an' de Debbil's ole ooman git mad an' chase 'er ter de top o' de groun' ergin. W'en she git up, she 'low she gotter hab somers ter lib, an' so she went ter wuhk, dat ole witcher-ooman do, an' she dig 'er out er mighty nice cave in de banks ob er mighty deep crik. De do' ob dat cave wuz unneat de watteh, honey."

"Why did she have the door underneath the water, Aunt Mymee?" inquired the little girl, eagerly.

"She wuz feard o' de Debbil's ole ooman, honey, an' so she want dat do' whurs nobody ain't gwine ter set eyes on hit. Dat de why an' de whahfo' ob dat doin's.

"I thought," pouted the child, as soon as her curiosity about the door was satisfied, "that this was a musquito story."

"Honey, ef yo' keep a-pullin' me up dat shawt (short) I gwine ter hab er sore mouf. Des th'ow de lines loose an' lemme gander (wander) down de road des 'cordin' ter de gait dat I want ter go at. Yo' kyarn' drive er ole hoss wid er sha'p-crackin' whup an' er stiff bit an' git ter de eend ob de road de quickes', chile. Gin de ole hoss er free line."

This metaphor Tow Head understood to mean that if she wished to hear the musquito story, she must not interrupt the narrator. She was displeased, and evinced her displeasure by puckering her brows into a frown, but, noticing the firm closure of Aunt Mymee's lips, concluded, after a moment's hesitation, not to indulge her temper at the expense of her curiosity, and effaced the frown with a smile badly wrinkled at the corners.

"I'm afraid to speak again, Aunt Mymee," she said, "so do go on without being asked."

Aunt Mymee chuckled faintly and proceeded.

"Putty soon, dat raskil ob er witcher-ooman hab heap o' chilluns. She ain't lub dem chilluns much ez some mammy do, an' she don't nuss um wid milk, she feed um wid— *blood!*"

" O—oh ! " exclaimed Tow Head, hugging her bony little
body in her bony little arms in her delight (her taste, like that
of many another, running to that which would " give her
the horrors "), " oh, Aunt Mymee! what sort of blood—
people's ? "

" N-nuh, deer's, at de fust, den all sorts ob de turr crittehs'."

" Did she shoot them and then give the blood to the children ? "

" No, suh ! she des slip up ter er critteh dat she ketch out
by he lone se'f and den she mek rings on de groun' an' she say
de cha'ms dat she know, an' dataway she conjer 'im so's he
kyarn't stir laig nur huf (leg, or hoof).   Den she fetch out dem
blood-suckin' young uns o' hern, an' dar dey stick on dat po'
critteh twell all de blood done drawed outen 'im an' he fall
down daid.   Dat de way huh an' dem mizzuble young uns does."

" The nasty, mean things ! "

" Dat ole witch keep dat up long time.   At de fust, she
mighty skeery an' keerful, but arter w'iles w'en de ole debbil-
ooman don't ketch 'er, she des ez bole ez brass.   She quit
a-skulkin' arter de lone crittehs an' go right mungs de crowds
evvywhurs.   My! hit wuz des er scannel (scandal) de way she
clean out de beasteses, kase, all de time, de chilluns gittin'
biggeh an' hongrieh.   Dey wuz so, an' dey c'd eat all de way
roun' fum sun up ter sun down an' back ergin.   Hit des seem
lak nuttin wid red blood gwine ter be lef'.

" At de las', de po' crittehs dat *wuz* lef' putt dey haids tergerrer an' say sumpin boun' ter be did an' dat mighty quick.
Dey tork an' dey tork, back an' fo'th, an dey ain't sottle down
ter nuttin.

" Den up jump Misteh Fox an' say—

" ' Laze an' gentermens, scuse me ef Ise too forrid, but I
boun' ter gin out my pingin (opinion) dat hit time ter wake
up Grey Wolf an' git 'im terr putt er eend ter dis hyeah blood-
suckin'.   He bin sleepin' off de tiahdness ob all de cunjerin' an'

fightin' he done mo'n er yeah now ; I 'low he got he nap out
an' I got de mine ter call 'im up.'

" Dey wake 'im up.

" He kyarn' do nuttin dis time.

" Dem po' crittehs des gin right out.

" ' Nemmine,' sez Ole Grey, wid 'er grin, ter 'courage um,
.' de Debbil er mighty big man, mighty big, but, suhs ! he—am
—er—*merried* man !—des putt dat in yo' pipe an' smoke hit.'

" Sho nuff ! dey done fegit dat, but now dey ree-mine (remember) dey 'courage some. Dey 'courage mo' w'en Ole Wolf,
he say he sen' Fox an' Badger ter fine Ole Miss Debbil an' ax
'er ter he'p um.

" Fox an' Badger, dey sot out, and dey rammle an' dey
scrammle plum 'crost de yeath 'fo' dey fine 'er. Arter long
w'iles, dough, dey kim up wid 'er an' tole dey tale. My ! w'en
she hyeah all dat, she des r'ared an' pitched, she des natchelly
did, and den she axt de place whah all dem gwine-ons wuz.
Dey tole 'er, an' she rid dar, in des no time, on er streak ob
lightnin', an', in dess less time den yo' kin holler ' Ow,' she kilt
dat ole witcher-ooman wid er club o' fiah. W'y, dat club hit
wuz so hot dat it buhn dat ole ooman *all* up. Dey wuzzent
e'en no ashes lef'.

" W'en dat job done, she tuhn roun' on de chilluns an' lay
off ter kill dem too ; but dat ain't no use. Dem chilluns, dey
wuz ha'f debbil an' hit wuz on dey daddy's side. No, no, dey
ain' no killin o' dem, but shuh ! dat ain't balk her. She des
swivel um up inter skeeter-bugs, and dar dey is ter dis day.
Dey feel des ez mean an' hongry dis day ez dat, but dey *li'l*
suckers now, an' dat sholy sumpin.

" Ole Miss Debbil, she mighty sot up wid dat wuhk, but she
git huh come-uppunce, she do ; she laff outen turr side o' huh
mouf toreckly, kase Ole Jay Buhd—de ole t'ief am allus
a-tattlin'—he tole de Debbil, an' de Debbil he wuz dat mad
'bout de chilluns ! (He ain't keer none 'bout dey mammy, he

sick o' huh). He wuz dat mad dat he tuck an' tuck Miss
Debbil's big cunjer-bag dat wuz chockfull o' balls dat c'd tork,
an' pipes an' whustles an' de laks o' dat, an' mungs um wuz dat
mos' 'tickleres' lil whustle dat she play on ter call up all de
snakes in de worl', wunst er yeah, w'en she gun um de pizon
dat 'bleege ter las' um twell de nex' yeah. Dat wuzzen' bad
dough, kase dat yeah er snake bite ain't no mo'n er ole hen
peck. Oh, yes ! but de nex' yeah, mine yo', honey, de Ole Boy
an' de Ole Gal mek up, an' de snakes wuz rank pizon an' de
skeeter-bugs, dey wuz t'ick in de worl' ez lies."

"Is that all ? " asked Tow Head

"In co'se, honey. De eend am boun' ter be de las', ain' hit ? "

"Didn't you leave out something, thinking I wouldn't know
the difference ? " was the next question, severely asked.

"Nuttin 'tall, honey," protested Aunt Mymee. "Aunt Jinny
ain't say nair nurr wuhd den de ones dat I des tole yo'."

"Then tell what Big Angy told about the lightning-bugs."

"Hit mos' de same tale, chile, but hyeah 'tis—

"One time, dey wuz er orfle big stawm. De win' riz, all on
de suddent, an' de t'undeh boom an' de lightnin' fling hisse'f
roun' de yeath, an' de big rain come down, an', a-ridin' on de
lightnin', wut yo' reck'n kim down wid de rain ? "

"Oh ! what ?—what, Aunt Mymee ? "

"Dey wuz er witch a-ridin' on de lightnin'."

"A witch ? "

"Yessum, dey wuz er witch, shoh nuff."

"Oh, Aunt Mymee ! was the lightning greased ? "

"Not ez I e'er hyeah tell un, honey. Wut putt dat noshin
in yo' lil haid ? "

"Why, the other day, when Uncle Adam was breaking the
grey colt, Granny said he wouldn't fall off, he could ride a streak
of greased lightning."

"So he could, honey, ef somebody ketched hit foh 'im, I
boun' yo', but, de lan' sake ! dat witcher-ooman c'd ketch de

lightnin' an' ride um too, leas'ways, she rid um wunst, an' den she lit on de groun', an' w'en de stawm go by she des whirl in an' buil' huhse'f er house, er mighty nice house, outen de fresh green tree lim's."

"AN' A-RIDIN' ON DE LIGHTNIN', WUT YO' RECK'N KIM DOWN WID DE RAIN?"

"I wish I could have a house like that. You must build me one, Aunt Mymee."

"Suttinly, honey, dat des wut I a-layin' off ter do. Dat de berry reason I name um so 'tickler unter yo', but lemme wine up dis hyeah tale 'bout de lightnin'-bugs fust."

"Well ! why don't you keep on till you finish it ? You just keep fooling to worry me, I know you do. If you don't quit it, I'll call you a 'pusson,' like Granny did one time."

"Don't yo' das ter ! ur nar nurr tale yo' gwine ter git outen me fum now twell de nex' week arter nebber ! " exclaimed Aunt Mymee, with a flash of the eye that was for Granny, not the child. "I 'clar' ter grashis, de impunce o' dem Ole Feginny niggehs am 'nuff an' er plenty, medout dey a-spilin' de mannehs ob all de chilluns on de place. 'Call me a pusson ! ' —de chile I nussed !—de chile I far riz (fairly) fum de grabe ! Well, suhs ! *I* ain't gwine ter be s'prise wid nuttin fum dis out."

"I didn't say it, I only said I would if you didn't hurry," protested Tow Head, seeing the promised story vanishing. as the fire-flies do when a too-eager little hand is stretched towards them. "How can I say it if you go on talking ? Do go on, Aunt Mymee. If you don't I *know* I'll cry, and if I cry I'll be sick again, and then you will feel—*awfully.*"

Aunt Mymee was subdued.

"De witch stay in dat lil house, des lak er owl, an' mo' wusser too, kase de owl run roun' in de night, but de witch don' do dat, ef de moon a-shinin', she des set fo'th w'en hit wuz ez brack ez er stack ob brack cats. Den, how she go ? She des slip thu de woods mo' quick'n de win' an' she shine fum top-knot ter toe-nail lak she all afiah.

"Arter w'iles, she got er lot o' chilluns, an' dey shine dataway too. Dey look mighty fine, but she ain't a-keerin', she ain't sot on um (devoted to them) lak urr (other) mammies. She ain't gin um no milk, she gin um blood, de blood o' de putty deer. She cha'm dem deer, she do, an' dar dey stan' w'iles dem fiah-chilluns hang on dey neck an' suck out all dey life. Dis hyeah go on twell de wolves git ter noduss dat de deer a-gittin'

mighty skeerce. Den dey rowge up—wolves mighty fon' ob
deer-meat—an' dey say—

"'Shoh ! we kyarn' stan' dis, noways ; we fine de deer
a-stannin' up des ez daid an' dry ez fodder-stalks, and dey ain'
fit ter eat, and dey ain' no libe uns skusely lef'. We boun'
ter stop dis bizniz ef we ain't want ter mek oweh nex' winteh
sassidge-meat outen oweh own tails.''

"Dey ain' wanter do dat, foh sho," continued Aunt Mymee,
enjoying the litle girl's amusement, "so dey git er deer an kill
hit an' dreen out all de blood. Den dey fill it up wid sumpin
dat look lak blood, but 'tain't ; hit sumpin' dat de Ole Boy
kyarn't do nuttin 'bout. All de wolves kin mek hit, an' now-
an'-'gin, dey play turr'ble tricks wid hit. Wut 'tis, dis niggeh
ain't know, but hit turr'ble. Dey putt dat in, dey do, an' dey
cha'm dat deer so hit go lak it a-libbin'. Hit go up ter de
witcher-ooman, an' she lay de han on it, and she fetch one
squall, an' dat de eend o' huh gwines-on. She swivel (shrunk
up, shrivel), she do. She swivel an' she swivel. She git ter de
size ob er lil ooman, lil chile, lil baby, lil pig, lil cha'm, lil pea,
den she gone ! No blood, no bone, no dut, no nuttin. Goo'-
bye, ole witch !''[1]

"What became of the little fire-children ? "

"Hole yo' hosses, honey. De chilluns, dey see dey mammy
go, an' off dey run. Dey ain't tech dat cunjer-deer, but hit got
de strenk ter pesteh um dough. Hit swivel um down ter
lightnin'-bugs, an' so dey is ter dis day, an' if yo' watch um,
yo' kin see um, wa'm nights, a-huntin' roun' foh de mammy
dey los', but, yo' hyeah me, dey ain' ne'er gwine ter fine ez
much ez de string ob 'er petticut."

" *What* are you stopping for ? "

"Dat's all, honey. I done fetch up ergin er bline wall."

"Oh, pshaw ! Why don't you have long stories."

---

[1] This strangely resembles the artificial story of the *Kalevalu,* made by the
evil ones (wolves), whose first act is to kick over and scatter a fire.—C. G. L.

"I hatter cut my coat 'cordin' ter my cloth, honey. Ef I got shawt news, I boun' ter tell um shawt."

"Tell something else, then. Do you know any other bug stories beside skeeter-bug stories and lightning-bug stories ? "

Aunt Mymee pondered, and her anxious expression was reflected in the countenance of her young friend. Finally, her serious, not to say care-worn, look was replaced by a smile that came on gradually like a sunrise and, in time, was a very brilliant illumination indeed. Tow Head marked, understood and laughed aloud in pleased anticipation.

" Tell it."

" Hit 'bout dese hyeah hoppehgrasses."

" Oh ! I know that. Granny told me."

" Dat mighty fine. Mebbe, dough, hit aint des zackry de se'f same tale. Des name it ovveh, chile."

" I'll sing it," said the little girl, gleefully. In a weak little voice she chanted—

> " Hoppeh-grass a-settin' on er sweet-taleh vine,
> A-kickin' up he heels an' a-feelin' mighty fine.
> 'Long come er gobbler a-steppin' up ahine.
> ' Scuse me, hoppeh-grass, I boun' foh ter dine.'
> An' picked 'im off dat sweet-taleh vine."

" Shuh ! dat tale ain't de one dat I wuz gwine ter tell, ain't ez much ez elbow-cousin unter hit, dey ain't no kin 'tall. Nemmine, dough, I ain't fo'ce no tale inter nobody's yeahs."

" Who said you would ? "

" Dey's mo' ways den one o' sayin'."

" I don't care if there's a bushel of hundreds ! I can't be teased about them—the doctor said so—and if you don't go on, I'll let my *two* bare feet get cold and I'll be sick again. There ! "

Aunt Mymee felt the force of the threat, and without delay began the tale of the grasshoppers.

" In de ole, ole times, dem dat wuz ahead ob de mos' ob de ole times, dey wuz er turr'ble witcheh man, an' dat witcheh-man, he mammy wuz er witch an' he daddy, w'y, honey, he des wuz de Old Boy hisse'f. Dis hyeah witcheh-man, he des natchelly 'spise all de folks in de worl', kase he wuz de mos' uglies' man in de worl', wid er whopple-jaw an' er har'-lip, sidesen er lop side an' er crookid laig an' one eye dat wuz des lak fiah an' one dat was daid."

" Oh, my ! "

" Uh-huh ! dat wuz de troof, an' he wuz mo' full ob meanness den uggyness, an' he wuhk her heap o' sorrer an' debbilment ter folks an' dumb crittehs, an' de grass an' de greens too, but de wust wuz 'bout de chilluns."

" What did he do to the children ? " queried Tow Head, languidly.

" Et um."

" No, no, Aunt Mymee ; he didn't eat the children, the poor little children, he didn't ! " cried the child, excitedly.

" He did, honey, foh troo," said the story-teller, " dat am, he cotched um an' sucked dey blood an' chawed um up an' spit um out in de grass."

" Didn't anybody come along and bury them ? "

" Nuh. Kase w'y, dey wuzzen' dead, dey wuz moggerfied (transformed). Dey wuzzen' daid, but, my lan' ! dey own daddies an' mammies ain't know um fum er side o' sole-leather. Dey hop up an' they jounce roun', but dey ain't look lak chilluns, dey wuz des hoppeh-grasses."

" What a shame ! I shouldn't like to be a hopper-grass and Papa and Mamma not know me."

" Dat wuzzen' de wust un hit," continued Aunt Mymee, solemnly ; " dem chilluns wuz Injun chilluns, an' dey daddies an' mammies, dey druv um inter hollers an' ketched um in bags an' den roasted um an' pounded um inter dus' an' mek um inter cakes an' *et* um—dey own chilluns ! "

" O—oh ! the poor little children were eaten twice ! "

" Some un um wuz, sholy, an' mo' un um would a-bin ef, one

time, er ole ooman, dat wuz a-huntin' roun' foh choke-churries an' a-squattin' down dat low dat he ain' see 'er, ain' seed '*im* spit out er chile an' seed de chile fly up er hoppeh-grass.   My !

"AN' DEN SHE TUCK DE CHU'N AN' PO' OUT DE WHOLE MESS ON DE YEATH."

she wuz des all in er trimmle an' goose pimples, but w'en he go on, she mek out ter run home an' tell dem bad nooze unter all de folks.   Dat wuz mighty bad, mighty bad.   Dem po' folkses, dey dassent kill no mo' hoppeh-grasses, kase dey don' kin tell noways de sho-nuff hoppehs fum de chilluns, an' so dem mischevyous lil crittehs des et up de whole face ob de yeath. Dey wuzzent er blade o' grass in de medders, ur er leaf on de trees, ur er plum, ur er berry, ur nuttin. De po' folks an' de beasteses wuz des styarvin' out. Dey wuz dat desput dat dey go plum ter T'undeh-Lan' an' ax de witch un hit ter sen' er big stawm an' kill off dem hoppeh-grasses, but she ain't keer none, she des druv um off. De Jedgment Day a-comin', dough, comin', comin'. Dat ole witcheh-man am dat sot up an' free-feelin' fum high libbin' dat he spit dem hoppeh-grass chilluns cl'ar 'crost T'undeh-Lan' right inter de ole witcher-ooman's front do'. Dat rile 'er. She tromple dem hoppeh-grasses down an' den she fetch out de chu'n-dasher an' de big ole chu'n, an' she chu'n up the bigges' stawm dat e'er wuz, an' den she tuck de chu'n an' po' out de whole mess and drownded out dem hoppeh-grasses, an' she fetch de ole witcheh-man er lick wid er streak o' lightnin', an'—goo'-bye ole witcheh-man, f'revveh mo'!"

"Then what?"

"Den, w'en de stawm sottle, de trees an' de grass an' de collahds [1] an' de inguns grow 'gin an' de folkses an' de beasteses git fat."

"But the little children—the poor, eaten little children—didn't they come again like Little Red Riding-Hood?"

There was a long pause.

"Didn't they come?" insisted the child, anxiously.

"Honey," said Aunt Mymee, slowly and regretfully, "dem chilluns ain't ne'er yit come back."

The little girl was so distressed and disappointed at this unhappy ending of the story that Aunt Mymee thought it advisable to cheer her with a little music, and without further ado, sang, to a wild and rollicking air, these words which had

[1] *Collard*, a kind of cabbage.

often roused her ire when any of the late partners of her
joys and sorrows had presumed to serenade her with them—

" Ez I wuz gwi-in up de hill,
I met de Debbil's wife.
I grab my hat an' mek my bow,
Kase I don't want no strife.
    No strife, no strife.
    Kase I don't want no strife.

' Howdy, Miss Debbil,' I holler out,
How am yo'se'f, dis day ?
Dis weddeh mighty good foh cawn.'
Not one t'ing do she say.
    She say, she say.
    Not one t'ing do she say.

De Ole Boy mus' a-tied 'er tongue.
Wish my wife done lak dat.
Oh ! I would spread my jaws out wide
An' tek on streaks o' fat.
    O' fat, o' fat.
    An' tek on streaks o' fat."

XVI.

SNAKE STORIES.

THE contrast between the rosy light flung over the cabin from the fire-place and the cold white moonlight without was so great that, as Aunt Em'ly said, "hit fa'r (fairly) mek er ole ooman blink," and so confused her vision that when she caught sight of a bit of rope, the property of Tow Head, lying at her feet, she uttered a frightened scream of which she was, the next moment, ashamed.

"Ise gittin' rickety, sho nuff," she said, apologetically. "Dat am twiste dis night dat I bin fool o' gittin' skeered o' snakes."

"Snakes in de winteh!" giggled Aunt Mary.

THE CABIN.

"Yo' gotter look shahp! Dey am er inmy arteh yo', unner hans," growled Big Angy, in warning. "Dat seein' whah dey ain', am *comme* de dream."

"Lor!" exclaimed the frightened Em'ly.

"Ef dat count, w'y ain' hit count ter stop um de same ez ter stop de libe snake fum a-bittin' by a-sayin', 'De seed o' de ooman shill bruise de sarpint's haid'? Ef yo' keep a-sayin' dat, de snake ain't hatch yit dat kin ha'm him dat say hit; dat

we kin prube, pintidly, den whyso aint hit good foh ter kyore
de bad dream ? " Granny interrogated, with an anxious and
deferential look at Aunt Mymee.

" Dunno," was the short answer.

"Dey's some luck in de snake," said Big Angy, encouragingly. " Dar's Gran'daddy Rattlesnake, dat bin sence de fus'
day an' am de king ob de Snake Kyentry. Me *connai* de tale
o' de boy dat go ter dat kyentry an' 'joy life dar."

On being importuned, Big Angy told the following—

There was once a little boy who had a bad stepmother. She
whipped him every day. One evening, when he was late in
bringing the cows home, she went out to meet him, and picking
up what she thought was a stick lying in the road, she struck
him a blow she thought would be very severe. The supposed
stick was in reality a snake. When she discovered it, she fled
screaming. The snake was left in the road, badly bruised.
The little boy stooped over it with words of pity. " We have
suffered together," said the snake, " we will recover together.
Come to the Snake Country. I will make you known to the
king. He will treat you better than that stepmother does."

The boy was not sure that it would be wise to go, but he was
desperate and went, reckless of consequences. The change was
for the better. Once he went home for a visit, and every one
saw that he was fat and dressed in fine clothes. Nothing could
persuade him to remain long in his father's house, he would go
back to the snakes and he would not promise to make another
visit.

" I know mo' biggeh tale den dat, 'bout de Snake Kyentry,"
cried Aunt Em'ly.

" Tell hit," said Big Angy, glumly.

Aunt Em'ly was too eager to practise her usual deprecatory
politeness, and at once told the tale of *her* little boy.

" Wunst on er time, hit wuz de ole time, *berry* ole, dey wuz
er lil boy dat los' he mammy. He daddy ain't noduss 'im

much, kase w'y he bin er gret hunteh an' he t'ink de mo' ob
de beasteses he ketch an' kill den he do o' dat peakeddy,
(peaked, or pale and thin) pindlin lil chile, so dat lil boy, in de
ways it fall out, des bleege ter be timbehsome (timorous) an'
low in he mine ef he don't mek no fr'en's mungs de crittehs,
kase in de woods dem's all de comp'ny dey is. Now den, the
crittehs, dey all know he daddy an' dey 'feard foh come roun'
an' ax 'im howdy an' pass de time o' day. Po' lil boy, he go
set on de big flat rock by de crik ; set dar an' cry kase he ain'
got no frens, no mammy, no nuttin.

" Snake-docteh ¹ come a-flyin' by.

" ' Wut de matteh, lil boy ? ' Snake-docteh ax.

" Lil boy cry so de don' kin spik out 'tall.

" Snake-docteh try 'gin.

" Lil boy sniff an' snuff, shake an' heabe. Bimby, he git out
de wuhd—

" 'I got no frens, I got no comp'ny, Ise honin' arter gittin
whurs my mammy gone ter.'

" ' Shuh ! ' say de snake docteh, ' yo' heap too young, foh
torkin' dat away. All yo' a-needin' am some un dat kin fall to
an' 'muse yo' wid de gwines-on ob de neighbehs, ur er (or a)
tale ur two 'bout somewurs, ur nowurs.'

" At dat de lil boy sorter kinder wipe de eye an' cock up de
yeah an' look lak he wanter hyeah mo' bout de case.

" 'Dat des all yo' a-needin, in de pints o' fack,' say de snake
docteh, sorter a-balluncin' hisse'f, lak he gwine ter fly off, 'but
ef yo' don't keer foh dat, in co'se dat yo' bizniz an' none o'
mine.'

" Den de lil boy, he sorter fetch er lil oneasy grin, an' he 'low
he lak some comp'ny ter tok (talk) wid fust-rate.

" ' My 'quaintence,' say de snake docteh, kinder fizzin' he
wing, lak he des a-stahtin', ' am mungs de folks dat I doctehs.
Dey's snakes, in co'se. Now, Ise gwine inter de Snake Kyentry

---

¹ "Snake-doctor"—Dragon-fly.

16

dis minnit. I bin sont foh in de bigges' kine ob er hurry,' sez 'e, sorter struttin' up an' down in de a'r, 'but den dat's nuttin. Dey allus 'low dey kyarn' git 'long bedout *me* ef dey's po'ly (poorly). Oh, yes, I bin sont foh (sent for), an' I got my bag o' yarbs, and I got my medsum pipe, an' I got my cunjer-bones 'long o' me, dis minnit, I has so. I gwine dis time ter de fust fambly, shoh nuff ; I bin sent foh ter Ole Gran'daddy Rattlesnake's ol'est son's younges' darter's, I is. One o' de chilluns is mighty bad, dey tells me, but dey 'lows I kin fetch um thu all right, yessuh ! an' dat why I in sech er big hurry.'

"Dat soun' mighty fine, but de lil boy, a-studyin' all de time whah *he* come in. He wiggle an' he twis' an' he open he mouf an' he shet um 'gin, an' he feel sorter sheepy 'bout axin' queschins, but w'en de snake docteh keep on a-wizzen' he wing an' braggin', wizzen' he wing an' braggin' an' lookin' lak he gwine ter be off in er seckint mo', hit come obeh 'im so strong dat he (was) a hyeahin' heap o' tork an' a gittin' no news, dat he git desput, an' he whirl in an' say—

"'Oh, say, Misteh Snake-Docteh, is yo' a-wantin' me ter go 'long an' tote de yarb-bag an' mek de 'quaintence o' de fambly dataway, ur is yo' gwine ter fetch some un um back wid you ? '

"'I wuz a-studyin' 'bout fetchin' some o' de chilluns hyeah,' sez de snake docteh, mons'us stiff an' sollum. 'Ef ye' c'd a-waited twell I wuz thu wid my disco'se, you'd a-larnt dat same, but, lan' sakes ! grown folks, speshul de ole, dey gits de wuhd snatch right outen dey mouf, des days. Dat wuzzent de way my mammy fotch *me* up, dat hit wuzzent !

> 'Spik w'en yo spoke unter,
> Come w'en yo' call.
> Ef yo' jump 'fo' I show yo',
> Yo' git er bad fall.'

Dat wuz de princerpul *I* wus fotch up on. Dat de mannehs wut she larn me, an' I was *bleege* ter foller um, chile.'

" Oh, dat snake docteh wuz mad l He mek lak he gwine now, foh suttin.

" Lil boy 'gin ter cry.

" 'I wuzzent meanin' ter aggervax ye,' Misteh Snake-Docteh,' he whimple out ; ' I dunne no betteh'n ter tork so. I ain't got no mammy ter larn me nuttin. Prease, suh, don't fly off. I ain't gwine do so no mo'.'

"Well, suhs l dat sorter pacify de ole snake docteh, but he say he bleege ter be a-gittin' 'long, all de same, but ef de lil boy be in de same place bout sundown, he gwine ter come' long wid two likely snake chilluns, an' dey des plum full ob fun, an' dey'd go in wid 'im foh raisin' all de ruckshin he kin study up. Hit tuhn out des dataway too. Dem young snakes des ez fat an' slick an' sassy ez young shoats in er cawn-fiel'. Dey tell 'im riddles, dey 'splain he dreams, day teach 'im de chahm dat ketch de buhds an' de molly-cotton tails, dey gin 'im whole han'ful ob snake-rattles foh ter tie up in he ha'r to keep off de haidache an' de sun-struck, w'en he run roun' in de hot noon sun. Dey mek 'im sly, dey mek 'im sha'p, dey mek 'im gaily. De lil boy feel mighty good. He laff, he sing, he mek de laughin' tale hisse'f. Bimeby dough, he get a-studyin' 'bout de tales dem two rattlesnakes tell 'bout der own kyentry, kase hit wuz dishaways : sometime dey play wid de boy, but off an' on dey wuz in dey own kyentry, an' den w'en dey git back, dey wuz tellin' de big tale bout whah dey folks lib, an' 'bout de king o' dat place wut hab hawns (horns) on he haid an' er gole crown wid red spots onter hit, an' he eyes wuz big ez waggin-wheels, an' dey roll roun' an' roun' in de sockuts lak de wheels too, an' de fiah spahks fly out en um. De ole king got er tongue lak er pitch-fawk an' des ez big too, dey tell, an' he kin spit de yalleh pizon er mile, an' de scales offen he las' yeah's skin, dey kin chahm off de swamp-feveh an' de rheumatiz. Oh, yes ! dat wuz er big tale dey tol dat lil boy, dough I hain't name but des de leas'es' lil smidgin ob hit. Hit des 'stractid dat boy, an' he

baig an' he plead ter see dem t'ings, twell de snakes dey sorry
foh dat honin', an' git 'im er eenvite ter mek er stay in de
Snake Kyentry, an' dey gran'addy, he writ 'im er pass on er
dock leaf wid de eend o' he tail. He writ hit on de leaf, an'
he wrop hit up in grass, to-be-sho, but hit wuz er good pass,
an' tuck de lil boy 'long des ze slick ze grease on de waggin-
wheel. W'en dat lil boy git ter de aige o' de kyentry, suhs, he
wuz s'prise, an' dat ain't s'prisin. Dar de big brack snakes wuz,
all a-stannin' on dey tails des ez stiff an' straight ez de rushes
a-growin' 'long de side ob de ma'sh. Dey bat de eye at de lil boy

LIL BOY AND THE SNAKES.

an' don' stir, but ef dey ain't see dat pass dey'd a-quile (coiled)
roun' 'im an' squoge de bref o' life outen 'im. Dey do see de
pass dough, an' dey bat de eye an' dat mean, ' Go 'long.' He
do go 'long twell he see de king an' de king' fambly an' all de
turr folks, an' dey wuz dat nice an' 'gree'ble dat he mek up he
mine dat he tek up he stan' dar foh good, so he des go ter de
cave ob de rattlesnakes an' mek hisse'f homefolks dar."

"How did he make himself homefolks with snakes?"
queried Tow Head, looking rather incredulous.

"Totin' wood an' fetchin chips an' runnin' arrints an' tendin' de baby, I s'poge," said the narrator, with an assumption of loftiness amusing even to a child. "Leas'ways, dat wut I reck'n," was the qualifying afterthought; mildly expressed, "but, nemmine, ennyways. Dar he wuz an' dar he stayed, an' at de fust he daddy ain't miss 'im. Arter w'iles he' gin ter mirate some, an' den he 'gin ter 'quire an' ax roun' mungs de trees an' de grass an' de criks—he ain't ax de crittehs, kase w'y dey up an' git too quick—ef dey seen sumpin o' dat triflin' boy. He sorter s'pishin dat de chile fall inter de crik nigh de cabin an' drownd hisse'f ter def, but de crik 'low dat ain't so, kase ef 'twuz, hit 'ud a-knowed it. Dat crik know mighty well whah dat boy gone, but 'tain't gwine ter tell kase hit none o' hit's look-out.

"De trees, w'en dey bin axt, 'low dey got dey 'tenshun way up in de sky an' dey ain't noduss no boys.

"De grass—shuh!—de grass boun' ter tell ur die; hit des bleege ter tattle an' pack de news eroun', ur else dry up an' blow off, so hit up an' tole de man de whahbouts dat boy use ter set a-gassin' wid de snakes, 'an',' says dat grass, des a-wavin' an' a swingin', hit feel so biggetty wid er tale ter tell, 'de ebenin' dat boy go off, de whole passel un um, boy an' snakes, wuz des a-kyarin' on high, twell dey go off seput ways.'

"W'en de man hyeah dat, he wuz pesteh in he mine. He ain't pay no 'tenshun ter de boy hisse'f, but he 'spise ter b'liebe dat de snakes et 'im, so he ax de way todes de Snake Kyentery. No un own up dat he know, so de man, he watch he chance an' ketch er snake wid er slip-knot. Man ax bout de boy.

"Snake say—

"'Yo' knows well nuff dat he go on lil ja'nt ter de Snake Kyentry. He come back w'en he git he bisit (visit) out.'

"Man ain't b'liebe dat.

"'Show me de way ter de Snake Kyentry,' sez 'e.   'Show it
dis minnit!   I boun' ter git dat boy back.'

"I show yo', in co'se', sez de snake, mighty sorf, ' but, Misteh
Man, I ain' kin trabble in nuttin lak dat hurry (de man wuz
des a-zoonin' er long), I bleege ter go slow, kase I ain't got no
footses.'

" ' Yes yo' is,' sez de man, sez 'e ; 'yes you' is got footses an'
Ise de one ter show um unter yo',' says 'e, an' wid dat he gin
de slip-knot er swing an' lan' de snake on de fiah—dey wuz er
good fiah o' bresh right dar handy—an', bress de goodniss! de
footses des comed a-stickin' out, an' de snake comed a runnin'
out o' dat fiah, quick ez er squirr'l and quickeh.

" ' Now den,' say de man, ' I foun' de footses, now yo' bleege
ter fine de hurry.'

" An', mon, suz, de snake do fine de hurry, an' dat mighty
suddint, an' so dey git ter de aige ob de Snake Kyentry in des
no time 'tall, an' dar wuz de snakes a-stannin' on dey tails, an'
'fo' dey c'd do nuttin, de man he holler out—

" ' Hi, dar! ef yo' come a squeegin' roun' me, des dat minnit,
I pull de haid offen yo' bruddeh hyeah dat I got a-holt ob,
mine dat!   Lemme thu ter fine my son, ef yo' know wut's
good foh de healt' o' de fambly.'

" So dey seen how 'twuz an' lef 'im thu, an' he went
a-huntin' an' a-huntin', up an' down, right an' lef', foh dat boy,
an' all de time, mine yo', he.wuz a-holin' dat snake by de neck
in de slip-knot.

" Bimeby, he fine de ole king an' he tell he tale, an' he lay
he gwine ter grab de haid offen dat snake he got in de slip-knot,
ef he die foh hit de nex' minnit, ef he don't putty soon ketch
sight o' dat boy.

" ' Come on,' sez 'e, ' come on ; but I lay dey 'll be one daid
snake 'fo' I fall in my tracks ! '

" At de wuhd, de ole king, he call up de crowd in de rattlesnake den, an' dey fetch de boy up 'long wid um.   Gorry ! dat

wuz er sight! dat lil boy mungs all dem wigglin' fawk-tongues! but de man, he stan' he groun' an' keep fas' a-holt de one in de slip-knot.

"Den, w'en dey all git sottle down, de ole king say unter de lil boy—

"'Yo' feggittit ter tell yo' daddy goo'-bye, an' so he come a-follerin' arter yo'. Is yo' gwine back wid 'im?'

"Boy look at he daddy, daddy say, ''Howdy.' Boy say nuttin.

"'Dat boy bin chahm,' say de daddy.

"'No, I ain' chahm,' say de boy, 'but ef so be I is, wut yo' a-keerin'? W'en I home yo' ain' spik unter me wunst er munt. De buzzuhds mought er picked me an' de wolfses gnyawed my bone an' yo' ain't noduss. I lay (I declare) I s'prise dat yo' miss me now. Goo'-bye, daddy.'

"Wid dat de boy staht off.

"'Come back, oh, come back, my son! I gwine ter treat yo' mo' betteh fum dis out. Come back, oh, come back!'

"'Goo'-bye, daddy, goo'-bye,' say de boy, a-lookin' obeh he shouldeh. ''Membeh me ter yo' gun—dat am mo' yo' chile den I is. Goo'-bye.'

"Wid dat de boy go cl'ar off an' de man ain't see 'im no mo'.

"De man go back outen de Snake Kyentry, an' de brack snakes, dey lef 'im go out w'en he leggo de snake in de slip-knot, an' dat time wuz de las' time dat de boy seen 'm ceppin wunst w'en he wuz a-bisitin' de snake docteh. He see de ole man, but de ole man ain't see him, kase he wuz wrop up in er snake-skin. De ole man ain't see 'im, but he hyeah 'im laff wunst an' stop, an' lissen.

"'Shucks!' sez 'e, arter a-lissenin' wid he han' ter he yeah, 'Ise gittin' ole an' weak in de haid. Wut *is*, I kyarn't hyeah, an' wut *izzent*, soun' ter me plain. Dat soun' wuz de echo a-mawkin' (mocking) fum de hill yondeh, dat I know, dough de soun' fool me at de fust.'

" Wid dat sayin', he pass on, an' de boy go back ter de Snake Kyentry an' he git de folks ter sew dat snake-skin onter 'im. He ain' nurr tek hit off no mo', so ef yo' see 'im yo' ain't gwine ter know but dat he am des lak de comp'ny he foun' in, an hatch ri' spang out (directly out of) en er snake-aig."

" Go on," said Tow Head, after a pause.

" Dat all, honey."

" Hit er mighty fine tale," said Granny. "I desh wush ter de Lawd dat I know one half dat fine, but all de same hit 'mine me o' sumpin."

" Les hyeah tell wut dat 'mindin, am, ef so be yo' mine ter faveh de comp'ny, Aunt Jinny."

" Hit des de lil foolish tale ob how one time Miss Hawk bin lub-sick foh Misteh Rattlesnake. Hit er foolish tale," continued Granny, turning her bright eyes on Aunt Mary, and inhaling tobacco-smoke with a long-drawn sigh—" hit mighty foolish, but hit got er lessun too foh some folks, ef dey des tuhn dey 'tenshun ter heedin' de same."

" Dat de tale we want, dat tale wid er lessun (with a moral). De Lawd know, we po' ooman-folks a-needun' all de lessun we kin git," cried Aunt Mymee, with unusual good humour in her tones, and unusual malice in her glance.

Madame Bougerau agreed with both the speakers, and so did Aunt Mary, presumably, for she nodded several times, and doubtless would have spoken if a paroxysm of giggles had not rendered it impossible.

" Dis de tale," said Granny.

" One time dey wuz er putty hawk—not one o' dem speckle kine—dat kine dat 'pear some w'ite an' some ash, wid er tetch o' green flung on ez ef yo' wuz a-lookin' at 'er thu er bottle. Shuh ! yo' know de kine *well*—one dem lil hawk, de coleh (colour) ob de young tree bahk. Dat wuz in de ole time, w'en all de crittehs—a-countin' in de beasteses longer de buhds an' de bugs, an' de snakes an' de bees an' de trees, an' all de turr greens—wuz mo' fr'en'ly-spurriter tergedder den dey e'er dar' ter be dese days. Well den! Miss Hawk, she fr'en'ly wid all de neighbehs, an' mo'n dat, dey wuz fr'en'ly wid huh—mo' speshul, de *he* ones, kase, mon, she wuz *putty*. She wuz de putties gal in de sottlemint, an' she de one dat knowed it, kase all de turrs tole 'er so, an' de half o' de men-folks ax 'er ter merry um.

"'Shuh!' sez Miss Hawk, sez she, ' my time ain't come yit. Ise bleege ter yo' gemplums, but I ain't see no call ter gin up my fun an' go ter cookin' vittles an' packin' fiah-wood, stiddier (instead of) settin' in de front room wid beau-ketchers in front ob my yeahs an' all my bes' close on, de wiles de boys draps hunks o' sugah an' churry-gum in ter my lap. Bleege ter yo', sholy, but I ain't fegit how mammy hatter (had to) wuhk.'

"Dat de way she go on wid 'er foolishniss, but, nemmine! huh time a-comin', comin' suddint, too! She fall in wid er lazy, wuthless, triflin', young, speckildly ratttlesnake, wid squint eyes an' er oller front tooth. De minnit she clap de eye on im she gone! Gone cheap, too! foh dat wuthless cuss, he put in de time a-swallerin' de chilluns ob Miss Fiel' Mouse an' Miss Toad an' Ole Man Rabbit—dat wut *he* lub, an' he lub um mo'n de sweet looks ob all de hawks in de kyentry. W'en he sees dat foolish gal, dough, wid er eye wall at 'im an' 'er pin-feddehs all a trimmelin', he *look* mighty sorf' an' pleasant, an' dat des tuhn 'er haid cl'ar roun'. She fa'r t'ink de groun' not good nuf foh 'im ter crawl on. She'd orteh knowed betteh'n dat," continued Granny, warming with her subject, " but, lan' o' Goshin! she des foh all the worl' lak some o' de oomans o' de prisin' time, dat dunno w'en dey well fix, but am des ketched an' spiled wid her grin ur two, lak er fly in bilin' 'lasses."

Aunt Mary laughed so long and loudly, that Tow Head grew indignant at the interruption, and stamped her little foot.

"'Tain't no use ter stomp, honey," said Granny, with melancholy sternness, " no use 'tall. Ef er ooman dat am got

ter de age ter know betteh am gwine licketty-switch down de
road ter sorrer, she *gwine*, dat all l But de time come l de
time come, sartin shore [Granny grew quite oracular], w'en
she gwine ter laff outen de turr side o' huh mouf, an' de soun'
ain't lible ter 'sturb de comp'ny ef dey got sumpin ur nurr ter
tell de res' o' de folks dat mo' sot on wuhkin' dey mines den
bustin' de windehs wid de haw-haws."

Aunt Mary instantly became grave and apologised most
politely.

Peace was restored and the story went on.

" One day dey wuz er big dinin' at Miss Hawk's house. Huh
pa gin dat big dinneh-pahty, an' dey wuz er heap o' eenvites
sent out, an' Miss Hawk, she see unter hit dat Misteh Rattlesnake git de berry fust one. Suhs, dat wuz er hongry rattler
an' he wuz on de groun's de fust one, an' he stay on hans
twell all de res' done putt on dey t'ings an' gone 'long home.

" Miss Hawk, she wuz mos' tickle ter def w'en she noduss
dat. She ain't kyurl de corndehs ob huh mouf so high, dough,
w'en de fambly come a-runnin' wid de wuhd dat one o' huh lil
sissies wuz a-missin', All han's dey s'arch an' dey s'arch an'
dey run 'cross ter de neighbehs an' ax is dey see 'er, an' won't
dey fine out is de chile stray off wid enny o' de comp'ny.
All dat ruction no use. De lil sissy gone, *clean l* Dey kyarn
fine hide nur ha'r un huh.

" Den Miss Hawk, she up an' 'low, she do, dat Ole Man
Owl, dat all de worl' know kin eat mo'n he wuth enny dey in
good vittles dat hit am er shame ter putt inter 'im, done et up
dat po' chile.

" She ain't wunst tuhn de S'pishin ob de folks pun Rattlesnake.

" Arter dat, all de frens ob de family semmle an' mou'n wid
de hawks, an' 'fo' de Lawd ! de mo' dey mou'ned de mo' dey
hatter, kase de lil hawks all a-gwine, one arter nurr. De ole
folks, dey ain't 'cuse nobody, at de fust, but Miss Hawk, she

keep hahpin' (harping) on dat one string 'bout Ole Man Owl twell dey all tek hit up an' go off de hannel an' up an' tax 'im wid hit 'fo' de whole crowd.

" Dat huht Ole Man Owl' feelins, hit do, but he hole hisse'f down an' tork back mighty ca'm, an' say he ain't de one ter play no sech tricks on dem dat treat 'im right, an' he gwine ter fine out who done dat meanness by de day he name—I done fegit des wut day 'twuz, but 'twuzzent' fur off—an' ef he ain . fine out who de one ter blame den he gin um leabe ter hang 'im in de fence-corndeh lak her aig-suckin' torm-cat."

" Just as Granny did the poor black cat that broke up the speckled hen's nest ? "

" Des de same way, honey, des zackry de same, an' all de hawks say dat er bargain, an' so he sot hisse'f a-watchin' an' a-spyin'."

" Did he catch the thief ? " questioned the little girl, with an air that indicated that she took an affirmative answer for granted.

" Not at de fust, honey, not ri' slam-bang at de fust off. Dat se'f-same day, nurr hawk wuz missin'."

" Then what did he do ? "

" He des gun out de wuhd (gave out the word) dat he wuz sick in baid fum bad luck an' trouble."

" Was he so sick ? "

" Nuck. He wuz des a-studyin' up pun de case, an w'en he mek up he mine dat he dunno nuttin 'tall, den he go a-slippin' off unter he granny dat lib 'way deep in de black oak woodses.

" Ole Granny, she mighty glad ter see 'm, but she fuss at 'im mighty strong foh not gittin' dar mo' sooneh. W'en she git dat offen huh mine, she tuhn in an' 'low she know who a-bustin' he wuthless hide wid hawk-meat.

" ' Den foh de pity sakes, Granny, tell me I Ef yo' ain't a-honin' ter go ter my hangin' tell me quick ! '

" I gwine ter let yo' tell yo'se'f, my son. Hit 'u'd be er po' 'scuse foh her owl ob oweh (our) fambly dat hatter be tole.'

" Den he git up. He frumple he feddehs an' blink he eye an' say he er plum fool, he know, an' he boun' foh ter die, kase he granny 'spise 'im too much ter let 'im lib.

" At dat she scole some mo' an' den she fall ter wuhk an' tell 'im how ter ketch de one dàt et de fambly.

" Arter dat, he cock up he haid an' whustle er chune, an' I boun' yo' he'd a-darnced er jobilee ef he footses wuzzen' so big. Den he fly back whah he come fum, an' dar wuz all de folkses soun' ersleep. W'en he done noduss dat, he tek seb'n lil strings an' he tie um roun' de laigs o' de seb'n lil hawks dat wuz lef', an' den he tie de turr eend o' de strings ter er good stout hick'ry pole dat he foun' druv up nigherbouts.

" All dat done, he crope ter baid an' res' hisse'f, and wait foh he game ter git in de trap.

" He ain't hatter wait long. Nex' mawnin', nurr hawk gone. Whooh ! wut er ruckshin dat raise ! Now dey boun' ter hang Ole Owl, sholy.

" He let on lak he mos' skeer ter def.

" ' Come, tek me by de han',' sez 'e, 'an' lead me ter de place whah dem young hawks is, an' den yo' kîn hang me, ef de t'ief I promuss yo' ain't ketch dar.'

" So dey lead 'im dar, an' den dey 'mence ter twust er rope an' ter fetch de planks.

" ' Shuh ! sumpin's fegot,' sez 'e. ' Count dem hawks dat's lef'.'

" Dey count um, an' w'iles dey a-countin', dey noduss how dey all fluttin' an' floppin' an' all tankle up in de strings.

" ' Huh ! wut dis ? ' dey say. ' Whah all dese hyeah strings come fum ? '

" At de same time dey see dey fas' ter de pole.

" Owl, he count de strings at de pole. One, two, thee, fo', fibe, six, seb'n. Seb'n strings. Den he count de budhs. One, two, thee, fo', fibe—six ! Six budhs !

"'My frens,' sez 'e, 'las' night, dey wuz seb'n strings tied unter seb'n budhs, an' de turr eend tied unter dat pole. Dis mawnin' seb'n strings am tied unter dat pole yit, an' des ba'ly (barely) six buhds am in sight. Dat seb'nt' string am still on de pole ; des feel roun' an' see wut am on de turr eend un hit.'

"So dey all went ter wuhk, feelin' 'long dem strings, an' 'twuzzen' no fun wid dem strings all tangle up mungs dem floppin', squallin' young ones.

"Rattlesnake, he look sorter quare de fust minnit, an' he 'low 'twuz er shame ter pester dem po' chilluns so, an' he ax leabe ter cut dem strings an' free de po' t'ings 'fo' dey git huht. He wuz a-slippin' eroun' an' a-axin' ter borry er knife 'fo' dat, kase he ain't got none, but he ain't mek out ter git one yit.

"Dey ain't nobody pay no tenshun, dey too much tuck up wid tracin' up dat odd string.

"Suhs, dey foun' out !—an' my !—ob all de hollerin' sence de worl' wuz made !

"Dat — string — wuz a-hangin' — out—o'—de—jaws—o'— Rattlesnake's own se'f !

"Putty Hawk, she holler lak de booggers (bogies, ghosts) got 'er, but w'en she git 'er bref an' come to, don't she sottle 'im ! "

"What did she do ?"

"She et 'im," said Granny, solemnly, and looking, not at the child, but at Aunt Mary. "She et 'im, she sholy did, an' dat whah she show huh good sense an' mannehs, stiddier 'lowin ob 'im ter rune huh an' all de whole fambly. She flewed onter 'im an' she hit 'im er clip twixt de eyes. Dat stonded 'im, an' den she tuck 'im up, she did, an' she flewed wid 'im up onter er daid sycamo' lim', an' dar she des natchelly tored 'im strip fum strip an' den she et 'im. Dat mo' sense den some folks got, speshul w'en hit come ter snakes-in-de-grass."

"Dey do say," said Aunt Em'ly, with a desire to keep the conversation from becoming too personal, "dat ef er pussen— dat am, er lady, ur er gen'mun, ur er chile too—kin kill de fust snake dey see in dey life, dey kyarn't ne'er git huhted by snakes arter dat."

What Granny would have answered will always be a matter of conjecture. She opened her mouth with an air as oracular as that of a pythoness, but the "tum, tum, tum" of a banjo at the door caused her to shut it without giving forth one word.

" Tum, tum, tum," went the banjo, keeping time to a dismal chant with which Uncle John serenaded Aunt Mary, "tum, tum, tum ; tim, tim, tim "—

> "Now hit's once to you
> My lub was true,
> But now-ow I keer nuttin erbout you.
> Foh yo' parrients treated me wid scawn—
> Sech conduc' do delay me !—
> Now I'll come no mo' widin' yo' do'
> Ter tell yo' dat I lub you.
> So I tuhn my back an' scawn erway-ay-a
> No mo' time ter tarry.
> No, nevveh will I ma-a-arry."

" Tum-tim, tum-*tim*."

XVII.

MORE SNAKES.

SNAKE AND OWL.

"E tale o' Aunt Jinny, turr night, 'mine me ob de tale o' Owl an' Bracksnake, and wut dey do o' de aigs," said Big Angy, absent-mindedly reaching for a " filling " of Granny's tobacco instead of replenishing her pipe from the pouch tucked under her girdle.

" Tuhn loose dat tale, do so," cried Aunt Mymee, authoritatively.

Aunt Mymee had just "charmed" a " misery " out of Big Angy's knee, done it for a price that even the unhappy possessor of the " misery " considered reasonable, so it was well to oblige her with a tale that cost nothing.   Angy therefore related this :—

In the old time—not the very oldest, when all things were very friendly—Owl and Blacksnake were not great favourites with the other creatures.   In consequence of this, they were to a great extent dependent on each other for society, and many were the rehearsals of evil gossip they had, as they sat together on a claybank or the low, dry limb of some stunted tree.   They talked much, and always unkindly, of their neighbours.   They were companions, but not friends, for whenever they met, each slily tried to make the other tell

her secrets while withholding her own. They were both
sorceresses of great power and malignity. Truly each was
worthy to be the other's only associate. While they were
plotting and planning together against their acquaintances,
and bringing bad luck to the harmless and unfortunate, they
were also secretly considering how they could do each other
great wrong. Above all things, Blacksnake wished for some
owl-eggs, for next to the hot and quivering brains of a rat
nothing could give more power for conjuring ; but she did not
long for them more ardently than did Owl for a meal of snake-
eggs. Owl was getting old and rheumatic, and had tried the
ointment made of black dog's grease without having her
youthful suppleness and vivacity restored. Only snake-eggs
could make her young and active once more. The two talked
and talked, and paid each other deceitful compliments, and
all the while they were burning and tingling to get at each
other's nests.

One day Owl found her opportunity. Blacksnake had gone
to a great meadow of tall, rough grass to hunt young rats, for
it was the season when many were to be found, if one looked
in the right place. Scarce had she glided away when Owl,
blinking in the dim light (it was a cloudy day, else weak as her
eyes were she could not have been out at all), came searching
about for the coveted " medicine." She soon found the eggs,
tore open their tough envelopes, and ate the " meat " with
great satisfaction. This done, she flew away, saying to herself
as she did so—

" That is a great matter settled for me, and no one can ever
know. Certainly, Blacksnake, if she has any suspicions, will
fasten them on Weasel, or Ferret, or, perhaps, Gopher. Yes,
she is likely to think that Gopher, stirring around where he
was not wanted, destroyed them as readily from a love of
mischief as the others would from the pleasure they have in
sucking eggs."

Two things she had forgotten—to wipe her foot as well as her mouth, and to consider that a fragment of shell can tell a tale better than a whole egg. While she was eating she had spilled a portion of the "egg-meat" and stepped in it. She did not notice that this left a print of her foot beside the rifled nest. The other silent witness was the shell. There were no tooth marks such as Weasel, or Ferret, or Gopher would make on its tough edges. Either accuser was enough, but she flew away without reckoning on even one of them.

When Blacksnake went home she was almost broken-hearted. She could not at first discover any clue to the robber; her suspicions were confused and contradictory. When she became calmer she carefully examined the ground and found Owl's footprint. Then she became very quiet. She coiled herself up under some leaves and meditated on vengeance.

Next day Owl made a call, looking as innocent as she could.

Blacksnake was not at home.

Owl waited a little, but as Blacksnake did not return, she went home when the sun shone out.

The next evening, when her mate relieved her of the care of the nest, she went back.

Still no Blacksnake!

A third and a fourth visit she made, and still Blacksnake did not make her appearance.

Owl did not know whether to be relieved or doubly apprehensive. Either Blacksnake had grieved herself to death or she had gone into some secret place to work spells of divination or cursing. The case called for serious thought. Owl set out for home feeling very serious. As she passed an old hollow tree, on which she and Blacksnake had often held meetings, she heard a faint voice calling her name. The voice sounded from the large limbs, and evidently was Blacksnake's. In another moment the snake's head appeared at a knot-hole.

"Is that you, my cousin?" she called to Owl.

17

Owl feigned great delight at seeing her, and said—
" What can I do for you, dear Blacksnake ?   Truly, I have
feared these last days that you were lost or killed."

" Almost have I died," answered Blacksnake.   "Now, I pray
you, go quickly and summon the snake doctor, for I am still
very ill.   The other day I came up here to get this fine nest
of young woodpeckers, and was taken suddenly ill—too ill,
indeed, to move.   You should have the birds if I could get out
of the way (they are behind me).   Find the snake doctor, and
when he assists me to get away you can get at the birds, which
I will willingly give you for your trouble.   I have lost all taste
for them, my one thought is to get home and see if my eggs
are hatching.   It is now time for that."

Greedy Owl cared nothing for Blacksnake's illness, but she
was anxious to obtain possession of the young woodpeckers.
She was thrown off her guard too by Blacksnake's ignorance
of what had befallen the eggs, she therefore set out with alacrity
for the pond where the old snake doctor lived.

She found it a long way to the pond, but she reached it at
last, told her errand, and, without waiting for the doctor to
bear her company, started back.   When about half way to the
tree, whom should she meet but her husband, flying towards
her in great agitation.

She screamed with fright at sight of him, he with joy at
sight of her.

" What has happened to the nest ? " she shrieked.

" What has brought you to life ? " he cried.

When they came close to each other there was a strange tale
to tell and to be heard.   Blacksnake had gone to Father Owl
and told him his wife was lying almost dead upon the river-
bank, and wished much to see him ere she let her life slip
through her nose.   Poor Father Owl was never a very wise
bird, he was not a sorcerer, he knew none of his wife's tricks,
so, as Blacksnake promised that she would look after the nest,

" SHE SCREAMED WITH FRIGHT AT SIGHT OF HIM, HE WITH JOY AT SIGHT OF HER."

he set out for the river, but having lost his way was nearing the pond instead.

Owl shrieked with fury and dismay. No shovel jammed into the fire could have stopped her voice that night, no matter how many people tried to put the spell of silence on her in that way. Well she knew she should find a ruined nest and no friend Blacksnake watching over it. No, no I she did not expect to see Blacksnake again, but neither did she expect to hear her call from a secret place beneath the desolated home—

" Another time, my wicked enemy, you would better cover up your tracks, unless you wish to prove that what one can do another can do, and the same measure can be used for berries or meal."

" You haven't told us anything about their berries or meal," complained Tow Head.

" Dat am des wut yo' ma' call er allygateh," explained Aunt Mymee.

" Mamma never, in all my life, told me an alligator story ! "

" Oh, yes, honey I oh, yes ! She done tole er tale outen de big Bible an' call um er allygateh."

" Allegory," corrected Tow Head, with fine scorn.

" Hit all de same," said Aunt Mymee, cheerfully, " an' now les go on ter nurr snake tale. Aunt Jinny, tell dat ole laughin' tale 'bout de hoop-snake."

" I done tell dat tale o'er twell hit gittin' plum frazzle (worn) out."

" Le's ha' 'er wunst mo'."

" Ise 'greeble unter dat, ef Miss Boogarry tell dat tale fust dat she tole 'bout nurr owl an' de snake she tuck ter fetch up. Dat tale sorter half in an' half outen my membunce lak er rag in er busted windeh. I boun' ter git um stuff back 'fo' I kin sottle down ter tellin' sumpin."

" He git back, *dat* gwick ! " exclaimed Big Angy, grinning and snapping her fingers.

This is what she put back into Granny's " membunce "—

THE SNAKE-EGG.

There was once a young owl who was very kind. She was the daughter of a witch, and could have been one herself had she wished ; but no matter for that ; there was no harm, no unkindness in her. She was as sweet in her nature as a wood-dove, and always ready to do any one a good turn.

One evening, in the spring, as she was flying around to rest her wings—she had been on the nest all day, and felt cramped —she saw in a place where the earth had been disturbed a very pretty little egg.

" Alas ! " said she, " some cruel creature has destroyed a nest and scattered the eggs around. This one will I take to my nest and hatch with my own eggs. Perhaps some day I may be able to restore it as a nestling to its disconsolate mother."

So saying, she carried home the egg, and in due time hatched it out along with the little owlets. Unfortunately, it proved not to be a pretty little bird, but a tiny wriggling snake. Owl was disappointed and sorry, but was too compassionate to throw it out of the nest. She warmed it against her own bosom ; she fed it as she did her own children ; she cared for it in every way as if it were one of them ; so it throve finely.

When she went off one day to search for food, she had no thought that she would return to an unhappy home ; but so it came to pass. On her return home she found one of the owlets missing. She inquired where he was.

The other owlets did not know. They had been asleep. Only the snake had been awake. He told his foster-mother that he had seen a terrible winged monster swoop down and carry away dear little brother owl.

That night snake could eat no supper, so grieved was he over the loss they had sustained.

The next week the poor owl lost a daughter while she was away from home.

Only the snake saw the little sister carried away by the same monster who had taken off the brother.

Again he grieved so sorely that he could not eat his supper.

The mother-owl, suffering terribly from grief and wishing for his sympathy, drew near to him and laid her claw on him.

Oh, terrible! she felt an owlet's head! In an instant she understood all. She was as quick to act as to understand. She tore the deceitful little snake apart and rescued her daughter. Her son, alas! she never saw again.

Since that time owls have never taken strange eggs to hatch, nor have they allowed them in their nests.

"Now foh dem tarnil hoop-snake."

"We hab mos' nuff snake," said Big Angy, thoughtfully, as she stopped a sneeze by pinching her upper lip till she looked not unlike a crotalus herself. "Dey ain' de bes' o' companie any times, dough dey be dem at t'ink so, but no ter de tase o' me, e'en ef I kin git de craft, de sottlety fum um. Me brer, he wuz turr way. 'E play wid um, tork wid um, hab um in de baid—rattlesnake, coppeh-haid, rasseh-bleu (blue-racer), bracksnake, j'int-snake, glass-snake—de w'ich hab two laig. (All snake hab laig, to-be-sho, but de res' kip um tuck out o' sight.) Den he *ami* wid de hoop-snake, too. Dey don' roll on *'im*, oh, but no! 'E des han' an' glub wid um."

"I ain't de one dat 'sturb 'im in *dat*," said Granny, with emphasis. "Ise seed one o' dem crittehs des wunst, an' so Gord he'p me out! I gwine ter let dat las' me twell de Jedgmint Day."

"Dar yo' is, fa'r stahtid on dat tale we all honin' foh! Des go ri' on now, Aunt Jinny."

"Dat hoop-snake I seen, I seen a-rollin' ercrost de perarer, an' de way *I* putt ercrost dat perarer wuz er sight ter mek er race-hoss tiuhd (tired). I des far (fairly) split de win'! I jump in de do' w'en I git home, and I slam de do' shet, an' I ain't

open um foh lub nur money twell Ole Mistis, she sont some
un out ter look, an' dey fotch in de wuhd dat he done roll by,
an' he done clean gone, an' he ain't nowurs roun'."

"Mebbe," suggested Aunt Mymee, just to be provoking, for
she believed in Granny's tale as firmly as did Granny herself—
"mebbe"—and she gave her eyebrows and chin a comical
twist—"hit wuz one o' dem light coleh (coloured) weeds dat got
er lil root dat break off easy, an' den de win' blow um, hitter
an' yan, 'crost de perarer."

"'Twuzzent no weed!" cried Granny, indignantly. "T"ink
dat one dat hed the 'speunce o' life dat I bin thu, an' dat so
mighty ole inter de bahgain, don't know er blowin' weed fum
er trundlin' snake! Nex', yo' gwine ter say dey ain' no diffunce
'twixt er haid ob er lady ur gemplum an' er punkin wid er
toller-dip eenside."

Aunt Mymee's leer was the very spirit and essence of aggra-
vation.

"Dey ain't so mighty much diffunce, to-be-sho," continued
Granny, breathing hard and sweeping the audience with a
significant look that added point to the thrust—"dey ain't so
mighty much ef all wuz lak some, but, bress de Lawd! dat
ain't de case wid me. W'en I sees weed, I know um weed ;
w'en I sees snake, I know um snake. Dis hyeah de way it
wuz," she continued, with a change of tone : "Ole Mistis, she
done sont me 'crost der fiel' unter Ole Miss Poteetses foh er
settin' o' Polandeh aigs—dem speckle-top-knot kine—dat Miss
Poteet, she promsus Ole Mistis she kin hab des w'ene'er we
git er hen dat show dat she 'sturb in huh mine 'bout settin'.

"Well, den ! I went 'crost de fiel', an' I met up wid Miss
Poteet's Joe, an' ax 'im is Miss Poteet in de house, an' he say
she am ; an' I go 'long an' wait in de kitchen an' sen' in er
gal ter ax 'er kin I see her 'bout Ole Misteses arrint ; an' Miss
Poteet, she sen' wuhd dat I mus' come in de settin'-room, an'
I go in dar whah she a-settin' a-knittin' er sock foh Bobby, an'

I mek er curchy w'en she ax me howdy ; an' den, w'en I ax am
she well an' how am all de chillums, an' say *we* all tollible,
t'ank 'er, *den* I tell dem se'f same wuhds dat Ole Mistis say I
mus' say : dat, ef 'twuzzent ancunvenyuns, will she be dat kine
dat she sen' dat settin' o' speckle-top-knot hen-aigs dat she
done promiss us some time back, kase oweh ole domminickeh
des boun' ter set 'aig ur no aig, but ef 'tain't des ez 'venient ez
nuttin 'tall, why, she mussen' t'ink o' sennin' no aig 'tall.   An'
den, Miss Poteet, she mos' cry, she do, an' she 'low she mighty
sorry, an' she wouldn' a-hed dat happen foh de worl' ; but de
troof an' de fack o' de matteh am dat she gun de las' settin' o'
dem aigs, des de day befo' yestiddy, unter dem folks dat lib up
in de Nish Bottom.   Den, she sorter chuck up, she do, an'
smile an' say she 'membeh now dat she got er half er settin' o'
dem aigs lef', an' ef I kin come back a-Sattiddy—dat · wuz
a-Chuesdy, mine yo'—she kin mek out er settin' foh me ef de
skunks an' de weasels don't git dey bid in de hen-house fust.
Den she gin me de fust ripe martis (tomato) dat I seen dat
yeah, an' I et um wid er lil salt, an' den I tuck out foh home,
an' I went thu de young o'cha'd, an' I sorter skyurtid roun' de
strip o' woods, an' I wuz a-takin' er shawt-cut 'crost de perary.
I wuz gwine 'long, gwine 'long, easy-lak, an' a-gropin' in my
pottit (pocket) foh my pipe.   I knowed dat pipe wuz in dat
pottit, kase I emp de ashes out an' putt hit in dar, des de
las'-mos' t'ing 'fo' I staht out, but I kyarn' fine um right off,
so I grope an' I grope.

   (No wonder it was necessary to " grope an' grope," for
Granny's pocket held almost as large and varied a collection of
useful articles as did that famous bag of " The Swiss Family
Robinson.")

   " I grope, an' I grope, an' I grope, *an'* I grope, kase I feel
lak gittin' er whuff ur two ter sottle dat martis, but tuck up
wid dat pottit ez I wuz, all on de suddint—de Lawd on'y know
de w'y an' de whahfo'—I look ahine me.   I look ovveh **my**

shouldeh, an', bress Peteh ! de bad luck was a-follerin' me, *dat* quick ! I wuz des in de middle ob de perarer, an' de grass wuz high an' all tankle up tergerrer in sorter bunches mos' evvehwhurs, but des whah I wuz, wuz er sorter high roll o' dat perarer, an' up dar wuz sorter dry an' bar', and' des ahine me on de bar' place, des a-comin', wuz dat hoop-snake. I knowed wut 'twuz de minnit I laid eyes on him.[1] Lawd o' mussy ! I reck'n I wuz 'bout ez ole ez de olest libbin', but de way dis niggeh lope out wuz er shame unter er race-hoss ! My ! how I do run ! De knots in de grass ketch me. Nemmine, ain't got no time ter tarry ! Lope on ! De stumps in de new fiel' stump my toe. Nemmine, ain' got no time ter tarry ! Lope on ! De bresh beyant de fiel' scratch at me. Nemmine, ain' got no time ter tarry ! Lope on ! Git out in de big road. De ruts am deep an' rough. Nemmine, ain' got no time ter tarry ! Lope on ! Meet er drove o' hogs. Man holler out, ' Don' scatteh dem hogs ; turn out ! ' Nemmine, ain' got no time ter tarry ! Lope on ! Man holler an' cuss, hit me in de back wid er big clod. Nemmine, ain' got no time ter tarry ! Lope on ! Come ter de bars. Dey ain't let down. Jump de fence. Nemmine, ain' got no time ter tarry ! Lope on ! Dawgs run ter meet me. Stumble o'er pup. Mammy m: d t'ar my dress. Nemmine, ain' got no time ter tarry ! Lope on ! Ole Mistis a-stannin' in de do' o' de Big House, holler at me. Nemmine, ain' got no time ter tarry ! Lope on ! Git in de cabin ! Bang de do' ! Set down on de flo', an', w'en I kin git bref, des holler an' squall lak er sinneh at er camp-meetin'. Mo'n dat, I ain't open dat do' foh coaxin' nur cussin', twell Ole Mistis, she come down an' tork ter me, an' den, w'en she get de eensight o' de marter, she sen' out de boys an' de dawgs ter hunt de critteh, an' den, w'en dey come back an' say hit gone foh shoh, den I open dat do', an' Mistis, she lead me ter de house—she tuck

---

[1] The hoop-snake is poisonous, and very much dreaded. It is believed to make itself into a circle or ring, and roll with great speed.—C. G. L.

me by de han' an' hole me, ur I won' go—an' gimme er big sup o' de currend wine dat she mek wid 'er own han's. Arter dat wine wuhk, den I tell ALL de tale, fum fust ter las'—wut I tole wid de do' shet ain't got de 'ticlers—an' *she* ain't laugh, I boun' yo' !

" My ! dat wuz er ja'nt (jaunt) !

" De nex' day I wuz dat squeaky in de j'ints dat I'd a-bin baid-rid shoh, ef Aunt Mary ain' rub me good wid de grease ob er brack dawg."

" De grease ob er rattlesnake bin betteh," said Aunt Mymee.

" Sholy, sholy, but den I hed de dawg-fat, an' I ain' hed no snake-fat—dat de diffunce."

" Ay-ee.   De fat o' de brack dawg mighty good foh heap o' t'ing."

" So 'tis, Miss Boogarry, so 'tis. Hit kyore de bres'-kimplaint (consumption) ef yo' eat um, an' de misery in de back an' de rheumatiz an' de stiff j'int, an' mek de ole ooman soople ez er gal ef yo' rub um on.   Dat er fack ; I done prube um.   Tur-kumtime (turpentine) ain' nowurs 'longside."

" De w'ite dawg de dawg foh me," announced Aunt' Em'ly.

" Rattlesnake haht de bes' foh bres'-kimplaint," cried Aunt Mymee, finishing the fugue almost with a scream.   " Swaller um libe an' hot, right outen de snake."

" De snake-breens is good ef yo' wanter git strenk in yo' haid foh cunjerin', Ise hyurn tell," added Aunt Mary.

" So's de breens ob er rat, ez we done name afo'. I done seen hit wuhk ! oh, I done seen hit wuhk ! "

The others, awestruck, not so much at her words as her significant expression, made haste to turn the conversation back to its original channel, Big Angy, for a wonder, taking the lead.

"Spik 'bout dem hoop-snake," said she, with a polite wave of her hand towards Aunt Mymee. " Me *young* brer, he hab sontmint (sentiment) at dem snake same ez A'n' Jinny hab, an' he hab de bad time too. Chooh ! Lissin ! A'n' Jinny, he hab de time o' werry dat mek 'im medit (immediately) er ole man, an dat in de parf (part) dat go fum de fur-trader house ter dat lil cabin wur he ooman bin. Helas ! he don 'hab no dawg-fat ter mek 'im young arteh dat. *D'ou vient il ?*—Whah am yo' gedder dat fat, A'n' Jinny ? "

" Hit de fat o' Jody's dawg," replied Granny, candidly. " He wuz er vigrous dawg, yo' mine, an' he ain't ne'er hed no fren 'cep' Jody. W'en de mowehs wuz in de harves' fiel', des back o' dat time I see de hoop-snake, dat ole dawg—an' de name un 'im wuz Lion—he crope up ahine one o' de mowehs an' bit dat moweh in de calf o' de laig, an' dat moweh, he ain't so much ez tek de time ter cuss, he des up an' mow de haid offen dat dawg wid he sife (scythe). Dat's des wut he do, an' sarve ole Lion right too ; but Jody, he wuz ez mad ez er nes' o' yaller-jackits, but he kyarn' he'p hisse'f. Dat dawg *daid*, an' dey ain't no gittin' he haid on ergin. So Jody, he hatter mek up he mine ter dat, an' so he tuck er spade an' dug er sholleh (shallow) grabe an' bury Lion—me an' Mary a-lookin' on, an', suhs, we des hed baig an' 'pled foh de fat o' dat dawg, an' Jody, he 'low he des ez soon gin us de fat o' he daddy, pre-zackry, wid dat arnser we boun' ter be sati'fy, but suhs, *dat dawg ain' res' easy in he grabe.*"

Granny ceased her narration, and laughed long and silently. The rest of the company smiled knowingly.

" G'long, Aunt Jinny."

" Aunt Mary an' me, we putt in de mos';o' de night arter dat funil (funeral) a-tryin' out brack-dawg grease in dat lil kittle we mos'ly biles greens in. Lor ! lor ! I wusht I'd a-seed yo' brer dat time, I'd a-gin 'im dawg-grease, an' weckom."

" He sho need'n' um vaire bad," said Madame Bougerau, shaking her head, " vaire bad. Dat time he see no one hoop-snake, wid tail in mout,' rollin', rollin', wid spahks flyin.' 'E see hunnet, mille-ye (hundreds, thousands) ! "

" He wuzzent drunk, wuz 'e ? " questioned Aunt Mymee, cautiously.

" Ah I but no. Hit happen dat wunst dat 'e staht home
vaire straight. 'E 'ab been at de stow (store) an' 'e git de grey
jug fill an' staht back vaire sobre. He tek lil tasse wid fren,
to-be-sho, but drunk lak pig—not 'tall ! "

(Oh, Big Angy, how impossible to reproduce that dialect of
thine !)

He set out to ride that small three miles between store and
cabin, on a little pony, and thought nothing of it. He started,
he went one mile, perhaps, and then getting in a hurry to
reach the supper he knew his wife would have ready, he left
the " big road " and took a short-cut (path) that led across the
Sauk Prairie. All went well for one mile, then the pony
jumped sidewise and threw the brother off, then he gave a
snort and away he ran. The dismounted rider was very, very
much surprised. He had not supposed the horse lived that
could throw him. He looked this side, he looked that side, he
scarce could believe his senses. Chut I a little pony to play
him a trick like that ! Well ! he must make the best of it
and walk home. Never mind I a mile is nothing of a distance
to walk, but to be thrown !—and by a little pony, at that !
Ptt I He takes a few steps, then suddenly he understands the
case. He runs like the pony, only, if there is a difference,
faster. He has found himself at a snake-dance, sure enough !
Millions of snakes—hoop-snakes I They roll this way, they roll
that way. The poor brother runs here, runs there, trying to
get away. They head him off, they try to roll on him. He
dodges, he darts about trying to get out of such company and
reach home. Indeed, he runs like the deer themselves, but the
snakes keep all that from counting for anything. They keep
this up till the sun goes down, they keep it up in the dark,
and oh ! the sparks that fly from their wicked eyes make light
enough to see the poor man they are tormenting. They keep
up this torment till the moon comes up, they keep it up, this
torment, till the moon goes down. They keep it up till day-

break. Then, when the poor man is nearly dead and they think he will soon be theirs, a sudden thought comes to him to say an *Ave.* He says it and a *Pater Noster,* he squats and spits. Then he recalls these words of the seed of the woman. He says them. At one and another of those good spells the snakes get frightened. They roll away and he sees them no more. He tries to say one more " Hail Mary," but the words stick and he falls like a dead man. The people find him like that in the middle of the day, when the children go home from the berry-patch and say they have seen a dead man. When the men and women go to him, they rouse him. His children are with the others. To them he tells this tale, all the rest hearing. Then he goes home.

" Did he leabe de jug ? " asked Aunt Mymee, with deep interest.

" No, ma mie, 'e tek 'im home, but lil use, kase w'en try tek de sup, dat jug git nuttin in hit."

" Dat wut I s'pishin," said Aunt Mymee, in almost too cordial acquiescence.

" He ain' drink um," cried Big Angy, angrily. " Fum de time 'e fall fum de pony he got no chance. Kin 'e drink wid dem snake arter 'im ? No ! de cawn-cob jam in de jug foh cawk all de time."

" Dar yit, w'en 'e git hit home emp'y ? "

" Suttin. De snakes mus' a-cunjeh de *eau-de-vie* out m'dout pull out de cob."

" Cose dey did," said Granny, soothingly. " I kinceit (fancied) dat fum de staht. . My ! my ! my ! dat wuz er speunce ! "

" Troof dat ! " assented Big Angy, subsiding into complacency.

" I gotter snake tale dat I hyeah 'way down in Tennessee," burst in Aunt Mary, very unexpectedly.

" Den ef yo' got de tail, dror um 'long twell we see de haid," chuckled Aunt Em'ly, proud of her joke.

"Hit tail an' haid too, an' er mighty quare (queer) weed inter de bahgin."

Aunt Mymee was on the alert.

"Fetch on dat tale, honey, dis minnit! I gotter go ter de House putty soon."

"Dey wuz mo'n one snake, an' my mammy say, w'en she tell hit, 'Hyeah de tale o' De Snakes an' de Quare Weed,' an' den she go 'long lak dis—

"Wunst, in de ole times, dey wuz er man a-gwine 'long de road, des at sundown. Hit wuz harves'-time an' he hab he sife (scythe) in he han'. 'Long he come, a-whustlin' an' a-honin' foh he suppeh, w'en he see de putties' lil snake dat evveh wuz a-layin' dar in de road."

"Wut kine o' snake, Aunt Mary?"

"Mebbe 'twuz er glass-snake, glass-snake mighty putty. Shuh! wut I a-sayin'? Hit wuz longeh nur er glass-snake. Hit wuz dis long, my mammy say," said Aunt Mary, measuring about twenty inches on her arm.

"Mebbe 'twuz er strawberry-snake, dey mighty putty *foh* er snake, wid dey red streaks an' speckles."

"Yuh! Wut yo' reckin er strawberry-snake a-doin' in de road? Dey hides in de strawberry-leabes, dey does."

"Green vipeh, mebbe."

"'Twuzzen' no green vipeh," declared Aunt Mary, beginning to grow impatient. "'Twuzzent no green vipeh wid hit jaws puff out lak er gopheh's. Hit wuz er putty snake, wid er w'ite belly an' er speckle back lak er trout, *dat* de kine o' snake hit wuz. Dar now! Lemme 'lone twell I get thu wid de tale I gwine ter tell."

"Aw ri', Aunt Mary, des rack on twell yo' git ter de eend o' yo' road. Now we git de queschin o' de faveh (favour—appearance) o' dat snake sottle, *I* ain' de one that gwine ter th'ow nuttin in yo' way. Des rack on, rack on," said Granny, poetically.

" Dat's mannehs, sho," said Aunt Mary, still somewhat ruffled. " Howsomedevveh, I ain' de one ter kimplain, dough I mos' fegit whah I git ter, I bin haul up so shawt free ur fo' times. Oh, yes ! De man, he wuz gwine 'long de road an' he see dat snake an' he ain' keer ef dat snake putty er not. He des tek dat sife an' he mek er lunge an' he cut dat snake in two. Hit wuz des at sundown he cut dat snake in two, so, in co'se, hit die right off."

" In co'se. All de 'varsil worl' know dat no snake kin die w'iles de sun up, nemmine ef yo' cut um in hunnert pieces."

" In co'se, but den '*twuz* sundown an' de snake, hit die an' de man, he mighty glad, kase he des hate snakes lak rank pizon. He kill de snake an' he noduss hit daid an' den he go 'long. Bimeby he look back an' he noduss nurr snake des lak de fust, a-crawlin' fum out de weeds in de fence-corndeh. He sorter tuhn back w'en he see dat, an' he say—

" ' Good nuff ! I gwine ter hab two snakes cl'ar offen de face ob de yeath stiddier one. Dis wut I calls good luck.'

" Wid dat sayin', he mek at un, but de libe snake ack so quare, he boun' ter stop an' see wut hit up ter. Hit wuz a-kyarin' er big piece o' green weed in's mouf. Hit wuz er branchin' piece o' weed, so I hyurn tell, dat de snake wuz a-kyarin' in he mouf, wid er heap o' leabes onter hit. Dat suttinly do look mighty, mighty quare, so de man, he wanter see wut dat snake gwine ter do wid dat big branchin' weed, so he step ri' dar in de road an' keep de eye on dat snake. Den wut happun, ye reckin ? "

" Dellaws ! Aunt Mary, wut ? "

" De snake dat kyarin' de weed, hit ain' noduss de man 'tall, hit des crawl, crawl, crawl, twell hit git whah de pieces o' de turr snake am. Hit crawl right up 'longside de tail-piece an' hit sorter gin um er nudge, den it crawl up ter de haid-piece an' gin hit er nudge, an' dat sorter fetch dem two pieces a-jindin (ioining). Den, beholes yo' I hit sorter bresh dat weed crost de

pieces an'—whoop !—dat snake des ez gay an' libely ez deday hit
git outen de aig. Dat done, de two un um slip ri' quick in de
weeds an' de man ain' see um no mo'. Wut he do see am de
weed dey lef' ahine um. He pick dat up an' he look an' he
look. Hit ain' lak no weed dat he bin use ter see a-growin'
roun' in de pasters an' corndehs. Hit er green branchin' weed,
he say, an' hit smell sumpin lak tansy an' sumpin lak ' ole man '
(Southern-wood—*Artemisia abrotanum*), but 'tain't tansy an'
'taint ole man."

" Snake-weed, I boun' yo'."

" Nuh. 'Tain' no snake-weed ne-er. 'Tain' de kine o' weed
dat button snake-weed am. Kase w'y, snake-weed, she grow up
slim, on de perarer, des 'bout so tall "—measuring about two
feet from the floor with her hand—" an' snake-weed, she grow
straight an' she ain't branch an' she got de buttons at de j'ints,
she got de putty lil bloom 'bout de purple coleh ob de iun-weed,
but dis hyeah turr weed wuz mos' 'ticlerly er bunch weed an'
er branchin' weed. Wut de name dat weed ? W'en yo' ax
me, yo' got me dar, I own dat up pintedly. De man, he
kyarn't call um no name, nur no turr man kyarn' in de worl'.
De man dat seen all dat done, he tuck dat weed, he do, an' he
staht 'long todes home, kase now hit a-gittin' late. Ez he go
'long, he look an' he look at dat weed an' he tuhn um roun'
an' he smell um—mebbe he tase um, I dunno, kase I ain' hyeah
tell—an' he mirate how dat weed kin ack so mighty cu'i's.
Hit look so simple but hit ack cu'i's, sholy. Ez he go 'long, go
'long, in er sorter trottin' step, an' miratin' ez he go, all on de
suddint er toad hop out. De man, he wuz a-studyin', an' dat
toad, hit s'prise 'im an' mek 'im jump, an' oh, my lan' ! he got
de sife-blade roun' he neck, so he kin hole de weed an' look,
an' he sorter stummle, an' dat sife-blade, hit de mos' cut de
neck un 'im cl'ar in two. Dat mought a-bin de eend o' 'im,
but de good luck hab hit dat ez he fell he putt up de han' wid
de weed in hit at de place whah de sife-blade cut thu."

Aunt Mary stopped as if the story were ended.

" Den wut ? " asked an auditor, impatiently.

" Dat marter sottle mighty quick. De man fall down, daid, an' git right up, well. De weed done dat good wuhk an' 'twould a-bin so he couldn' mek out but dat he dremp hit, ef 'twuzzen' foh de blood on he shuht-colleh. Yessir l dis er true tale ez Ise er libbin critteh, kase menny an' menny's de time mammy, she go an' he'p de man hunt foh dat weed."

" Kyarn' dey fine none ? "

" Nuh, nurr smidgin (not a bit). He putt in all he spar' time a huntin' dat weed, fum dat time fo'th' but he ain' ne'er foun' none. He los' dat piece he hab, wut's wuss."

" Huccome dat ? "

" Los' um w'en he fell down daid. Den 'twuz dahk an' de road mighty dusty. He hunt turr'ble but de dahk done come on an' he don't fine um. In de mawnin' he go hunt 'gin an' he mos' 'stractid, but dat don' he'p out, kase he ain't see hide nur ha'r o' dat weed ter he dyin' day."

Big Angy was the first to announce her approval of Aunt Mary's story, and, after the others had enthusiastically echoed her compliments, she went on to say that it reminded her of that old tale, which everybody knew, of the daughter of Old Grandaddy Rattlesnake, who was changed into snake-weed by her angry brother. Being importuned by Tow Head for particulars, she stated, concisely, that once, in the very earliest times, Old Grandfather Rattlesnake was going away somewhere, she really did not know where, and he left his son and daughter in charge of the world. Now, the son was very malicious and bad-tempered, and he charmed men and beasts and made them come close to him, when he at once bit them and infused enough poison into their veins to kill them.

" Hole on l hole on l " cried Aunt Mymee, " dat ain't de son, dat Ole Grandaddy he own se'f yo' a-tellin' on."

" *No.*"

" Yessir ! dat de way de snake-darnce come, darncin' roun' de Ole Gran'daddy ter git strenk 'dout (without) pizon."

Big Angy inexorably proceeded with her version of the story. The world would soon have been without anything in it but rattlesnakes, had not the daughter of Gran'daddy been of a very different nature. She was as kind as he was cruel, and imme- diately healed all those whom he had poisoned. This went on for a long time, the son biting, the daughter curing. At last he discovered why his efforts to rid the world of those whom he hated were unavailing. When he found that his sister was foiling him, he fell into a great rage and said a mighty charm which changed her into a plant, and so she remains to this day, and people call her and her children " snake-weeds." Fortu- nately, her healing properties still belong to her and her descendants. If you are bitten by the most venomous of reptiles, and at once drink a tea made of snake-weed and rain- water, and at the same time bind on the wound a poultice of snake-weed and milk, you will soon recover from the bite.

" Mighty quare how crittehs kin change eroun ! "

" Quare how dey git merried an' raise up quare chilluns, too," said Granny. " Dar am dem snakes 'way down Souf, whah I wuz wunst, wid wings. Dem snakes de chilluns ob sho nuff snake an' snake docteh."

" Dar now ! dat news ter me," said Aunt Em'ly.

" Torkin' 'bout dat toad dat hop in de road an' mek de man kill hisse'f, 'mine me o' dat ruckshin [1] Old Rattlesnake mek at Miss Toad's pahty," said Aunt Mymee.

" Toad gin er pahty ? Shuh ! dat do beat all. Gin us dat tale right now, Aunt Mymee."

" Ole Miss Toad, she bin a-layin' off ter gin er pahty e'er sence cawn-plantin', but de mo' she projeck on hit de mo' sumpin happun dat she kyarn' gin none. Fust, de baby choke hisse'f wid er hoss-fly dat wen' down de wrong way, den 'er ole

---

[1] Riot insurrection. Irish, *ruction.*

man git tromple on by er cow w'en he go out in de medder foh
ketch er mess o' young hoppehgrasses foh suppeh, den lil boy
kyar off de oles' gal in he pottit an' keep 'er dar er week ur mo',
an' all de res' o' de fambly a-ginnin' 'er up foh daid an' mos'
feerd she er hant (ghost) w'en she git back, den one t'ing come
up, den nurr, twell 'twuz mos' time foh w'ite fros'. Den Ole Miss
Toad, she noduss cole weddeh a-comin' on fas' an' she des r'ar
an' pitch an' she 'low she gwine ter gin dat pahty ef de whole
fambly up an' die de day bee-fo' ; she done sot huh foot down
on dat, she tell um all, an' dat sottle hit. So den ! she gun hit,
an' I boun' dat satify huh foh some time, an' dis hyeah am de
w'ys an' de whahfohs :—she git out de eenvites airly in de week,
but de time bin sot foh Sat'd'y in de ebenin'. She ax all huh
kinfolks an' 'lations an' all *dey* kinfolks an' 'lations, she ax all
de neighbehs an' *dey* neighbehs, she ax hyeah an' she ax dar,
but she ain't ax Ole Gran'daddy Rattlesnake. Deah suhs, but
he wuz mad !

"'Oh, yes ! ' sez Old Daddy, sez 'e, 'I reckin Ole Daddy am
heap too ole foh gwine out ter git some o' dis hyeah lil snack
dat Miss Toad a-aimin' ter fix up ter stay de stummicks o' de
folks twell dey kin git back home an' eat dey regler suppeh,'
sez 'e.

" (Miss Toad, she suttingly wuzzent er mighty fine provideh.)

"' Uh huh ! co'se Ole Gran'daddy too ole,' sez 'e, ' but, all de
same, I lay he gwine ter hab he own 'musemint outen dat
pahty an' he gwine ter git er big suppeh outen dat pahty too.
De res' un um kin eat de snack,' sez 'e, ' an ' den Ole Daddy
kin go roun' by de back do' an' lick up de crum's,' sez 'e, a-
lookin' lak he knowed sumpin cu'i's, ' an' w'en he thu nobody
gwine ter 'spute dat he got mo' in he braid-bastet den dem dat
got dar foh de fust table,' sez 'e.

" So hit tuhn out, zacry, too. Dem wut got de eenvites
slick deyse'f up de bes' dey kin an' git ter de pahty yarly ez dey
'low dey spectid, an', arter dey hang roun' de do' an' peek an'

dror back er time ur two, dey mek out ter git in, an' den dey laff an' dey giggle an' dey tork an' dey chat an', bimeby, de gayes' o' de young uns git ter darncin' an' a-playin' games wid walk-erouns inter um. Oh, 'twuz er sassy crowd I Nemmine, dough I nemmine I some un um a-doin' dey las' hoppin' eroun' an' hit wuz dishaways hit tuhn out dataways—Ole Gran'daddy Rattlesnake, he keep dat 'p'intmint dat he mek wid hisse'f, an' w'en dey done et up de suppeh an' drink up de bug-juice (whiskey) an' feel mo' pearteh den dey done yit, den *he* come. He come des lak he say he gwine ter, roun' by de back do', an' he creep an' he cr-r-r-eep, an' he go thu de back do' an', he come pun de trundle-baid whah de chilluns bin putt ter baid soster git um outen de way. He stop dar, but he ain't stir up dem chilluns an' say ' howdy,' he don't say nuttin, he des retch out he mouf an' he tek um inter hit. Fus' one, den turr, he tek um. He gin one gulf, dat one gone I gin nurr gulf, nurr gone ! an' he bat de eye an' he grin dry, an' so he keep dat up twell Miss Toad, she outen all dat big fambly ain't got nair one chile an' she don't know hit yit, but she gwine ter, oh, she gwine ter I

"De nex' off ob dat Ole Gran'daddy wuz ter creep an' cr-r-r-eep inter de settin'-room whah de ole folks wuz a-settin' roun' an' a-swappin' dey ijees. He mek out ter gulf one un um, but de res', dey holler an' run, an' dey ain't got no time ter gin wa'nin' (warning) unter de young folks in de parlo', dey mek de scattimint so fas'. De young folks, dey a-hoppin' an' a-darncin' an' a-cuttin' up so gaily dat dey don't hyeah nuttin but dey own racket. Dat bein' de case, he creep an' he cr-r-r-eep in mungs um, a-keepin' closte ter de shaddehs an' he mek out ter git 'bout fawty-leb'n gulf down 'fo' de res' noduss an' cl'ar out. W'en dey *do* noduss, dat de finishmint o' dat pahty. De folks, dey putt an' run bedoubt dey hats an' bunnits an' nobody ain't mine dey mannehs ter say ' ebenin', Miss Toad.' Dey run, dey did, but des 'bout half o' dem dat hed de eenvites wuz et up,

an' hit mos' sholy wuz de case ez he say hit gwine ter be, dat
Gran'daddy hab de bigges' suppeh dat wuz et in de settlemint
dat night. Yessir I an' dat w'y Miss Toad, she done gin up
pahty-ginnin."

"Me nuttin 'stonish in dat," said Big Angy. "Gran'dad, he
de one dat mek all 'fraid, nah but wut 'e git he come-uppunce
awso. He mos' time git ahaid, but, chut I de bigges' hog in de
poke git ter de sassidge-choppeh one day. Dataway Grandad,
he too much chilluns—mo' speshul de gran'darter hat (that)
wuz er owl."

"Shuh I shuh I shuh I—dey's allus sumpin ter larn. Dat's
de fust I hyeah tell dat he got chilluns dat ain't snakes."

Big Angy sniffed a little at the ignorance of her audience,
and then proceeded to enlighten it by telling the story of—

THE SNIPE.

In the old times there were no snipe among the other birds.
Afterwards they were plentiful, and one has only to listen in
order to find out that it all came about through the agency of
an owl who was taught magic by her grandfather, old Rattlesnake. This owl was a very great witch, greater in magic than
her wizard husband, who was also an owl. So much wiser was
she that she hated him for his silliness, and he, in turn, hated
her because her tricks made him suffer. Each sought an
opportunity to kill the other. As one would expect, she
succeeded. One night her evil charm worked and killed him.
In a very secret place between hills she buried him under
a stone. The stone she fastened down with a spell, lest some
one should let his ghost out to worry her. She need not have
gone to this trouble. No one took notice of his death or cared
that he was no more seen. After awhile she cared, for she
found herself very lonely. All shunned her ; even her grandfather, Rattlesnake, did not care for her society, and took not

the same notice of her that he did of his other grandchildren. Soon, therefore, she began to say—

" A bad husband is better than no husband at all."

So lonely did she become, that if her magic had been strong enough to lift the stone and bring her husband back to life, she would gladly have used it, but, alas ! it was *not* strong enough, so she looked about her for another mate.   She looked every-where, but no one would have her, which, indeed, was quite right ; if husbands had come to her easily, no doubt she would have had many, and killed them as soon as she found they had faults.

When she had made many efforts and failed in them all, she retired to a quiet place to think.   This is what she resolved on at the end of her meditation :—

" I will watch my chance and get me a very young husband.   I will train him in my ways, and we shall both be very well content."

So she watched her opportunity, but for a long time caught no young husband.   All the parents

" THIS OWL WAS A VERY GREAT WITCH."

were watching her, that was the reason of her failure.   She perceived this, and promised Hawk a strong medicine if he would harry the parents when they took the young birds out to teach them how to fly.   She knew that if some one created confusion at this time she could fly off with a husband at once.

Hawk did as she paid him to do, but she did not catch a husband flying.   She saw a fine young quail hide under a leaf while his mother looked out for Hawk.

She took the little creature home.   He was very small, a baby only.   She pulled his legs till they were very long, longer than his father's, longer than any quail's that ever was seen.   She also pulled his bill till it was very long, longer than his father's, longer than any quail's that ever was seen. This strange deed she did so that if his mother should meet him anywhere she would not know him. Poor fellow ! he looked large enough to be the husband of any witch, but he was only a very young quail, as foolish as any other baby, but still he had sense enough to remember his mother, his poor mother who grieved for him night and day. To be sure, she often saw him, and if she

"SHE PULLED HIS BILL TILL IT WAS LONG."

had talked with him might have recognised him by his voice, but she never suspected that the long-legged bird was any relation of hers, so she passed him by in silence. As for him, he was young and heedless, and did not see her at all. If he had he would have spoken.

Once, some of the mother's friends heard the witch talking to the young husband, and heard him reply. Immediately they went to the mother, and told her that surely the new bird with the long legs and bill was her son. She refused to believe it. They insisted it must be so, that he, doubtless, was enchanted—an easy matter for a witch to accomplish.

Still incredulous, she started on a round of calls for the purpose of asking other acquaintances for their opinions.

She asked Mole.

Mole said—

"I cannot see, but undoubtedly the bird has a voice like your son's."

She asked Rattlesnake.

He said a little of this and a little of that, and, after all, his words meant nothing at all.

She asked Prairie-Dog.

Prairie-Dog pitied her, and said—

"Yes, my cousin, that is your son. The witch has pulled him into that shape so that you may not know him. He makes her a pleasant husband."

"Husband of a witch my son shall not be ! "

"How can you help it, cousin ? "

"That you must tell me. You are shrewd and kind-hearted. For the sake of a poor mother can you not coax him into your dug-out as he goes by, and keep him there until I come ? "

"No, no, cousin. The witch, his wife, is always along when he walks about."

"Then what shall I do ? "

"Do not fret, cousin, that will not help."

"You must help. Your head is stronger than mine."

"My advice is, steal him while the witch is asleep."

"When does a witch sleep ? "

"Soundest at sunrise. Now go. Get ready to steal him in the morning."

She did as he advised. She went to the cave where the witch slept, and stole him and hid him in a slough.

When the witch found he was gone, she made a great ado, but could not come at him for the water of the slough, so she asked Gran'daddy Rattlesnake to help her.

He did not care for her, but he wished no one to thwart a member of his family, so he started to drink the slough dry. When he was half through, he found that the water, which was very dirty and dead, was making him sick. He said a charm, and kept on drinking. By and by he was so awfully sick that he vomited himself out of his skin, and had to go off and hide till a new one grew.

Since that he has always hated his owl relations, and has shed his skin once a year.

As for Quail, he stayed in the slough till he was old enough to take proper care of himself; then his mother brought him out, but his brothers and sisters made so much sport of his shape, which no art could free from the witch's enchantment, that he went back to the slough, and can seldom be coaxed out. How he and his children lost the name of Quail and took that of Snipe no one knows ; but no matter for that, the weight of a name breaks no one's back.

"Lor! lor! lor! dat tek de rag offen de bush," cried Granny, admiringly. "I gin up on de snake queschin fum dis out. Ef I git axt ef I know er snake tale I gwine ter tell um no."

"Me too," said Aunt Emily.

"Hit knock de socks offen *my* tale," added Aunt Mary.

What could Big Angy do but tell another story ?

"Yo' all hyeah 'bout de cow-suckin' snake ? "

"Dem ez mek de cows gib bloody milk ?—Sholy. I ain' des seen um, but I seen de bloody milk, menny's de time."

"De milk prube de suckin'," said Granny.

"Ow-ee, hit do. Ef yo' kin hunnerstan' buhd-tork, dough, Buntin' gin yo' wa'nin' (warning) 'bout de snake."

"Dar now, Miss Boogarry, dat news unter me."

Big Angy was glad to hear so eminent a scholar in the lore

of the fields as Granny acknowledge this, so she at once related all she knew about—

THE COW-SUCKERS AND BUNTING.

There was once a poor old woman who had nothing in the world but the cabin in which she lived and three nice cows, the sale of whose butter and milk provided her with such necessaries as she had to buy from the cross-roads store. Every day she drove her three friends—the only friends she had, truly—from the clearing where the cabin stood, along the narrow path that was broken through the underbush so crowded by the selfish tall trees. Through the forest with the brush scrambling and tangling about it, she drove her cows to the open prairie where the sweet, rich grass grew thick and tall. There, in the middle of the prairie, very near the little lake and its tributary stream, she left them until sundown. Then she went to the edge of the wood and called them home.

Usually they went gladly, not running like pigs, to be sure, called from the mast of the oak-forest to a supper of corn, but going with a quiet, steady step that allowed time to gather a sweet mouthful of leaves, now from this side, now from that, as they advanced along the path. When they reached the cabin door, they stood calmly and cheerfully to be milked ; not switching the flies too hard, lest they strike their mistress or the little cow-buntings who were often so intent on picking off flies and ticks that they rode quite home on the backs of the amiable animals. This was pleasant for all, but, alas ! there came a time when all the pleasantness was ended. The cows became morose and unfriendly. The old woman sighed and wept.

" Helas ! " said she, " I am afraid I shall freeze to death this coming winter. How can I knit stockings and petticoats for myself if I have no yarn ? How can I have yarn if I have no

milk and butter to sell ? Too bad, too bad ! My food I could
get very well with plenty of birds and rabbits to trap, and
plenty of dead wood to be picked up when one wished to boil
a pot, but how can I manage about yarn ? Too bad, too bad !
just as butter has gone up to five cents a pound, and milk to
five cents a gallon, too. Oh ! I could soon have all the yarn
I should need for years if those cows of mine were not in such
bad plight. Their milk has been too bloody to use these ten
days past, and it gets no better. How this has happened I
cannot tell. I have been very careful not to kill any field
crickets, and only crickets have power to avenge themselves by
sending bloody milk—excepting, of course, the witches. Truly,
a witch must be abroad, but who can it be ? "

She never thought to inquire of the cows what was wrong.
This was a mistake. If she had asked them privately, when they
were at home, what had gone amiss, they would have told her.

Day after day she drove them to pasture. Night after night
they came home drooping and sad. She saw this, she saw also
that they were glad to come home and unwilling to be driven
forth, but she did not reflect as to what might be the cause.
No wonder she was always poor. A woman who does not put
this and that together until she knows all about a business will
never thrive, no matter how hard-working and saving she may
be.

(If your eyes are good for something besides seeing flies in
the milk [1] and knots in the yarn, thank the good God, and if
you can piece out something besides calico, thank Him twice !)

At last, the cows' friend, Bunting, could stand the trouble
in silence no longer. He flew back from the pasture one
morning, and spoke softly to the woman, saying that he had
it on his mind to tell her a secret the cows dared not speak of.

" To the point at once, then, that is my way," said the
woman. " I never beat around the bush."

[1] " Je cognoys bien mouches en laict."—*François Villon.*

"Here is the news, then, my mother," said he, "there is a family of snakes down by the stream that runs into the lake, and these snakes are sucking the milk of the poor cows, and filling their bodies with torment."

The woman screamed piercingly. She had heard before of snakes treating cows like this, but she had put so little faith in the one who told her that the whole story had gone out of her mind.

"Is it the terrible joint-snake who is doing this thing?" she cried. "He is ready for any evil deed, and so very hard to kill, inasmuch as he grows together again as fast as you can cut him apart."

"Not so bad as that, my mother. The mischief-workers are blacksnakes. They are the real cow-suckers. The cows, poor things! run and run till they almost run themselves to death, trying to shake off these villains who rise up out of the grass and snap hold of the teats. Helas! they cannot shake them off. Do you go rescue them, else will they soon go dry and for ever remain so."

When he had finished this warning Bunting flew away.

The woman took in her hand a spade with a long handle, and, saying a charm as she went, set forth to seek the cows.

She soon found them, and it was a bad sight to see the poor things, each with four snakes clinging to her. The first she reached was red cow, and the woman struck the four from her with the spade and said the charm, and they lay wriggling on the ground unable to rise and choke her in their folds, as is the way of blacksnakes. The charm said over and over made them helpless ; no wonder they were easily killed.

Then the woman went on a little way, with the red cow following and looking less sad.

She came up to white cow. She struck the snakes and said the charm. The snakes fell wriggling to the ground, and she killed them and went on with the red cow and the white cow following.

Soon she came up to black cow. She struck the snakes and said the charm. The snakes fell wriggling to the ground, and she killed them, and went home with the red cow and the white cow and the black cow following.

Next day the woman took them to a new pasture, a long way from that unlucky place where they had been ; she took them to a fine place where rushes, calamus, and sweet-pea grew as thickly as the grass, and that was the end of the trouble, for she taught the cows the charm that conquers snakes, as they went along together. It was that old charm : " The seed of the woman shall bruise the serpent's head," that she taught them.

She should have done this long before, but then she was not very smart.

After the cows had learned the charm by heart, she asked them—

" Why did you not tell me what was troubling you ? Is not your trouble my trouble always ? "

The cows said—

" True enough, all that, but some things we are not permitted to tell you hoofless creatures unless you ask."

Aunt Em'ly roused from a reverie. Evidently she had not heard the woes of the cows.

" De way I hyeah dat tale o' Owl wuz diffunt," she said. " De way I hyeah hit, Owl, she *do* hab heap o' young hubsums (husbands) an', w'en she git outdone wid um, she kilt um in dey sleep an' tuck out dey hahts and sucked up de strenk ob um. Dat kip up too, twell she kill Rain Crow w'ich wuz de kinfolks o' de big T'undeh-Buhd dat lib in de mountins 'way out yondeh at de eend o' de perarer. De willer tree see Rain Crow kilt, an' seen 'im flung in the crik mungs de big flags too, arter he haht wuz out. De flags wuz w'ite, but dat cole kyarkiss mek um

so cole dey tuhn blue an' dey tell hit ter de willer tree dat see
de trouble. De willer tree tell de maple dat hit sholy wuz er
buhnin' shame dat de flag git sarve dataway, an' de maple tell
de cotton-wood, an' de cotton-wood tell de plum tree, an' de
plum tree tell de warnit, an' de warnit tell de hick'ry. De
hick'ry ain't 'feard o' nuttin, an' 'buse dat witch out an' out,
an' holler 'crost de woods ter de ellums ter tell de oaks ter tell
de pines ter tell de whole meanness ter Ole T'undeh-Buhd
hisse'f. Dataway de trees all tek up foh Rain Crow. My!
T'undeh-Buhd (Thunder-Bird—Eagle) wuz mad an' up an'
a-gittin', but he ain't git up fas' nuff. Er lil traipsin', wuthless
puff-ball, a-rollin' hyeah an dar, hyeah all de ruckshin an' tole
Miss Owl an' she des putt foh huh gran'daddy, Ole Rattlesnake.

"Ole Rattlesnake, he tuck an' hid 'er in he den, an' Ole
T'undeh-Buhd an' he chilluns, dey hunt an' dey hunt, 'fo' dey
fine 'er. At de las' dey mek out whah she a-scrouchin', an' dey
say—

"'Bust open, den!' an' de den bust open, but, lo an' beholes!
dey ain't ketch 'er yit. She seen um a-comin' an' flewed down
Ole Grandaddy Rattlesnake's thote.

"Dat dis'pint de T'undeh-Buhds mighty bad an' e-er sence
dey 'spise de snakes. Dey hatter go home bedout killin' Owl,
mo' am de scannel (scandal), but nemmine! Rattlesnake git he
pay. Owl, she flusteh roun' twell Rattlesnake, he git dat sick
dat he fling 'er up an' fling he own hide off inter de bahgin
(bargain), an' he dat mad he go hide, an' good nuff foh de
vilyun! he kep dat up wunst er yeah e-er sence."

Aunt Mymee jumped up with a yawn that threatened to
rend her countenance in twain.

"I 'low I hyeah snake tale nuff ter las' me de res' o' my
bawnded days," shè said. "I reck'n I betteh git 'long up ter
de House."

Nobody interposing any objections, she went. As she disappeared, the other aunties heard her singing, or rather growling, this uncanny song—

" De Debbil, he spit an' he spit out snakes.
　　　　Snakes, snakes.
De wood-choppeh chop an' he chop out snakes.
　　　　Snakes, snakes.
He hitch up de cattle an' he snake out logs.
　　　　Snakes, snakes.
De wood-choppeh drink an' he drink up snakes.
　　　　Snakes, snakes.
De Debbil git he kyarkiss, de Debbil git he soul.
　　　　Snakes, snakes."

XVIII.

"JACKY-ME-LANTUHNS" SOMETIMES CALLED "WUL-LER-WUPS"—ALSO "PAINTERS" AND THEIR VICTIMS.

Big Angy and Aunt Em'ly arrived at the cabin door together. Both were agitated and both were anxious to conceal the fact. They laughed a great deal and talked so rapidly that Granny told them candidly that they were "kyarin' on lak er half-sled

THE JACKY-ME-LANTUHNS.

in er snow-stawm." This uncomplimentary remark moved them to explain that they "plum fegittit dat twuz too cole ter onbine dem wuller-wups, an', in consequence, each had mistaken the other's lantern for that dreaded emissary of the Devil's wife. They had flung themselves down on the snow and

272

stopped their ears and waited thus until they were almost frozen. Finally, they had courage to look up, then, as they saw that the lanterns had gone out, they spoke. In another instant they were on their feet, the lanterns were relighted, and they finished the walk across the fields together.

"Ise er big fool not ter t'ink 'bout de crittehs bein' hilt fas' by de cole," said Aunt Em'ly, with another foolish laugh, "but, Gord know, I des ez liefs meet up wid er painter (panther) ez er jacky-me-lantuhn (jack-o'-lantern), dat's de natchel troof."

"Hit come ter de same t'ing, honey," said Granny, with her most oracular air. "Ef yo' meet de painter yo' git et up ; ef yo' meet de jacky-me-lantuhn—an' hit's de se'f-same beastis ez de wuller-wups—yo' git drownded. De onles way in de bofe case am ter fling yo'se'f down flat an' shet yo' eyse an' hole yo' bref an' let on lak yo' daid a'ready. Mo'n dat, yo' boun' ter stop up yo' yeahs too, kase ef yo' hyeah sumpin yo' gwine ter git up an' foller fust t'ing yo' knows."

"I ruther o' some git drownded nur et up," said Aunt Mary, with emphasis.

"Hit dishaways," said Granny, with a serious and judicial air, as she presented the "points" of painter and jacky-me-lantuhn, "de painters, dey's debbils. Dey git yo', dey eat yo' meat an' dey gnyaw yo' bone an' dey chahm yo' spurrit so hit boun' ter follow 'um an' sarve um.[1] De jacky-me-lantuhns, dey ain't des zackry debbils, dey's gostes an' dey in de clutch o' de Debbil's ole ooman. Dey drownds yo' sholy, but yo' spurrit, hit go free ter de place hit 'long unter. Sidesen dat, drowndin' am sorter easy-goin', wiles gittin' tored inter smidgins an' den all mess up in de pluck ob er low-down debbil-varmint am sorter hahd, e'en medout ter hafter sarve dat critteh, too."

"Dat wut *I* say. Gimme drowndin' in de bog, but don't gimme up foh sassidge-meat unter er painter !"

[1] There is the same belief in India as regards the tiger.—C. G. L.

"Dey's er charnce," said Aunt Mymee, with cold and cruel emphasis, "dat yo' git ter be er jacky-me-lantuhn yo' own s'ef."

"Not ef I 'have myse'f," cried the usually amiable Aunt Mary, stung into sudden fury. "Not ef I 'have (behave) myse'f! an' ef I tek ter doin' dirt,[1] den Ise willin' ter be jacky-me-lantuhn —an' sarve me right, too!"

"Troof too," said Granny, pretending to think Aunt Mymee was bent only on enlightening her friend; "ef yo' ain't do no dirt, ur ef yo' sorry yo' did, 'fo' yo' git drownded. Yo' safe fum · dat. Dem dat stick ter dey own podner (partner, husband) am gwine ter go off 'bout dey own bizniz wen dey daid in de bog ur outen hit, but dem dat's bin a-traipsin' arter yuther folkses podnehs dey ketch hit, *good*, ef dey git coax in an' drownded, yessir! W'en dey daid, de Debbil's ole ooman gwine.ter ketch up dey spurrits an tie um up in big blathers (bladders) an' light um up an' tuhn um loose in de bogs an' sloughs so dey fool turr po' sinnehs an' 'tice um inter de bogs an' sloughs fum a·t'inkin' dey see er man ur er ooman wid er lahntun. Dat de jacky-me-lantuhn bizniz, ter fool de folkses on an' on, but yo' kyarn' tuhn jacky-me-lantuhn *on*less yo' bin a-doin' dataway I name. Yo' kin slip down in de mud and slosh (ooze) an' die dar, but yo' ain't boun' ter be er jacky-me-lantuhn. No suh!"

"Dey's man-jacky an' ooman-jacky," said Big Angy.

"In co'se," said Granny. "Dat's de way dey tolls folks on. Ef er man gwine 'long in de night lose de road, den he see afront 'im wut 'e des sho an' sartin am er ooman wid er lantuhn. He see de lantuhn plain an' he sho he see de ooman, dough he kyarn't see er good, an' he foller an' he foller an' he kyarn't he'p hit, an' he t'ink he hyeah 'er say sumpin, dough he ain't kin tell des wut, an' he foller on thu de mud an' down in de slosh an' he kyarkiss, hit ain't gwine ter get out o' dar twell de Jedgmint Day. Ef er ooman lose de road, den she 'magine she see er man, an' she des 'stractid ter ketch up an' *she* foller an' foller twell down she go."

---

[1] To do dirt, to act immorally.

"De onles way," said Aunt Mymee, so interested in the discussion of the "jackys" that she forgot to be insulting to the aunties of greater fascinations for the opposite sex, "am des ter fling yo'se'f down an shet yo' eyes an' hole yo' bref an' plug up yo' yeahs."

"Des wut I say unter Mary," said Granny, with rather austere politeness.

"Me git fool dataway wunst," said Big Angy, grinning and blushing till the red blood showed in the bronze of her cheek.

"HE SEE DE LANTUHN PLAIN."

"How way?" "Dis night?" asked her auditors with gratifying interest.

"Nuh, no dis night. Hit bin dishaway :—me gwine 'iong de road, *rapidment*, kase 'twuz late an' de slough wuz dis side, an' de Injun grabeyahd wuz dat side. I lose no time, nuh, a-stoppin'. I wuz half-way 'long pass de slough, w'en in de front me eye, dar in de road, a-bouncin' un' a-jouncin', er jacky-me-lantuhn!

Me fling me down, me holt me bref, me squinch, me shet de eye, me putt me de finner (finger) in de yeah.

"Bimeby, sumpin me hit. Hit lak hoss-shoe. Me tr-r-rimmle, tr-r-rimmle. Say nuttin. Stir not. De finnirs wuz in de yeahs, but some t'ing I hyeah, de t'ing dat soun' lak horse snort an' r'ar an' shy, de t'ing dat soun' lak w'ite man cussin'. Den me hyeah de soun' lak sumpin joomp unter de groun', an' me veele (feel) sumpin ketch me a-holt pun de shouldeh, put de han' pun me chis'. Me hyeah sumpin tork—

"'Is yo' daid? Nuh, yo' issent daid, yo' dhroonk. Git hup!'

"Dat wuz kase me mus' breeve or bust, an' me breeve. Den me peep out de eye, me see man wid lantuhn, zo one me eye me pinch shet, one me flop op'n.

"De man bin de man dat lib in de medder lan' ahine dem ash trees. He hole up de lantuhn, he look, he say—

"'Damme! damme! damme!—Ole ooman, w'y yo' dar? Am yo' dat droonk yo' kyarn' git hup?—Yo' skeer de hoss, he t'row me. Spik, ef yo' ain' too droonk.'

"Me spik, me say—

"'U-uh! Misseh Smif, dat yo'?'

"'Hit me,' he say. 'Wut yo' a-sprawlin' in de dut foh?' he say. ''Fo' dis, me t'ink yo' decen' ole ooman.'

"'Misseh Smif, me no droonk. Me skeer. Me—ah—t'ink yo' er jacky-me-lantuhn.'

"'Wut o' dat?—Git hup.—Jacky-me-lantuhn nuttin cep rotten win'.'

"Me me try scuse (I tried to excuse myself). No good 'tall. He laff, he holler, he smack de laig. Den, sez 'e—

"'Ef so be me na (if I were not) sick a-laffin', me whup yo' foh mek de hoss shy. Hit spile good hoss, wunst 'e lahn dat trick.'

"Nemmine. I go dishaway. He go dataway, but nex' day he tell dat in de sto', an' w'en I go sell de mitten, all laff."

"Pester yo' heap?"

"Nuh. Dey buy de mitten an' gimme de lil sip o' *eau-de-vie*. Dat good. Me git de monnie an' de *eau-de-vie*, dey git de laff an' de mitten."

"Dat er f'ar trade, Miss Boogarry."

"Hit er f'ar trade, but 'tain't no reely wuller-wups ahine dat trade," said Aunt Mymee, with a languidly-bored air that would have done credit to a drawing-room. "Dar's er tale *I* kin tell, dat my mammy knowed, dat don' tuhn out no sech er w'icherways."

"Ef hit 'greeble unter yo', gin hit out an le'ssee."

"Hit wuz des lak dis:—Ole man, he got er lil gal. He ole ooman daid an' all he yuther folks daid cep dat lil gal, an' she all in de worls dat he got. He lub dat lil gal des lak de 'possum lub de 'simmon-tree. De man at de nex' place jindin (adjacent) des got one boy. Dem two daddy mek hit up dat de boy gwine ter merry de gal w'en she ole nuff. Meanw'iles, dat boy, he heap oler den de gal, he run arter a ooman in de holler. Er man dat lub dat ooman fine out dat ooman done tuck up wid de boy. He kill um bofe an' fling um in de quogmiah (quagmire). Huccome he kill de two an' dey don' kill 'im, huh? He kill de ooman fust an' fling huh in de slosh. Den he tek 'er shorl (shawl) an' wrop hisse'f up in hit. W'en de boy come 'long de parf an' see in de dim light ob be night dat shorl, he putt out de han', but, my gorrymighty! hit er man dat grip dat han', hit er man dat ketch he thote an' choke de life harf outen 'im an' den fling 'im 'way out in de mud, an' holler an' laff w'en de boy baig an' plead dat he reach 'im er pole ter git out by. Hit—oh, good Lawd!—hit er man dat holler an' laff w'en de boy go down in de brack mud an' watteh. Wuss'n dat, hit er man, dat man, dat mek de folkses t'ink dat boy an' ooman done runned off.

"Bimeby, dat man set up ter dat gal. She mad 'bout dat boy dat she t'ink runned off, an' she merry dat man kase she feel spiteful. Den she wish she ain't. She fine she cut off 'er

nose ter spite 'er face, dat all.   All de night long de jacky-me-
lantuhns rise outen de groun' an; jounce, jounce roun' de house.
Roun' an' roun' dey go, fust dis side, den dat side, roun' an'
roun' tell 'long todes day, den dey go sorter 'squitch!' an' den
dey gone.   Dey ain't go off, dey des nowurs.   Nex' night dey
back, dough, wuss an' wuss.   Den, w'en de mawnin come an'
dey gone ergin, de gal run home.

"'O, daddy!' she say, 'lemme in! lemme in! De jacky-
me-lantuhns so, bad at my ole man's I dassent ter stay.   Hit
'pear lak dey a-huntin' sumpin, kase dey bob roun' dar de whole
night thu.'

" So 'er daddy tek 'er in, an' he cuss an' he cry, an' den he
watch w'les she go sleep on de flo'.

" Arter w'iles 'long come de man.   Whoo! de ruckshin, de
fuss!   He pitch an' he r'ar, he scole an' he cuss, he coax an'
he lallygagg, he cry an' he promuss de big gif'.   He gib de lil
gal no peace, so, at de la;', she say—

" 'Ise all wo' out wid yo' baiggin'.   I'll go try de place wunst
mo'.'

" She go back ter try one mo' night.

" De nex' mawnin', beholes ! dat lil gal comes des a-puttin'
ter huh daddy.

"'O, daddy, lemme in!   Lemme in!' sez she.   'Ise mo'
feard o' de jacky-me-lantuhns now den yistiddy.   All de night I
see dem jacky-me-lantuhns an' dey's er man an' er ooman
jacky-me-lantuhns an' dey laigs is gone.   I kyarn't stan' dat,
daddy.   Lemme in! lemme in!'

" 'Er daddy tek 'er in, an' he cuss an' he cry, an' den he watch
w'iles she fall down sleep on de flo'.

" De man, he done set out yarly in de mawnin' he own se'f
an' he ain't git back home twell mos' dahk.   Den he miss de
lil gal.   He look one place, look turr place, look ev'whurs.
No lil gal.   Wait er minnit, den holler.   No un arnser back.
Den he go a-runnin' arter huh.   He fine 'er wid 'er daddy.

Her r'ar an' pitch, cuss an' t'ar, coax an' lallygag, cry an' promuss. Shuh ! lil gal, she thu wid 'im, all he good bref dat otter gone ter cool he vittles gone foh nuttin.

"'Go 'way,' de gal say, ' go 'way an' lemme 'lone.'

"'Come back. Yo' my ooman now.'

"'Nuh. Won't go 'tall.'

"'I kill yo', gal. Look out ! '

"'I gwine ter die hyeah, ef so be my time come.'

"Den de man staht off, an' he call back—

"'I staht out so quick dat I fegit de gun. Wait ! I gwine git dat gun. Den see me swage (persude) yo' an' yo' daddy ! '

"Wid dat he lope back ; he git de gun, he staht ter go back an' swage de lil gal an' huh daddy.

"Bimeby, he see de jacky-me-lantuhn, bibbery-bob, bibbery-bob hyeah she go. Now she front, now she 'hine, now she closte, now she fur. 'Way off yonder, nurr one bob, bibbery-bob, bibbery-bob, but dat un don't come anigh. My ! de sight tuhn 'im cole. He des hone ter tuhn back."

"But he kyarn't," said Granny.

"Nuh. He kyarn't . He footses, they sholy 'witched. He grab um wid he hans, he try ter hole um fas', but dey go, des lak dey wuzzent hissen, crossways ob de road an' thu de wet grass. On go de jacky-me-lantuhn todes whah de turr one a-balluncin', bob, bob, bibbery-bob ; 'cross de wet grass inter de shaller watteh mungs de roots, bob, bob, bibbery-bob ; 'cross de shaller watteh mungs de roots inter de t'ick mud, bob, bob, bibbery-bob. He foller. He up ter he shins now. Bob, bob, bibbery-bob. De mud gittin' t'in now, hit rope w'en de win' blow. He up ter he knees. Bob, bob, bibbery-bob. He mek er splunge. He up ter de wais' now. Bob, bob, bibbery-bob. One mo' pull. He up ter de neck. Bob, bob, bibbery-bob. Dem two jacky-me-lantuhns bofe closte unter 'im, one dis side, one dat. Bob, bob, bibbery-bob. Dey come ter gerrer. Dey sottle onter 'im. He shet de eye. He gone.

'Guggle, guggle—PLOM !' say de watteh. Bob, bob, bibbery-bob—'way go de jacky-me-lantuhns. Go asleep, lil gal, no man gwine ter kill yo' now 1 "

" Who saw that and told it ? " asked Tow Head, sceptically.

" Who see yo' ha'r grow ? " was the retort-discourteous.

" Nobody. How could one ? "

"Hit grow dough, des de same, an' same way de tale o' de jacky-me-lantuhn. Hit come, hit de sollum fact, an' no un kin tell nohow."

" Sholy, sholy, ez de chile kin hunnerstan', an' dat 'mine me ob er tale ob one o' dem jacky-me-lantuhns dat don't come outen de ma'sh, dey come outen de grabeyahd, an', stiddier drowndin' folks, dey git um stonded (stunned), an' den suck out dey blood an' lef um ez dry ez er cawn-shuck arter Crismus."

" Shuh, now 1 yo' des sorter projeckin'," cried Aunt Mary, uneasily.

" No, suh 1 hit de troof, dat kine o' wuller-wups, dey de wusses' ob all de jacky-me-lantuhns, kase dey grows fum suckin' all de life outen crittehs twell dey's tall ez de bigges' cottonwood trees. Mo'n dat, dem dat's sucked ter def gits up and stahts out in de same bizniz an' dey grows an' dey grows, but de wust ob all de mizzibleness am dat de life ob um's all on de outside an' dey hahts am cole ez def. Yessuh ! cole ez def ! "

Everybody shuddered visibly and with no effort at conceal-ment as the picture rose before her mental vision of this terrible icy-hearted " wuller-wup," shooting up from the grave like a mighty column of flame, and sweeping through the night in eager search for the warm life of humanity.

" But dey's er way ter gin dis hyeah jacky-me-lantuhn he come-uppunce," said Granny, with evident pity for the agita-tion of her audience.

She paused to give her consolation time to " work," then continued.

" Hit's dishaway," and she drove the poker into the heart of

the great fire before her until the sparks flew up the chimney
in a column tall as any wuller-wup, "des, dishaway : Ef yo' see
un un um a-comin' an' yo' squot right down an' mek er cross
in de dut an' spit in de middle o' dat cross, an' den jump up
high ez yo' kin, and poke yo' han' thu de light an' down de
thote o' Misteh Jacky-me-lantuhn an' grab out he haht, an' tek
dat haht an' peg hit ter de groun' wid splintehs ob de ash tree,
an' den pile up de leabes an' rubbidge an' set hit afiah an' buhn
dat haht up. Hit'll buhn mighty slow, an' tek er heap o'
kin'lin', dat haht will, but wunst hit buhn, dat jacky-me-lantuhn done wid, hit boun' ter des pindle down ter nuttin an'
ne'er git up no mo'. Ef dat haht bust loose, an' git erway
dough—an' hit try mighty hahd—hit gwine ter fly back back ter
whah 'twuz afo', an' den de jacky sholy be heap wuss'n 'twuz in
de fust place, an' yo' sholy will git sucked de fus' night hit git
er charnce at yo'." [1]

"Troof too," said Aunt Em'ly ; "but ef yo' scuse me, Aunt
Jinny, I tell yo' dat dese hyeah jacky-me-lantuhns dat riz outen
de grabe ain't allus lak de yaller light. In de daytime, an'
some in de nights too, dey des lak grea' big ole doted (dry-
rotted) trees."

"Is yo' e'er seed um, Aunt Em'ly ? "

"Nuh, I ain't des seed um my own se'f, but my mammy, she
seed um menny an' menny er time, dat she hez."

"Wut she say dey look lak, honey ? Wut kine o' trees, des
zackry ? "

"Des zackry lak no kine dat grow. Dey stan' up high lak
daid ole tree, dey got on no close, kase wy, dem dey wuz bury
in am too lil foh um now sence dey grow by de blood. Dey all
kivveh wid ha'r dat look lak tree-moss, dey yarms (arms) fell
down lak daid lim's, dey haid no mo'n er big knot-hole twell yo'
look mighty closte ter hit, den—oh, my !—hit awful ! De eyes,

---

[1] This is the terrible cannibal giantess of the Algonkin Indians, who cannot
be destroyed until her heart is completely burned up.—C. G. L.

dey so daid an' sickly dat yo' kyarn' skusely see um, de nose is all fall down, but de toofses, dey ain't all fall down ! No, suhs ! dem toofses des ez big ez de saw-toofses in de saw-mill. Oh, dey de awfules' paht ! Dey ain't no back-toofses, but dem front ones so strong dey kin bite thu folkses necks an' let all de blood an' de strenk out."

"Dem's booggers, dey ain't no wuller-wups," said Aunt Mymee.

"Sholo dey am wuller-wups," said Aunt Em'ly, firmly, "kase w'y ?—dey come up outen de groun', an' dey kin go roun' in de big blathers o' fiah ef dey wanter."

Aunt Mary forgot to giggle, and turned quite ashy.

"W-w-w-'y, Aunt Em'ly," she sputtered, "ef dey wuz lak yo' an' Aunt Jinny say, putty soon de whole worl' u'd git bit an' tuhn inter booggers, an' der won't be nuttin lef'."

"Dat mought happun, chile, ef so be 'twuzzent dat w'en dey gits bad in er neighbeh-hood, de folks, dey all tuhn out wid fiah-bran's an' hunt um down. De folkses safe w'iles dey a-lookin' at dey own fiah-bran's, an', fust t'ing dey know, dey hyeah—'squitch ! ' an' dey know one bus', an' dey git he haht an' buhn hit des lak Aunt Jinny say. Oh, yes ! dem kine 'feared o' fiah des lak some gostes."

"Some gostes choke yo' ef dey ketch yo' 'way fum de fiah, but fiah melt dey strenk, an' so 'tis wid dem kine wullerwups."

"Wut happun ef yo' see dem kine o' wuller-wups w'en yo' otter (ought to) look at yo' fiah-bran' ? "

"Yo' boun' ter run unter um an' git yo' neck broke an' yo' strenk tuck."

"My ! "

"' My,' sho nuff. Dem's mo' lak paintehs nur wuller-wups."

"Dey holler sumpin lak paintehs too. Dat am, dey holler so hit soun' des lak er young one dat's mos' cry hitse'f ter sleep. Ise hyurn um, an' de w'ite folks say hit de sobbin' o' de win', but 'tain't 'tall, hit diffunt."

" Dat same ez de painteh."

"Sumpin, sumpin, an' de painters suck de blood an' hole (hold) de spurrit too."

" Dey's cunjerers, dey is, an' dey kin go roun' lak folkses, ur lak beasteses, des ez de noshin tek um."

"Shuh, now ! Aunt Jinny."

" Yessuh ! an' I kin prube hit."

" Prube hit wid er good tale den."

" Mebbe so good, mebbe so bad. Hit de troof dough, an' hyeah 'tis :—

" Wunst on er time dey wuz er ole ooman in er lil cabin des set back lil way fum de big road w'ichaways all de movehs (movers, emigrants) go wid de big w'ite waggin——"

"Uh huh, dem big t'ing de w'ite folks call de ' perarer-schooneh.' "

" Wid de big w'ite waggin," continued Granny, loftily ignoring the interruption, " dat got all de chilluns an' de quilts an' de vittles an' de plundeh (plunder—baggage, household effects) an' de lil sheet-iun stove an' de ole ooman pack eenside, an' de dawg unneat' an' de cow a-follerin', an' de ole man a-walkin' 'longside ter goad de oxen. Dat de kine hit wuz, an' two, free, ur mo'n dat, pass by in de co'se ob de day, an' dat heap o' comp'ny ; and de ole ooman, she dig an' she sow an' she gedder in de crap an' she ain't lonesome 'tall. Oh, yes ! she closte ter de comp'ny o' de big road an' she got chilluns o' huh own, free nice boys, an' dem boys putty ez de sun an' moon an' stahs an' ez keen ez de aige ob er broadax. De oles' boy, she name him Nar, an' he got de brackes' eye an' ha'r in de worl'. De nex', he wuz Brune, an' he hab er yolleh eye lak er eagle, an' brown ha'r an' mo' red in he cheek. De younges', he wuz de pet lam'. He got de ha'r lak de flax on de spinnin'-wheel, an' de eye lak de flax w'en de blue bloom come an' skin lak de milk-w'ite buckw'eat floweh, an, oh, he so sweet an' kine ! He hab de pet deer an' de pet rabbit an' de pet 'coon an' de pet dove.

Dat mek he big brers laff. Suh ! he ain' keerin' none, he laff
he own se'f wid um."

"Wut yo' say de name o' dat boy?   I done fegit," said Aunt
Mary, with the intention of stimulating Granny's memory in
the most polite manner possible.

"I ain' say *yit*," answered Granny, with cold dignity. "I
ain' de kine dat mess up er tale. W'en I gits ter de right place
I tells, w'en I ain' got dar I holes back.   De name, ez I wuz on
de pints o' sayin', dough, wuz Blonk, leas'ways dat wut Miss
Robidoux say, an' she know de oomen dat know dat boy wid
de light curly ha'r. Yessuh ! he wuz name Blonk, an' hit gin
'im er heap o' werryment de way dem brerrehs o' hissen kill,
kill, kill all de woods-crittehs dey kin come at. He ain' kill much,
ain' Blonk, but he kin beat de worl a-shootin' ef he a-minter."

"Me kon dat tale !" cried Big Angy, with the pleased air of
meeting an old friend.

"Den yo' gin hit de finishmint, Miss Boogarry," said
Granny. "Ise got er frog in my thote dis night, an' I heap
sooneh lissum at dem ole tale den tell um."

"Me shill staht at de night dey foun' de gals?"

"Sholy."

"One night," resumed Big Angy, "hit bin dahk night an'
de cole rain sizzle down an' mck de fiah spit. All dem brerreh
an' dey mama sit at de ha'th foh kip wa'm. De rain fall slow
an' cole an' de fiah go 's-s-s-ss !' an' 'pip-pap ! ptt !' an' de
coals jump out in de flo'. De ole ooman an' de boys ver glad
dey in house. De deer, he stan' in shed by windeh ; de chuffy
an' de 'coon in de corndehs by de chimly ; de dove go sleep wid
haid unneat wing, 'way up mungs de raftehs. All go well.
De folkses roas' de tatehs in de ashes an' eat um hup. Dey
br'ile de meat on de coal an' eat um hup. Dey bile de bean-
meal in de pot in de chimly an' eat um hup. Den dey crack
de warnit an' pick de meat hout an' eat um hup. Arter dat
dey smoke an' dey tork.

"Bimeby come de cry. 'Hih! some un on de big road wid er sick chile, dis night,' say de boy.

"'Nah, nah, me son, shet de yeah, foh dat de painter. De painter cry, 'e call de folks. W'en dey come, he t'ar out de spurrit an' hole hit foh sarvint, den 'e eat de kyarkiss. Hole still, me son.'

"Cry come 'gin.

"Blanc staht hup.

"'Ef 'e painteh,' sez 'e, 'me kill um by light o' 'e eye dat shine lak fiah-coal. Ef 'e chile me fetch um in.'

"'Nah, nah, me son——'

"Ptt!—He grab de gun an' gone.

"Dey wait. Dey stan' in de do' an' hole de han' 'bove de eye an' try peek thu de dahk. Ah-ee! see nuttin thu de wet an' dahk, hyeah nuttin cep de 'sh-sh-sh' o' de cole rain comin' down.

"Go back in de cabin an' lissun. Hyeah no cryin'. Whah dat boy?—Kyarn' tell muttin.

"Bimeby, 'way in de woods, come de 'bim-boom' o' de big ole gun.

"'De ole gun hit sumpun,' de boys say.

"Hit do, sholy. Putty queek dey hyeah de bresh a-cracklin, an' de stomp, stomp, stomp o' er man dat got er big load on 'e back. Putty queek arter dey hyeah 'pat, pat, pat' 'longside de stompin'. Den Blanc, 'e come wid er daid painter on 'e back an' 'e fling um down 'fo' de fiah an' look ahine ter see wut foller. De turr boys look. Hit mek de haht melt. Dar de two putties' gals in pe'cuts o' fur an' necklash o' claws, an' dey tork sorf (talk softly) an' hole out de han'. Wut dey say, personne kin na tell, hit sumpin outlandish, but de soun', hit sweet."

"I reck'n hit de tork I done hyeah w'en I wuz young, fum de wile niggehs des offen de boats," said Aunt Mymee, musingly.

"Mabbe, mabbe so. Enway dey tork sumpin, an' dey so

putty an' light, wid de eye lak the painter an' de pe'cut lak de painter fur, an' long, long ha'r retchin' down. Blanc, he say he foun' um in de wood. Dey run at 'im arter 'e kill painter. 'E mistrus' dey gwine fight an' 'e club de gun an dey foller 'long.

"Zo den, dem gal stay, an' dey eat an' dey sleep in de cabin

DE PAINTER.

wit turr folks. De ole ooman, she don' lak dem gal ; Rabbit, 'e don' lak dem gal ; Deer, 'e don' lak dem gal ; Dove, she don' lak dem gal. 'Coon, 'e de onles one dat lak um, an' 'e des er varmint 'e own se'f.

"Soon ole ooman die.

"Brun lub one gal, Noir lub turr. Two boy merry two gal.
"Blanc, he na keer 'tall, but de gals mek lak he do ter (their) two hubsums. Dey wuhk on de mines o' de —— fools an' mek um hab de jalousie. Noir, he lay de plan foh kill Blanc. Deer, he hyeah dat plan, 'e sorry, but 'e 'feard de gals an' don' tell Blanc. 'E tell Dove. Dove, she fly at 'e shouldeh an' tell de bad tale in 'e yeah. Blanc, he sorry, 'e go 'way.

"W'en Noir go 'way off on de big hunt, Blanc go back home, kase 'e lub de home an' de grabe o' mama.

"Den Brun, 'e hab de plan ter kill Blanc. Rabbit hyeah dat tale. 'E sorry, but 'e 'feard tell Blanc, 'e go tell Dove. Dove, she fly at 'e shouldeh an' she coo an' she coo, an' all dat time she say wuhd now'n den dat tell de bad tale.

"Blanc go 'way gin. 'E na kin tell wut 'e do. 'E hab nossin 'e kin lub, 'e berry twiste.[1] Dat wut 'e t'ink. Aha! de deer foller 'im w'en 'e donno, de rabbit foller 'im w'en 'e donno, de dove foller awso. W'en 'e stop for sleep dey come up, dey tork. 'E stop de cryin'. Nemmine! he got dem ter lub. He mos' glad ergin.

"Bimeby, de coon slip up an' den slip back. He t'ink dey ain' see 'im, but Deer 'e smell 'im, Rabbit, 'e see 'im, Dove, *she* see 'im. All tell Blanc, 'Hab de care.' Dove, she do mo.' She say—

"'Me boun' foh tell yo' dem gal des (are just) painters, dat wut dey am. We know all de time, but 'feard ter tell. Now we desput, we wan' dat yo' go back, git de close o' dem gal wiles dey sleep an' buhn um all hup. Dat kyore yo' trouble. Dem gal wan' kill you, will so, else, kase yo' kill dey papa.'

"'E slip back, 'e git de pe'cuts, 'e buhn all hup. 'E slip in de cabin in de night, 'e feel an' feel twell 'e git dem pe'cuts, den 'e run out wid um, an' w'en dey 'gin ter buhn out dar in the woods, dem gal staht up, dey scream lak painter, dey *is* painter.

"De hubsum git de gun, dey shoot de painter-wife. Dey

[1] *Triste.* French, sad.

ain' know dem de wife, dey call an' call. No wife dere, des
daid painter on de flo'.

"Dey t'ink Blanc got dem gals. Dey run, dey fine 'im rakin'
in de ashes. 'E fling dem pe'cut ashes on dem brerreh. De
cha'm broke! Dem brerreh lub 'im 'gin. All go back ter
cabin, all lib dere berry gay."

"Dat er good tale, shoh!" said Aunt Mymee, with un-
qualified approval." Dey ain't no tricks dem paintehs ain't git
up ter. Dey wus er man dat I know dat run arter painteh in
de night, w'en he t'ink 'e hyeah er baby cryin'. Dat de las' o'
him. He old ooman go out foh hunt 'im. Dat de las' o' *huh*.
He brer go hunt um bofe. Nuttin git 'im, kase 'e got er rattlesnake belt an' er duck-wing whustle an' er silveh bullit in he
gun. De painteh et he kinfolks, but dat de las' o' dat kine o'
eatin'. Dat painteh git kilt and et up hisse'f, an' he hide, hit
hang in de sun, but de gostes o' dat man's kinfolks wuz allus
a-perawdin' eroun' whah dat hide wuz."

"I knowed er man," said Aunt Em'ly, "dat kilt er mammy-
painter an' tuck de kitten home, an' dat kitten wuz ez fr'en'ly ez
er pup. Hit sleep wid de baby in de ole log c'adle an' hit lap
milk out en de baby's tin cup, but, all de same, w'en dat pet
kitty git big, one night, de man hyeah sorter guggle lak
chokin' an' sorter smack lak suckin', an' dat go on twell he
jump up an' light er chunk an' look in de c'adle. Gord! Dat
painter-kitty done cut de baby's thote an' suckin' hit blood!
He jerk de gun off de hawns (deer-horns used as a gun-rack)
an' shoot de painter, but wut o' dat? de poor baby daid. Oh,
mon! de paintehs is varmints, but dey's debbils too!"

The audience gloomily acquiesced, and mused and smoked in
silence until Uncle John "drapped in" and, on finding the
cause of the depression, plunged into description of a "festible"
he had attended a few nights previous.

"An' arter de chickens an' bile custahd wuz et," he went on
with growing enthusiasm, "de ladies all stud up, wid Aunt

Stacie at de haid un um, an' Misteh Hicks, he sot out ter
darnce dat 'shiny-eye' darnce dat am er sorter painter-play
too. My! hit mek my eye bat now, ter t'ink how fine 'twuz.
Misteh Hicks, he laigs des ez limmer ez willer-twigs, he des
kyurve roun' ez light ez er budh on de wing. He sorter
'vance an' sorter dror off an' den sail up ter de fust o' dem
thutty ladies a-stannin' in er row an' he say—

" ' Whah my eye ? '

an' ez she say,

' Shiny-eye ! '

he tuhn 'er roun' ez sorf ez ef huh footses bin mek outen
feddehs, an' den he go on ter de nex, an' de nex', twell he tuhn
um all.

"Den I tuck de stan', an' w'en I thu, de turr boys foller, an'
w'en all bin down de line, we wuz dat hot an' sweaty—scuse
me, ladies—we wuz all shiny-eyes. Dat lil Mose, he wuz de
las', an' w'en he come ter dat yaller gal, Hanner, dat wuhk at
de bodin'-(boarding) house, he say—

' I *foun'* my eye '

dat sweet dat hit seem lak de 'lasses wuz des a-dribblin' outen
de corndehs ob he mouf."

"Wut she do ? " asked Aunt Mary, bridling at Uncle John's
significant look.

" She let on lak she gwine tuhn 'er back, den she giggle an'
shuck 'er shouldehs, but all de time she puttin' 'er han' forruds
foh 'im ter grab. Shuh ! er ooman's er ooman, an' de mo' she
run, de mo' she gwine ter be dis'pointed ef yo' ain't got de spry-
ness ter ketch up."

" Dem's fools ez does," said Aunt Mary, suddenly sour.

" Does ketch up ? No, no, my honey, my lub, my turkl-dub.
De ladies is de meat on de bone, de sugeh in de dram. Yessuh ! Now, ladies, les all stan' up an' try dat 'shiny-eye.' "

20

Gemplum.—Whah my eye?
Lady.—Shiny-eye!
Gemplum.—Who got my eye?
Lady.—Shiny-eye!
Gemplum.—Am dis my eye?
Lady.—Shiny-eye!
Gemplum.—Who foun' my eye?
Lady.—Shiny-eye!
Gemplum.—I los' my eye.
Lady.—Shiny-eye!
Gemplum.—I *foun'* my eye!
Lady.—Tee-hee! -S-sh-shiny-eye!

XIX.

THE LAST GLEANING OF THE FIELD.

Tow Head had been off on what Granny was pleased to term a "jant," and had not seen her old friends for weeks. She insisted on the evening meeting being turned into a festival of rejoicing at her return. When everybody had inspected her small figure and assured her that she had "growed mightily," been missed "heaps," and "wouldn' skusely a-bin knowed ef met up wid on de big road," she had "comed on so," had expressed unbounded gratitude for her most astonishing and inappropriate presents, and had vowed to keep them "f'r evveh-nevveh an' amen," she demanded a story, "a nice one without any snakes or jackys at all."

"Hit am a-gittin' late foh tales. De icicles is down an' de fros' a-comin' up outen de groun'," expostulated Granny. "Hit fetch bad luck ter tell tales arter de lil booggers dat's bin froze up all de winteh gits loose an' goes a-perawdin' eroun' an' a-lis'nin'."

"It's awfully cold to-night," insisted Tow Head, trying hard to shiver. "Tell a bird story, do, or else I'll go off and stay until you won't know me."

"I reck'n we betteh gin in, ef dat am wut am afo' us. Tell 'er er tale, Aunt Em'ly, soster sabe de feelin's ob de fambly."

"Sure ! dat de wuhk foh yo' own se'f, Aunt Jinny."

"G'long wid yo'. Ise a-tuhnin' er tale roun' in my membunce an' a-huntin' foh de fust eend un hit, but 'tain't show out wid me yit. G'long, Aunt Em'ly, de w'iles I surter sort out dat membunce dat's a-gittin' so ole an' frazzly."

"Frazzly! Shucks! W'en yo' git frazzly I be plum wo' out, dar now! Ef hit 'bleege yo' dough, I tell de onles' tale dat's lef' me—ur is I tole yo' a'ready, de tale ob de two b'ars an' Ole Woodpeckeh?"

"Oh, no! you have not."

"Sholy?"

"Surely. You have told only of the *one* bear Old Woodpecker fooled out of his claws."

"Dat'n ain't de one. Dishaway dis urr tale go :—

"Dey wuz wunst er ole mammy b'ar dat wuz er widdeh-b'ar, an', ez she wuz gwine 'long thu de woods, one time—hit wuz 'long in de spring-time—she met up wid nurr b'ar dat wuz er ole maid. Arter dey ax one nurr howdy an' pass de time o' day an' say how dey feel lonesome now dey fambly all bruck up, dey sorter 'gree an' mek hit up dat dey keep house tergerreh enduin' o' de wa'm weddeh. So say, so do, an' dey settle down tergerreh des ez dey laid off, an' dey hunt an' dey fish an' 'vide eben (divide evenly) an' fa'r twell ole Miss Widdeh-b'ar, she tuck er cole fum a-gittin' 'er footses wet w'en she was out a-fishin', an' hit sottle in 'er eyes, hit did, an' bimeby hit putt um clean out. Dat wuz er bad time foh Miss B'ar. Dar she wuz, in 'er own house, but dat ole maid b'ar ain' fetch 'er nuttin but de bones ; all de good meat she don't eat right up she keep on de high swingin' she'f in de sulleh whah po' ole bline mammy kyarn' fine hit. Mammy, she sorter s'pishin' sumpin, but dar she am, an' no use ter say nuttin, but she git mo' leaner all de time, twell 'er bones rattle w'en de win' blow an' 'er hide flop lak er flag on de hill-top. Ef 'twuzzent foh Ole Woodpeckeh, ole mammy, she'd des natchelly a-gin up de gose, but he wuz a-knockin' roun' mungs de shingles on de roof an' he hyeah ole mammy snuffin' an' cryin'—de ole maid wuz out a-huntin' —an' he peek down de chimbly an' see des how 'twuz.

"'Nemmine!' he say, 'I fix dat.' Den he holler down, 'Hello, mammy! come he'p me.'

"She stop de cryin' an' say—

"'Who is yo'?'

"He holler 'gin—

"'Ise er po' lil boy got stuck in yo' chimbly.'

"Stiddier scolin' lak de ole maid 'd a-done, po' ole mammy grope ter de chimbly an' feel roun' ter he'p.

"OLE MISS WIDDEH-B'AR, SHE TUCK ER COLE FUM A-GITTIN' ER
FOOTSES WET W'EN SHE WAS OUT A-FISHIN'."

"'Po' chile,' sez she, 'Ise 'feard I kyarn' do much. Holler 'gin sost I kin tell des whah yo' is, kase Ise bline, honey.'

"He holler an' holler an' keep ole mammy a-feelin' roun' twell she des 'stractid. Den, all on de suddint, he fling er chahm spang in 'er face dat fetch back 'er sight dat quick dat she see Ole Woodpeckeh fly outen dat chimbly an' cl'ar out.

" She run ter de do' an' holler—

" 'T'anky, Marse Woodpeckeh, t'anky,' an' den she hunt foh vittles. She foun' um too, on dat high swingin' she'f in de sulleh, an' she et all de meat an' lay back de bone 'fo' ole maid git back.

" She ain't say nuttin.

" Ole maid see how 'tis an' *she* ain't say nuttin.

" Arter dat dey git 'long putty well, an' w'en dey tuhn in (turn in—hibernate) ole mammy wuz de fattes.' Dey don' keep house dataway, dey don't, de nex' spring, dough, kase ole mammy, she merry 'gin, an' wut come o' de ole maid I dunno."

" Maybe she went to the mountains, or, maybe, she went into the woods and, when the trees began to walk and talk at midnight, they killed her or pulled her tail off, or something," hazarded Tow Head.

" Mebbe so, honey, mebbe so, but le's gin 'er up now, an' git dat tale fum Aunt Jinny. By de way she bat 'er eye I kin tell dat hit's on han's."

It was " on han's," and, as Granny said, " dreened one po' ole ooman dry " of bird stories. It was of the bee-king, the shell-bark hickory and the bee-martin—less about the martin, indeed, than the tree and the king, still it would pass for a bird story.

" In de good ole times dey wuz times w'en de folkses wuz pestehed des lak dey is now. Dey wuz times w'en de chilluns git beans up der noses an' bugs in dey yeahs, an' de chimlies smoked, an' de butteh won't come, an' de kerridge hosses go lame, an de perarer fiah buhn up all de fences, an' de young crittehs lay down in de fiel' an' die 'pear lak des foh spite. Oh, yes ! dat allus bin de way, an' de ole bee-king he own se'f 'low nobody know de trouble he hab. Dat wuz troof too, he hin hab heaps o' werrimint wid de b'ars an' de mot-millehs (moth-millers) an' de humin' crittehs a-sneakin' arter de honey-comb, an' de buhd san' de toads, an' de fishes too, a-snappin' at de bees. Hit 'pear lak some day he des gwine ter fly clean off de hannel an' go plum 'stractid. One yeah, hit 'pear lak he des gwine ter lose de las'es' bee he got. Ole Bee-Martin,[1] he hab de big luck a-ketchin' ob um twell he s'prise he own se'f. De bees dey staht out in de mawnin' des ez spry, an' dey go a-hummin' an' a-buzzin' to'des de perarer-blooms an' de tree-tossels, an' dey don't ne'er git back no mo'. Dey des natchelly gone, cl'ar an' clean ez er gose (ghost) arter sun-up. Hit keep on dataway mos' all de summeh-time, an' Ole Bee-King, he study an' he study, an' he watch an' he watch, an' he ain' see nuttin git dem bees. Mor'n dat, he ain't s'pishin' nuttin ne-er. He see um sot out, he see um load up wid honey, he see um staht out foh ter tote dat honey home. Up, up dey go, den he don't see um come down. Dey *don't* come down. 'Sumpin a-ketchin' ob um,' sez Ole Bee-King, sez 'e. Den he look up an' shade he eye wid de han', dishaway, an' he keep a-lookin'. De sun so strong he wink an'—shuh! whah dem bees? Bees gone foh good. Mighty bad! King, he mighty mad. Nem-mine, at de las' he ketch de t'ief. He hole one eye open an' wink wid de turr. Den he hole turr eye open an' wink wid de fust shet. Dat way he see mighty trashy, long-tail brown buhd sneak outen de shag-bahk (rough bark) hick'ry tree leabes an' grab dem bees des ez quick ez lightnin' an' den fly back an' hide.

"'Uh huh!' sez Ole Bee-King, sez 'e, 'so dat's de way, am hit? Dat ole shag-bahk bin on de watch, an' de minnit dat I tuhn my back ur shet my peepuhs, he gin dat low down, ornery t'ief de wuhd (wood), an' he sail in an' eat my chilluns,' sez 'e. 'De owdashus ole squirr'l-feedeh! Ef I ain' stop he tricks an' gin 'im sumpin ter 'membeh me by inter de bahgin, den I dunno bees fum bug-aigs,' sez 'e.

"Fust, he t'ink 'e peterfack 'im, but den de ole shag-bahk's troubles 'd a-bin done foh good an' all. Shoh! he t'ink 'gin an' he ain't satify. Den he study some mo', an' den he git up

---

[1] A bird which preys on trees.

an' shahpen he fingeh-nails. Dat done, he run up 'gin de ole shag-bahk an' gun 'im sech er clawin' dat he leabe 'im wid de bahk all frazzle out ez 'tis ter dis day. Dat ain't satify Ole Bee-King yit. He tuck an' tuck er big straw an' suck all de sweetnin' outen de hulls o' all de nuts—dey wuz sweet ez plums 'fo' dat—an' den he tek de straw an' blow in some puckeh-juice (pucker, astringent, puckering the mouth) outen er mean weed.

" ' Now,' he say, 'lemme see yo' coax my bees ter come anigh yo'. Yo' sweetnin' gone foh good.'

"OLE BEE-KING HE TUCK AN' TUCK ER BIG STRAW.

" 'Twuz too. Dem hulls bitteh ter dis day. Dat mighty hahd ter stan', but wut mo' hahd yet wuz dat nuttin wuzzent done unter de bee-martin dat et de bees. To-be-sho, Ole Bee-King, he lay off ter gin 'im he come-uppunce, but den Bee-Martin, he so spry an' so sly dat he ain't ne'er gin 'im de charnce yit."

" Why didn't Bee-King petrify the hickory?" asked the child, with a disappointed air.

" I dunno, honey, no mo'n yo' own se'f, medout de ole king

thunk dat too easy 'bout stoppin' trouble, but de nex' time I sees 'im I gwine ter putt dat queschin pintedly."

" Pettifyin' dangis (is dangerous)," said Big Angy, and, as a proof of this, told of—

THE HAND OF STONE.

In the old time a beautiful girl came to the earth. No one knew where she came from, and she never would give any account of herself. All that was known was that one day some young braves standing near a village saw something fall through the air very swiftly and alight on a hill close by. They ran to the hill and found there the girl, unhurt, but seemingly bewildered. By signs they invited her to go with them to the village. She went willingly. The chief's wife would have kept her, but she would not have it so. She went to an empty lodge and stayed there ; she refused all presents of food, and went down to the river near by and called to the fish in strange words. When they came to the surface of the water, in response to her call, she gathered them up, one by one, using only her left hand, and ate them, bones and all. Soon she learned the language of the people, and talked pleasantly with them. The hearts of the young men turned to her, for no girl of the village was her equal in beauty and grace. She smiled on all, and all were her lovers. Many went to her lodge, and none came out the same as they went in. They went in men, they came out helpless children. This made the old men and the women hate and fear her, but the young men were bewitched, and would listen to no counsel—the sight of their foolish companions was no warning—they bitterly denied that the beautiful stranger had wrought the evil. Many plans were laid by the old men and women to destroy her, but they never came to anything, she was too wise and too wary. It was a young woman that finally delivered the people, a young wife whose husband had been turned from her. She secretly followed him to the stranger's lodge and watched. By the moonlight she saw the stranger withdraw her right hand from the folds of the robe where it was usually hidden. The light fell on it. It was of stone. With it she touched the breast of the faithless husband. Then she pushed him from the door. The young wife saw what happened, and in silence and sorrow led him home. All his pride and courage were dead. His heart was stiffened into stone by the hand that had touched him. The poor wife went to the sorcerers and told them what she had learned. When they heard they trembled, they could think of no spell strong enough to protect the village. Were all the young men to become imbeciles, and was the name of the people to be forgotten ? They deliberated a long time, trying to recall some old charm strong enough to overpower this supernatural woman. They fasted solemnly, and entreated aid from the spirit that had always helped them. After that they could only wait. For a time no help seemed coming. The woman went on doing mischief, but mischief was not to last always. One day she went as usual down a steep, high bluff to a narrow, low strip of bank where she was wont to look into the deep water and call up the fish. This time she called and none came. She called again and again. Finally, she stamped her foot and said words that would dismay devils even. Then came up a little fish like silver. She took him into her mouth and began to swallow. He began to swell. She choked, and vainly essayed to get him down her throat. When she could not, and he continued to grow, she tried to spit him out of her mouth. That she could not do either, so she took her hand and tried to pull him out. When she failed in that, she forgot all caution and, leaning against the bluff, pulled hard with both hands. Alas ! the fish stiffened into stone, choking her horribly. In agony she clutched her throat, she beat her breast, but her trouble was soon over, soon she was no longer a woman. All her body became as that evil right hand. The rocky bluff received her as a part of itself, and there she stands to this day, as many have seen as they floated down the great Missouri river. Thus were the people rid of her. Those of good mind and courage rejoiced, but those foolish victims, who were never cured of her enchant-

DE PELICANS.

ment, went about grieving for her and seeking her as long as they lived.

" Dat mus' a-bin de fish dat kilt Pelican," cried Aunt Em'ly, greatly excited.

" Mebbe," said Big Angy, rather sourly.

" Did a fish turn Pelican to stone ? " questioned Tow Head.

" No, honey," answered Aunt Em'ly, with a solemnity befitting the recounting of a tragedy, " hit bustid 'im, bustid 'im wide open, dat des wut hit do."

" Oh ! oh ! how did that happen ? "

" 'Way back yondeh in de ole times, Pelican, he wuz ez gay ez er flea in de cawn-shucks, but de folks in de lake dat wuz neighbehs unter 'im, dey wuzzent gay none, kase w'y, he des et um mos' all up an' de res', dey wuz spectin' ter go dataway mos' enny time. Po' t'ings ! Dem frogs an' fishes wuz 'stractid out an' out, an dey don't 'tall know wut in de wide worl' ter do. At de las', dough, dey wuz one big ole buffler (buffalo) fish dat say he 'low he go ax de mud-hens an' git um ter ax dey granny dat wuz de big witch unneat' de lake. De turr fish 'gree unter dat, an' he go ax de mud-hens wut all de folks in de lake gwine ter do an' won't dey ax dey granny.

" ' Sholy,' say dey, ' kase we 'spise Ole Pelican a-stannin' roun' on one laig an' a-blinkin' in de sun an' a-ketchin' up all de crittehs, an' ef he don' swaller um right off a-puttin' um in dat big yaller bag unneat' he bill.

" Oh ! dey tork servigrous (fiercely) an' dey go off an' dey ax dey granny ter he'p an' den dey come back unter Buffler wid er lil teenty fish des a-shinin' lak watteh in de sun, an' dey say unter 'im—

" 'Granny gun dat unter us, an' she say yo' mus' swaller um.'

" Buffler, he swaller um, an' den de minnit dat lil fish down Buffler, he grow turr'ble an' look mighty good. He swim up ter Pelican an' Pelican, he gulf 'im down quick. Whooh ! Buffler, he grow an' he grow an' he grow twell he bust Pelican wide open. Den he go home an tell all de frogs an' de fish an' de tadpoles, an' den, big ez he am, he tuhn mighty sick. He git so sick he frow up, he frow up dat lil w'ite, shiny fish. Den he feel betteh, but he swink up twell he des de size he wuz 'fo' he et um, an' dat de way he stay."

" What became of the little white fish ? " asked the child.

"He dove down ter whah de witch wuz, an' dat all I know 'bout 'im."

"Dat na all 'bout Buffler," said Big Angy. "Dey wuz er man come fum T'undeh-Lan', kase Pelican got kinfolks dar, an' he shoot t'ree arreh, one in de sky, hit snow ; one in de groun', hit freeze ; one in de lake, hit go dat cole an' solide dat all de fish die—Buffler mungs um."

"Troof dat," said Aunt Em'ly, placidly, " an' de lake bin solid ice yit, mebbe, ef Ole Rabbit ain't cross um gittin' home fum er pathy an' he drap he luck-ball dar an' de lake melt dat quick dat Ole Chuffy wuz nigh a-gittin' drowndid."

"That's all horrid," pouted the child, " why don't you tell a bird story ? "

"Ain't Pelican no buhd ? " inquired Aunt Mymee.

"He isn't a nice one like woodpecker, or even Blue Jay."

"Troof," grunted Big Angy, pleased with the commendation of her favourite. " Me tell de nice tale un 'im now."

WOODPECKER AND THE YOUNG MAN.

One time there was a young man named Young Moon going along a trail through the woods. He went along thinking of what the old men told him and troubling nothing. At last he was roused by a cry of distress, and something fell at his feet. It was a very young woodpecker. He took it in his hands, and as he did so he saw a great black snake gliding down the tree from which the bird fell. He dropped the bird, seized his bow and a keen little arrow, and shot the snake in the neck, pinning it to the tree. Almost instantly, however, the terrible thing pulled loose, and flung itself at the youth, darting fire from its tongue and hissing horribly. Nothing daunted, he fought it fiercely, using knife or hatchet as he could. They fought a long time, and the young man was almost killed by the poison spit into the air and the burning breath of the serpent. Finally, he gave a last despairing thrust, and it rolled over dead. For a long time he could not move. When he could he was in haste to get away, but the pitiful voice of a child stopped him. He looked all around. Finally, he saw a little red baby sitting among the leaves where he had dropped the woodpecker.

"Do not leave me until my father comes," entreated the little one.

The young man was frightened. He saw that he was with a child of the sorcerers, and knew not what to do. The child

HE SHOT THE SNAKE.

smiled to reassure him, and asked to be set on the trunk of the tree. The young man lifted him, but before he could place him on the tree a terrible voice said—

"What are you doing to my child?"

The young man had not a word to say, but the child answered—

"He saved me from the great snake, your enemy. Being a man, not a sorcerer, he could kill it. Here it lies, dead."

At this there came through the undergrowth a little red

man dressed in a fine bonnet of eagles' feathers stained red, and an embroidered black blanket. He looked pleasantly on the young man as he strode up to him and took the child from his hands. He said no word, but ran with the child up the tree. When he was just disappearing into an opening high up on the trunk, he turned and flung down a black feather marked with white and twisted like a ringlet.

"Keep this always," he said, "and it will do you more good than you have done me."

At once he went out of sight.

After waiting a long time to see if he would reappear, the youth went home.

From that time he prospered exceedingly. All the girls loved him, all his enemies feared him, he had the greatest number of horses, he killed the most game, he had the strongest children. He thought he owed it all to the feather, and was careful of it. When he grew old he became vain, and changed his mind. He had the feather loosely twisted in his hair one day, and a sudden gust of wind blew it away. That night enemies burned the village, carried off his horses, wives, and children, killed his friends. He escaped in the darkness, but what of that? Better be killed with your friends than be eaten up by wolves.

Tow Head almost groaned. "I want to hear a story that will make me laugh," she complained.

"Is I tell yo' 'bout Ole Jay Buhd's brack bahs (bars) on he blue coat?" asked Aunt Mary.

That sounded promising. The child encouraged Aunt Mary to tell all she knew about the black bars on the blue coat.

"One dem times w'en Ole Jay, he wuz a-gittin' in lub an' a-gittin' de big laugh on 'im foh he trouble, he go fall in lub wid er gal-buhd dat wuz ez sweet ez 'lasses todes Bluebuhd. I done fegit de name o' dat gal-buhd," said Aunt Mary, with the anxious look of a historian resolved on perfect accuracy.

"Hit mought a-bin Yellah-Hammeh, ur Sparrer, ur Buntin', ur Pea-Buhd, ur mos' enny name, kase Bluebuhd, he er mighty fayvorite wid um all."

"Never mind! I don't care for her name. What did Jay do?" said Tow Head, impatiently.

"He tuck hisse'f off ter de Ole Boy, dat wut he done, de nex' Friday, an' w'en he git thu a-flingin' down de san', he up an' ax, he do, ef he ain't done nuff ter 'zarve some pay. De Ole Boy bin feelin' peart dat day an' he sorter grin an he say—

"'I reck'n I done treat yo' well, but den I kin treat yo' betteh. Wut yo' arter now, ennyways?'

"Den Ole Jay, he ups an' sez, he do—

"'I wanter blue coat des lak Bluebuhd's.'

"Ole Boy, he study some, den he gin 'im de blue coat. Off go Jay des a-prancin'.

"Nex' week he come back.

"'De gal ain't set none by dat coat,' said he. 'Gimme er top-knot.'

"Ole Boy gin 'im er top-knot. Off go Jay des a-prancin' an' a-r'arin' up.

"Nex' week he come back.

"'Dat gal ain't set none by dat top-knot. Gimme gole laigs.'

"Wid dat Ole Boy wuz mad. He wuz a-br'ilin' sumpin at dat minnit an' he des up wid de hot gridiun an' he fling hit at Ole Jay, an' he hit 'im too—kerspang!—'crost de back, an' ef yo' ain't breeve dis tale, des look at Jay an' he chilluns. Ter dis day dey all got dem mahks, dem brack swinge-mahks o' de hot gridiun bahs on dey long feddehs, ez yo' kin see, plain."

"Folks an' crittehs an' buhds do all mighty quah foh lub" (act strangely for love), commented Big Angy. "Dey wuz wunst bin er eagle dat tuhn gal foh lub o' man."

"De lan' sakes! I ain' ne'er hyeah tell o' huh."

Angy did not suppose she had, and proceeded to enlighten her.

THE EAGLE WHO BECAME A GIRL.

In the old times, the great Thunder-Bird and his children lived on a high bluff. One of these children would not mate with another eagle. The reason was that she had, while sailing through the sky, seen a handsome young man sitting on the bank of the Missouri, the "Big Muddy" river, and watching for the great channel catfish which once every summer comes to the surface and talks and prophesies. From that moment the eagle loved the man, although she knew he could not fly, but must always creep along the ground. For a long time she was ashamed to speak, but when she saw him with a girl she could not endure it, and went to her father and asked him to bring to her the young man. This could not be, and her father, very angry at her foolishness, told her so. She entreated so vehemently that he finally said that she might go among men, but then could not set foot in Thunder-Land. She agreed to go, and he changed her into a girl—all but her feet, they remained eagle's claws, all his sorcery could not make them different.

"Let no human eye see your feet," he said, "or you will again become an eagle."

She heeded his words. She went among the people, she won the love of him she came after, she went to his house and was happy for a little while, only for a little while, for soon he began to wonder why his beautiful wife never took off her moccasins and leggings. For a time he said nothing, but after he saw her go through a stream and come out dry-shod, he was troubled, and tried to make her show her feet. He could not tell whether he had married a witch or a woman under an enchantment. When she would not take off her moccasins, he resolved to find out why, so he watched her until she fell asleep

21

and then cut a hole in one of them. He saw the dreadful claw. At the same moment she awakened, she looked at him with the fierce eyes of an eagle, she sprang up, her arms became flapping wings, and, as a storm struck the lodge and scattered its poles and painted skins, she rose in the air. He caught her by her long flowing hair, but it came off in his hands, and she flew out of sight. Since then no eagle has ever married a man or regarded him as anything but an enemy.

HE CAUGHT HER BY HER LONG, FLOWING HAIR.

" De way I hyeah dat," said Granny, " de gal kim in er big rain-drap w'en er stawm wuz gwine on.   W'en de drap bustid out she jumped.   W'en she tuck up wid de man she lub, she tole 'im plain dat she kyarn' go out do's w'en de sun ur de moon wuz a-shinin'.   He 'gree dat she go des w'en 'twuz cloudy, but after w'iles he fegit ; wunst, w'en he all tuckahd out (tired) arter huntin' he mek 'er go out an' git de game whah he flung hit unneat er ash tree. She don't wanter go, but he mek 'er, an' she git de tucky (turkey) an' de piece o' deer meat an' staht back. De moon come out des ez she git ter de do' an' de man see 'er sail up in de a'r lak er eagle. She drap 'er shoe, dough, an' whah hit fall—hit wuz one dem bead shoe dey call moc'sins—dey grow up er floweh des lak hit, an' dey call hit arter dat name."

" I've seen a moccasin-flower," cried Tow Head, in triumph.

" Dey wuz wunst er man tuhn inter er buzzahd for killin' he mammy," said Aunt Mary, but nobody paid any heed to her.

"Huccome doves [1] wuz fum lub," said Big Angy, and, poor a subject as she looked for the tender passion, as she sat there with the firelight playing over her angles, she told " huccome lub " with evident sympathy for the trials of lovers.

The Doves.

In the old times, almost in the beginning, were a boy and girl most beautiful. No one can tell how much they loved each other, but, alas ! a terrible sorcerer loved the girl and his daughter, a terrible woman with a hump-back and fiery eyes, loved the boy. The wicked ones swore by fire, water, wind, the ground, the blood of all things, and the poison of the snake-king to have these innocent young people for themselves, This the grass told to the poor young people and they ran away. hoping the sorcerer and his daughter could not find them. They fled through all the world, but the wicked ones were hard after them. All things would fain have helped the lovers, but they could do little against sorcery ; still, they could do something, so the vines flung out their branches to stop the sorcerers ; the birds called, " This way ! this way," when it was not the way the boy and girl took ; the grass sprang up quickly and hid all tracks ; the thickets closed round them when they stopped a little to rest ; the streams parted their

---

[1] How they became doves.

waters and let the lovers go through, but raged as torrents as the pursuers came up. All this helped a little, but not much, the sorcerer and his daughter gained on the others every moment. One evening the boy and girl reached the lodge of an old and great sorcerer who lived alone, and cared nothing for any spell. He was too old to walk, but he could see into the clouds and down through the solid rocks. He saw these people a long way off. He knew what he would do. He called fire and it came ; he poured magic herbs on it ; he sprinkled it with the dust of withered enemies. When the lovers came they could not speak, they entreated with their hands, they fell down at his feet. He heard the trampling of the sorcerer and his daughter and smiled. He took the lovers and flung them into the magic fire. The evil ones came up and tried to snatch them from the flames, but the boy and girl flew up to the tree tops singing. They were changed into doves. When the sorcerer and his daughter saw it they cursed and howled. The greater one kicked them away from him changed into stones. The stones rolled into a stream, the stream carried them to a lake, and there they lie, fast buried in the mud at the bottom of it.

"I know a better love story than that!" cried Tow Head, eagerly.

" Dar now ! "

" Yes, I do. It's about—

> ' Noah's weary dove
> That sailed the earth around,
> And not a resting-place above
> The cheerless waters found.

I'll tell it to you some time."

" Des hole on twell I tells dat ole Whip-po'-will kill he own brerreh foh lub ob er gal 'an' now he sorry an' ax yo' ter whup 'im, an, ef yo' don't wanter die, ef yo' hyeah 'im ax, yo' got ter th'ow fiah-coals at 'im. Dat done, Ise out o' wuhk. Yo' hatter tek up de bizniz," said Granny.

" Yo' hatter tek keer. Yo' gwine ter git scrouge clean offen de flo', ef yo' ain' watch yo se'f ! " cried Aunt Mary, strangling a giggle.

" Trooftoo," assented Aunt Em'ly. " De young folks crowd us, dey suttinly do, but den we ain't gals no longeh. We's gittin' on, Aunt Jinny, we's gittin' on."

" Dat's so, Aunt Em'ly, dat's natchelly so. De mo' ez I lib de mo' I feel lak I gwine ter quit de urr chunes an' stick ter ole' 'Sundown'. Hit des suits my case, an' ef yo' ladies 'll he'p out on de secon' lines, I'll strak up de a'r right now."

The "ladies " having agreed to " he'p out " as desired, Granny began to mark time, first with her feet, then with her hands, alternately clapping her hands together and against her knees. After a prelude of, perhaps, two minutes, she began to sing, or rather chant, in a high, thin, but still sweet, old voice, the sweetest of all negro hymns, " Sundown "—

" Ise gittin' ole, Ise gittin' ole,"

she sang, and the others in deeper tone responded—

" Ise lookin' todes Sundown."

How Aunt Mymee's glorious contralto swelled out on the night like the notes of an organ !—

" Dese po' ole bones, dey feel de cole.
Ise lookin' todes sundown.

Oh, Jesus, honey, deah good Lawd !
Ise lookin' todes sundown.
Oh, come er long an' loose de cawd !
Ise lookin' todes sundown.

Oh, break de bowl des w'en yo' will !
Ise lookin' todes sundown.
Ob dis vain worl' Ise got my fill
Ise lookin' todes sundown.

O, break de pitcheh at de well !
Ise lookin' todes sundown.
Des keep de pieces out o' hell.
Ise lookin' todes sundown.

Come, Lawd, come ! come arter me.
Ise lookin' todes sundown.
Come tek my han' an' set me free.
Ise lookin' todes sundown.

Sundown ! sundown ! We'll all git dar !
Sundown ! sundown, hit's comin' !
De trump o' Gabr'el shakes de a'r !
Sundown ! sundown ! hit's comin !"

FAIRY TALES OF THE NATIONS

ENGLISH FAIRY TALES.

Collected by Joseph Jacobs, President of the English Folk-Lore Society. Pictured by John D. Batten. 12mo . . $1 75

"The stories are all either new or told in new form, and the book as a mechanical accomplishment is one of the most admirable things that has come from the press for many months."—*Detroit Free Press.*

CELTIC FAIRY TALES.

Collected by Joseph Jacobs. Pictured by John D. Batten. Uniform with above. 12mo $1 75

"Mr. Jacobs relates their marvels racily and in a way to hold the ear of either a child or a student of this fascinating branch of folk-lore."—*Christian Union.*

INDIAN FAIRY TALES.

Collected and edited by Joseph Jacobs, pictured by John D. Batten. 12mo $1 75

"His works are always entertaining and valuable, aud his series of fairy books grows in interest with each new volumes."—*New York Post.*

CHINESE NIGHTS ENTERTAINMENTS.

Forty Tales Related by Almond-Eyed Folk. Actors in the Romance of "The Strayed Arrow." By Adele M. Fielde. With illustrations by Chinese artists. Uniform with above volumes. 12mo $1 75

(Ready May, 1893.)

G. P. PUTNAM'S SONS

<table>
<tr><td>NEW YORK</td><td>LONDON</td></tr>
<tr><td>27 WEST 23D STREET</td><td>24 BEDFORD ST., STRAND</td></tr>
</table>

POPULAR ARCHÆOLOGY.

primitive Man in Ohio.—By WARREN K. MOOREHEAD, Fellow of the American Association for the Advancement of Science, author of "Fort Ancient, the Great Prehistoric Earthwork of Warren County, Ohio." 8vo. Fully illustrated. . . . . $3 oo

This book, which is a companion work to Nadaillac's "Prehistoric America," is the result of the observations of the author and his collaborators in Ohio during a number of years; their deductions are made from the testimony of the burial-places, village sites, and fortifications marking various epochs in primeval man's existence. It is a comprehensive statement of their discoveries related without ornamentation.

prehistoric America. By the MARQUIS DE NADAILLAC. Translated by Nancy Bell (N. D'Anvers), author of "History of Art." Edited, with Notes, by W. H. Dall. Large octavo, with 219 illustrations. Popular edition, . $2 25

CHIEF CONTENTS.—Man and the Mastodon—The Kjokkenmöddings and Cave Relics—Mound Builders—Pottery—Weapons and Ornaments of the Mound-Builders—Cliff-Dwellers and Inhabitants of the Pueblos—People of Central America—Central American Ruins—Peru—Early Races—Origin of the American Aborigines, etc., etc.

"The best book on this subject that has yet been published. . . . for the reason that, as a record of facts, it is unusually full, and because it is the first comprehensive work in which, discarding all the old and worn-out nostrums about the existence on this continent of an extinct civilization, we are brought face to face with conclusions that are based upon a careful comparison of architectural and other prehistoric remains with the arts and industries, the manners and customs of 'the only people, except the whites, who, so far as we know, have ever held the regions in which these remains are found.' "—*Nation.*

"His book is one which no anthropologist should be without. It gathers into one critical and incredulous volume all that is most solid, sure, and trustworthy in the whole realm of American archæology."—*Pall Mall Gazette.*

The Customs and Monuments of prehistoric peoples. —By the MARQUIS DE NADAILLAC. Translated, with the permission of the author, by Nancy Bell (N. D'Anvers). Large octavo. Fully illustrated. . . . $3 50

G. P. PUTNAM'S SONS

NEW YORK   LONDON
27 and 29 West 23d Stree*   24 Bedford Street, Strand